NEITHER BOMB NOR BULLET

NEITHER BOMB NOR BULLET

BENJAMIN KWASHI:
ARCHBISHOP ON THE FRONT LINE

ANDREW BOYD

MONARCH
B O O K S

Published by **Monarch**
www.lionhudson.com
Part of the SPCK Group
SPCK, 36 Causton Street, London, SW1P 4ST

ISBN 978 0 8572 1843 8
eISBN 978 0 8572 1844 5

First edition 2019

Cover image © 2019 Ben Kwashi

A catalogue record for this book is available from the British Library

Printed and bound in the UK, November 2022, LH57

To Joel, Sam, and Charles

Your adventure awaits. Get going!

ACKNOWLEDGMENTS

My grateful thanks to Release International (www.releaseinternational.org) and my friends at Life Church Petersfield (www.lifechurchpetersfield.org.uk) for helping to make this book possible. And my thanks to my wife Seren for being my hyphen queen and encourager-in-chief.

We all have dreams. Helping Ben Kwashi tell his inspirational story was one of mine.

FOREWORDS

Baroness Caroline Cox, cross-bench member of the British House of Lords and CEO of the Humanitarian Aid Relief Trust

t is a privilege to write a few words about one of my greatest heroes of faith, who together with his inspirational wife, Gloria, is holding a place on one of the most challenging front lines of faith and freedom in our world today: Jos, in Nigeria's Plateau State.

Archbishop Ben and I first met after his deaconess, Susan Essam, showed him a copy of my biography by Andrew Boyd, documenting some of my work with people suffering oppression and persecution. That was the beginning of such a valuable and valued relationship that we have agreed that whichever one of us outlives the other will speak at the funeral (or memorial) service of the departed one. As I'm now eighty-one, I have reason to hope that it will be Archbishop Ben who will be doing the speaking!

So, what is it that has generated my profound admiration and affection for Archbishop Ben and Gloria?

Firstly, a wonderful Christian living faith. Whenever the Archbishop preaches or speaks about faith, the message is so inspirational that it helps me personally. His faith is "lived out" in a life that demonstrates the reality that faith without action is dead.

Secondly, courage: Ben and Gloria had to flee from their former home as the house was set ablaze by militants. Today, a three-dimensional picture frame contains the only remnants of that home: ashes and a cross twisted by the heat of fire.

Years later, militants attacked their home in Jos, intent on killing Ben. He was away, so they subjected Gloria to unspeakable torture and humiliation. Of course, Ben returned home as quickly as possible and sent an email which I will never forget. It included words such as these: "We praise God that we have been found worthy to suffer for His Kingdom; and we pray that God will use Gloria's pain, anguish, and humiliation for His Kingdom, His glory, and the strengthening of His Church."

Thirdly, compassion: I have indescribable admiration for the living faith and love exemplified in their personal lives. Currently, in their home are fifty-two orphaned or abandoned children, who live in a security and happiness they never knew before.

Gloria has founded a school for other children in great need. And she gets up at 4 a.m. every morning to cook food for them, which will often be the only food they will have that day. I always leave humbled and inspired. It's a saying in Britain that "behind every strong man there stands a strong woman". The testimonies to Archbishop Ben's achievements, supported by Gloria, are a glorious proof of this!

Archbishop Ben and his inspirational team are heroes and heroines of the faith and they worship with more joy than is found in many a church in the "comfortable Christianity" parts of the world. They know that churches are targets for militant Islamist jihadists and so many have been destroyed, sometimes by Boko Haram suicide bombers driving their car or motorbike into a service, leaving many dead and injured.

While I write this, the people of Archbishop Ben's part of Central Nigeria are suffering horrendous persecution. According to the Christian Association of Nigeria (CAN), 6,000 Christians were killed between January and June 2018, and many subsequently. More than 2 million displaced people have been forced to flee for their lives.

During my most recent visit to Archbishop Ben, we visited one of the camps for hundreds forced to flee from their homes by Fulani jihadists. Local churches and dedicated individuals were doing all they could to help, but conditions were dire: in a room the size of a small gymnasium, 800 women and children slept every night.

Archbishop Ben is calling for your prayers as, together with his courageous, grace-filled colleagues, they valiantly hold these front lines of faith and freedom.

St Paul, in his first letter to the church at Corinth, wrote about how when one part of the Body of Christ suffers, we all suffer. Therefore, we have a biblical obligation to be alongside our brothers and sisters in Nigeria (and many other parts of the world where there is persecution), and if not physically, at least with our prayer support. And, remembering that faith without deeds is dead, we should be open to God's guidance showing us any other ways in which we can provide support.

In these parts of Nigeria, shamefully off the radar screen of contemporary media coverage, the suffering is indescribable. But Archbishop Ben and Gloria, with faith, passion, and courageous commitment, are doing all they can, with very limited resources, to alert us all to the reality that persecution is not history but a contemporary living challenge.

I pray that we will be worthy of the price they are paying for our faith.

Paul Robinson, CEO of Release International

Several years ago, I heard Archbishop Ben Kwashi say these words: "If God spares my life, no matter how short or long that is, I have something worth living and dying for. So, I'm going to do that quickly and urgently. That kind of faith is what I am passing on to the coming generations. This world is not our home, we are strangers here, we've got business to do, let's get on and do it."

Those words reveal something of what has made Ben's life so special: a deliberate choice to devote himself fully to God, to lay down his own life so the life of God might be made real through him.

All true followers of Jesus Christ face the same choice. Will we call upon the grace of God today to live fully for Jesus Christ;

are we willing to count the cost of being His witnesses in this world; are we determined to lay down our lives in the service of God's kingdom, to love people as He loves them?

Ben chooses to live like that in a part of the world where Christians are severely persecuted for their faith in Jesus Christ. For many years, north-east Nigeria has been one of the most difficult and dangerous places for Christians to live. Persecution has come in many forms and has been relentlessly inflicted as groups such as Boko Haram and Fulani militants have sought to enact their influence and agenda.

I have seen persecution's effects first-hand: people have been mercilessly attacked, children and adults maimed and murdered by machete, beating, burning, or rifle. I have spent time alongside Ben with children as young as seven who bear the literal and savage scars of persecution in their bodies and in their minds. Right there, alongside those who suffer, Ben chooses to demonstrate God's love to the persecuted, and the persecutors.

Ben is one of the partners of Release International, which supports persecuted Christians around the world. In Jos recently, I overheard Ben greet some of his pastors with these words, "Welcome, my dead brothers." Later I asked what he meant. He told me, "In northern Nigeria we do not know if we will last this day but, live or die, we do all we can to help people find joy in Christ!"

In the face of imminent danger, Ben, his wife Gloria, and his team are willing to give their lives daily to joyfully serve God, knowing today could be the one in which they are attacked, injured, or killed. In making that choice, they are examples of what it means to be disciples of Jesus Christ.

As you read the pages of this book please don't fixate on Ben as a "great" person; observe how he has chosen to live fully for Jesus' sake, and let that inspire you to choose likewise. After all, it is not just in Nigeria that people need to become disciples of Jesus Christ, it's also right where you live and work.

CONTENTS

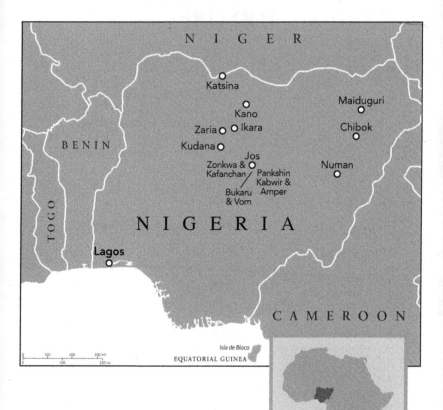

TIMELINE

Personal		National
	1806	Usman dan Fodio jihad, Sokoto Caliphate
	1901	Nigeria becomes British protectorate
	1907	Plateau State evangelized
Ben Kwashi born	**1955**	
Gloria born	**1958**	
	1960	Nigerian independence
Military School, Zaria	**1970**	
Nigerian army, Lagos	**1974**	
Ben becomes a Christian	**1975**	
Discharged from army, accepted into Theological College of Northern Nigeria (TCNN)	**1978**	
Posted to Numan for teacher training	**1979**	
Graduation from TCNN, ordination, posting to St Andrew's Church, Zaria	**1982**	
Ben and Gloria married	**1983**	
Posting to Ikara	**1986**	Nigeria admitted to Org. Islamic Cooperation
Posting to Zonkwa, Ben and Gloria's house destroyed	**1987**	Church burnings

Chaplain, Kaduna Polytechnic, TCNN	**1988**	
Rector, St Francis of Assisi Theological College, Wusasa	**1990**	
Consecrated Bishop of Jos	**1992**	
Gloria begins homeschooling	**1994**	
	1998	Lambeth Conference, Anglican fault lines appear
	2001	Jos Crisis begins
	2002	Miss World protests, riots in Kaduna, Boko Haram founded
	2004	Fulani crisis
Attack on Gloria, work with orphans begins	**2006**	Mohammed cartoon riots
Assassins return for Ben	**2007**	Riots in Jos
Appointed Archbishop of Jos	**2008**	
	2009	Boko Haram insurgency begins, churches attacked
	2010	Fulani Dogo Nahawa massacre
Address to Muslim conference in Jos	**2011**	
	2012	Boko Haram targets churches in Jos
	2014	Chibok girls kidnapped
	2015	Fulani named fourth-deadliest terror group
Ben's cattle rustled, neighbour killed	**2018**	
Appointed Gen. Sec. of GAFCON	**2019**	

THE ASSASSINS RETURN

They say that your life flashes before you when you are about to die. They had tried to kill me before but failed. But today I knew my time was up.

The assassins had returned. They had smashed their way into my house. There were forty of them. With guns and knives.

My killer stood before me, shaking. Adrenaline or drugs. Maybe both. "Man of God, let's go!"

They had marched me to my room to kill me. And I was saying my prayers.

Gloria, who had been raped and almost killed by them before, had prayed there would be no more bloodshed. My only prayer was they would spare Gloria and the children. The only blood shed that night would be mine.

Prostrate on my face on my bedroom floor, surrounded by my killers, I prayed: "Even though I walk through the valley of the shadow of death…"

They say your life flashes before you when you are about to die. What would I make of mine?

PART ONE

BENJI BOWS IN

The hands that hauled me howling into this world belonged to a missionary from Sheffield. But it was far from Sheffield that I was born.

I, Benjamin Argak Kwashi, emerged in Kabwir, Plateau State, into the modest mud-and-thatch building that was the first mission hospital in northern Nigeria.

The date of my birth was 23 September 1955 – and it was yet another feast day for my mother, Elsie.

Shortly before going into labour, Elsie had looked at her father, Gideon, the way that only an only daughter could and asked him whether he would kindly kill a ram for her.

In those days, the eating of meat was reserved for special occasions, but what could be more special than the occasion of your only daughter's first baby? How could her father refuse?

In our culture, we have a traditional way of preserving the ram. Elsie's father, Gideon, boiled the ram with onions and salt and put it in a grass basket with a bowl beneath to catch all the drips. When the ram had finished dripping, he tied it up, so Elsie could pick off whatever she wanted, whenever she wanted. Meat prepared this way could go for a week without spoiling, even in our hot climate.

So in the days before delivery, Elsie ate and ate. And she continued to eat until she had single-handedly devoured the entire ram. By now, Elsie was big with child and big with ram. And still she was hungry.

It was then that her father overheard Elsie saying what she would really like, what would be very nice indeed, would be a second ram to eat.

So Gideon went out and sacrificed a second ram, just for

his beloved daughter. As an only child, Elsie had a special place in her father's heart. In my country, daddies love their daughters, and their daughters can get away with almost anything.

Not that Gideon was Elsie's daddy, in fact. Not really.

I know. I've confused you, but this is Nigeria!

Gideon was in fact Elsie's uncle. Try to keep up while I explain.

Elsie's actual father, Mr Micah Nenpan Goyang, was the treasurer of the Colonial Office and the wealthiest man in the village. He lived in the only two-storey building in Pankshin and owned the only car.

In our culture, when you want to wean a child off its mother's milk, you separate that child from its mother and give it to someone else, just for a time. That someone else was Elsie's Auntie Bilhatu.

Elsie's actual mother was Keziah and Bilhatu was her older sister. When Elsie was still a baby herself and in need of weaning, her mother Keziah took her to her sister Bilhatu's house. That's where Elsie stayed and that's where Elsie thrived. It just happened that way. It was God's providence. So Elsie was brought up by her Auntie Bilhatu and her Uncle Gideon, who was a pastor. Elsie called them mother and father, and mother and father they were.

In our culture, a wife returns to her parents' home to have her first baby, so her mother can assist her. She leaves the house of her husband for up to six months, and all the other women come and stay and take turns, week in, week out, until the mother regains her strength. Then one of the older women remains with her until the sixth month. This is still our way.

New mothers are treated like queens. Everybody comes and dances round them. And Queen Elsie was a queen above queens. Elsie looked on her auntie and uncle as her parents and remained their only daughter for nearly twenty years, before my grandparents were blessed with their birth child, a son.

To ask for meat was special. And if you asked for meat and got it, then you too must be special. So, my mother asked for and got her second ram, prepared just so, in the traditional way. And my mother cried with joy and ate it, gave birth, and feasted on its meat while she was breastfeeding.

To call Auntie Bilhatu a capable woman would be to severely underestimate her. Bilhatu was nothing short of formidable. People used to drop off stray children at her house for Bilhatu to bring up. She raised so many orphans: we can number nearly thirty.

And even though Bilhatu was illiterate and couldn't speak a word of English, she was a trainer of missionaries. With the help of a Hausa dictionary she taught those missionaries everything they needed to know. They in turn would teach English to Bilhatu and Bilhatu would teach the rest. The missionaries came from Oxford and Cambridge and all over to live with Bilhatu and develop their language skills.

Today, there are at least five women in Jos, the capital of Plateau State, who lived with my grandmother and who still speak of her in hushed and respectful tones. Bilhatu was a great woman.

Even so, the thinking in those days was: why would you waste an education on a woman who will only go and get married? So my mother remained eternally grateful for growing up with her auntie, who sent her to school so she could at least learn to read and write and speak some English. And at home, Auntie Bilhatu taught her how to cook and keep home and to serve the missionaries and to be very, very polite.

These things Auntie Bilhatu built into this girl, who was precious to her. So, when Elsie married my father, John Amos Kwashi, he found in her a fitting wife, well prepared to look after his home and raise his children and speak to the missionaries in English.

Bilhatu did a great job of raising my mother. And my mother in turn did a great job of raising her children. One sister is a physician, another is a journalist. Both are living in the US. And my brother is a bishop – all this from a semi-literate mother who was raised by an illiterate mother, both of whom were thoroughly educated in the Bible.

Eventually, after her confinement, my mother took me home and back to my father, an educationalist, who had risen to become a senior civil servant. John Amos Kwashi was the warden of technical schools in Bukuru and Potiskum. So many people used to come and ask things of him, he acted like he owned the school. He had his own quarters with servants, and that's where I grew up.

I was the sixth of my father's children. His first was a baby girl he had with a beautiful Muslim princess from the ruling house of the Kanam kingdom. They never married. Then his first wife, Julie, gave him four more children before she died. Then I came along. I was my mother's first and for a time she couldn't have any others, so I became the centre of attention. Some of the missionaries were carpenters so I had the luxury of a wooden cot. I even had nappies, though we called them napkins. And that was very posh.

In the end, our family grew to three boys and six girls, and I was the sixth... until Bilhatu died, when my mother inherited some of her younger orphans.

Although my father was well-to-do, meat was still a rarity – certainly for children. When there was chicken it was exclusively for the elders of the family. The only parts permitted the children were the legs, the head, and the intestines. Not even the eggs. It was said that if children had eggs too early, they would enjoy them too much, and would steal all the eggs from the chickens – and then there would be no more chickens for anyone.

Not that the children missed out. The older people made sure they left enough on their plates for the children to scavenge, especially the bones. We would chew each bone decently, grinding that bone with our teeth until no part was left. We might not have had much meat, but we had plenty of calcium!

My mother was a pretty woman: black, petite, and very jovial. She was a woman of great joy with an infectious laugh, who loved to eat sugar cane.

My father was talented, with a good sense of humour. There were no degrees at that time in northern Nigeria but he was educated by the Church Missionary Society (CMS – now the Church Mission Society).

He was disciplined but not stern and passed that on with a certain dryness, which he had inherited from the British. He would look at you and weigh you up. If you washed a glass for him, he would examine the glass. And then he would examine you and ask you to do it again. He wanted things done properly, and there was never any compromise on decency, politeness, or the line between truth and lies.

He was a man with authority, a no-nonsense individual. Sometimes I wished he would just ease off, but it paid off, eventually. Later his children saw the value in it and admired him for it.

My father had more influence on my life than my mother. I love the truth. I like facts. I like to read. My father was a great reader. He devoured *Reader's Digest* for years. He kept his things decently – books especially. He revered books. You would get the beating of your life if you tore a book. His library was great.

He was a meticulous record keeper and finance manager. He kept everything in order. He was organized, and I like that. Those things he passed down to me, though I could never be as hard-working as he. This is a man who never owned a car, not because he couldn't afford to, but rather he simply didn't want one. Above all, he loved his dignity and respected himself.

He used to wear handmade kaftans of sparkling white, milk, or blue, and hand-embroidered gowns in blue, red, white, yellow, and green, topped off with a traditional northern hat, that looks like a pot, in a colour to match. We were afraid when it came to getting him gifts. We would travel far and wide to buy him clothes. Whatever he liked he would accept, but whatever he didn't like, he would just give back: "I thank you for this, but this one – no."

My father was 5 ft 5 ins and my mother was shorter still. But what Elsie lacked in height, she made up for in fashion. She wore a yellow top with a wrapper (a long wrap-around skirt), in light green, red, or deep blue-black. And her headgear was something else. This small woman would pop up in bright high-heeled shoes. High heels raised eyebrows back then, but Elsie's fashion sense told her that heels were fitting for a woman who was married to an educated man.

Even so, she used to criticize my father for being too flamboyant and expensive. My dad was very picky. His watches were unique. You could never buy him a watch. He would tell you specifically, "I want an Oris or an Omega." Even as a little boy, he bought me watches and a camera, which I kept on losing. They were expensive, and when they went missing my father would be angry, but then he would buy me another. He loved his son!

I was growing up at a time when Nigeria was searching for its own identity. My family was more English than Nigerian. My father liked all things English, even Marmite. His cologne had to be from England, even his soap. Anything that was not English-made he had little respect for.

Whenever my dad wanted to buy anything, he would look in his British magazines and order them. And in those days they would come in a fortnight – clothes, shoes, anything. We never wanted for a thing. My grandfather even bought me an English tricycle – the first tricycle in the village. All the village kids used to come and fight over who could push me. There was an efficiency in the colonial era that continued into the 1970s.

Our house was an old colonial home, with two bedrooms and a plain zinc roof. It was well painted and looked after, with a veranda and a garden and an area for the children to play. The floor was painted red and the bottoms of the walls were green, while a milky wash covered the rest of the render. We and the house were looked after by two servants.

All the neighbours were civil servants. Each house was surrounded by hibiscus. You would arrive down a dusty drive into the compound, set in the centre with a square of earth that acted like a roundabout, from which grew a strong, shady tree. There were flowerbeds full of African Never Die and red and yellow flowers. School was within walking distance.

By the time my father married my mother, most of his children from his first marriage had grown and left. So I shared a room with my older half-sister Saratu until she headed off for secondary school.

Saratu was five years older than me and beautiful as a berry. But it was me, Benji, who was the apple of my father's eye. I was spoiled and I knew it and I made the very most of it. I was a clever kid. I knew what I wanted, and I knew how to get it. I would tell on my sister to my dad or invent stories that somebody had beaten me, complaining with wide, sorrowful eyes: "I don't know what I did wrong!" And my dad would bend down to comfort me and say, "OK, sorry. What do you want?" That was the music my ears longed to hear.

My poor mother despaired of me. I was one of those children who could never do anything right. But I was her son. And at that point, I was still the only child she had. But slowly and surely, the days of my reign were numbered. Eventually, she became pregnant with my sister Caroline. Until then, I ruled the roost.

For a time we lived in Katsina in northern Nigeria. The first rains would delay until June, and after the rain would come the flash floods. When those rains came, they excited us as children. They were torrential. We ran and we jumped and we played ball in that rain.

One day, at least ten of us were screaming and leaping as those waters lashed down. I was almost five years old, and while I was jumping for joy, the flash flood came. It washed me away... I disappeared.

After the flood had gone, everybody was out looking for me. Everybody was saying, "Where's Benji? Where's Benji?"

My mother was beside herself, crying and screaming. She was so scared. She thought I had drowned. Well, I almost had. I had been swept into a well and passed out. Someone went into the well to haul me out and I vomited water and came back to life. They said it was one of God's miracles. After that, it became a law that whenever you dug a well, you had to build a wall around it.

My mother wrapped me in a warm blanket and sat me in front of the blazing charcoal heater. Her face was a picture of concern. She inquired: "Benji, what will you eat?"

In my most feeble and plaintive of voices, I uttered: "Mummy, a sardine…"

"And Benji, what will you drink?"

Somehow, I managed to lift my eyes and, in that same pitiful voice, struggled to reply: "A Tango…"

For two whole days I was plied with sardines, bread, and fizzy orange. I milked it. I got anything I wanted. I refused to get well. But then young Benji got bored and simply had to get back out.

From my earliest moments, I was a rebel. But mixed with my rebellion were the first stirrings of compassion.

§

It was soon after that I began to feel that not all was right with this world. It was when I began to see little boys like me begging for food. Today I know them as Almajiris. These are Muslim children whose parents send them off to Koranic schools. I'm sure some parents are motivated by faith, but for others, it is a convenient way of getting their offspring off their hands.

From first thing in the morning, these children learn the Koran and Muslim prayers, and then they are released into the wilderness of the world to beg for food. They return late afternoon for more schooling, before going off for the evening to beg again for food and anything they can get. Sending these children out to fend for themselves was part of the culture in those parts of the country. It still is. The school gave them neither breakfast, lunch, nor dinner.

I was upset. These were kids my age, begging for food, when I had so much. They didn't even have shoes. They had maybe a tattered shirt or a torn singlet. Some would be lucky to have trousers. All they had was this bowl or plate in their hands with which to beg.

I was confused by what I saw. I went into the kitchen and saw a plateful of my father's food, so I took some. One woman who spotted me from a distance called my mother and said, "I think Benji is taking food to the Almajiris." I knew it would get me into trouble, but I couldn't bear these children begging.

It began in Katsina, and went with me when my family moved to Zaria.

The Almajiris would come to our quarters pleading for food. And, bigger and bolder, because I was now aged five, I would follow them back to their madrassa.

Their schoolhouse was simply the house of their teacher. It was a world apart from my own home, which was plastered and had water and electricity. Their madrassa was a thatched mud hut, shared by thirty or more children.

The main compound was a room for one of the teacher's wives and then his own quarters, with a bathroom and toilet. But these children went to the toilet in the bush, along with the goats, sheep and donkeys.

They slept in an open parlour at the entrance of the house, littered all over it, some on the bare floor, some on mats. At my home I had a bed, a blanket, a bathroom – everything.

Their parlour was also their classroom. When they awoke in the morning, they did their Muslim prayers and began their classes right there. The teacher didn't throw me out, because he liked me. I was sharp and I knew where the kids could get good food. So they liked me too. And we could understand each other, because I could speak Hausa. We became friends.

I knew where to find the houses of senior civil servants, where there would be leftovers aplenty. I have been blessed with a loud voice, so I cried out for food in their language.

Then someone would call out from the inside, "Almajiri? Bring your plate." Had they seen this chubby, little, well-fed kid they would have picked me out from the Almajiris straightaway.

So I got food for the Almajiris and they would come, "Benji, Benji! Let's go begging!" And I would zoom off with them and not come back until late into the night.

I no longer cared for my own food. I would take my food and put it on their plates and eat with the Almajiris. My mother didn't know where I was so she used to give me a beating every night for coming in late. I would say, "Mama, I was just outside playing!"

She would say, "But I didn't see you!"

I'd say, "Mama, I don't know why."

There were these constant arguments. I was angry towards my father and mother for keeping our food to ourselves.

My Auntie Azumi eventually got wise to me and informed my mother this was what Benji was up to. "He's become an Almajiri, one of the street kids, begging for food."

It was my fault. I should have known better than to go to my auntie's house and pretend to be an Almajiri. I went outside her house and cried out for food like the others. Usually, you just put your hand round the door and without even looking, they would give you a dish. But her son, my cousin, told on me. And my auntie grabbed my arm and pulled me in. She had a cane waiting and gave me a spanking. Then she took me home and my mother finally understood why I had been coming back so late. I had been doing this for months.

To her horror, she found out I had been going to the madrassa along with the children and learning Islam and Arabic. I was also learning to pray along with the other kids.

At my tender age, the ragged lives lived by these children felt so unfair. I felt sure my father could have done more to help. I didn't understand that this was the life their parents had chosen for them. I couldn't understand why they had so little, while I had so much.

When I grew up, I later found out that my father had helped many Muslim men. One man of eighty told me that if my father had not helped him at the age of eight, he would have died. And he would never have had an education. Another had become a director in the Federal Ministry of Finance. He told me that my father had put him in school as a child and paid his fees. I later met many who testified to my father's kindness, generosity, and benevolence.

One of these was Joseph, who had served as our houseboy. My father trained him and put him through school and he decided he wanted to be a printer. My father put Joseph through technical school and he went on to become one of the top printers in the state.

It was only at my father's funeral that I became aware of his kindness. There were people from everywhere, of all races and religions, who spoke highly of him. One was an ambassador, another a manager, another a top politician. They sat me down and said, "Your dad was a good man. He put me through school. Now see what I am today." I had no idea.

All I knew back then was that when my parents found out I was turning into an Almajiri they sent me back home to my grandmother, Bilhatu, in Plateau State. And with hindsight, that was perhaps the very best thing that could have happened to me.

§

My grandmother was the one person who showed me what it really meant to know Jesus Christ. I had grown up on the *Book of Common Prayer* and *Hymns Ancient and Modern*. I thought that was Christianity. But over the two years I spent in my grandmother's house, I got to know her more closely. I saw in Bilhatu the discipline of a spiritual life.

Everything for Bilhatu was the Bible. She would wake herself early in the morning for prayer. You didn't swear and you didn't call the name of the Lord in vain. Hygiene was also a top priority. She had this presence about her. People respected her, because she carried something when she approached you. When she talked to you, you could be sure that what she said was not only reasonable and wise but would offer the way out. She had that gift. She spoke into people's lives, and so it was. I carried that with me, even as a non-believer. When Grandma said things, they would happen, and that would frighten me. Let me show you what I mean.

My two young sisters, Caroline and Anna, came from the city for the weekend. They said to their grandmother, "We want to eat bread." But there was no bread to be found in the entire village. So my grandmother took these two young girls and said, "Let us pray that Jesus will bring bread." So they did.

All day passed, but there was no bread. Then, in the evening, an uncle was coming from Lagos and drove up in his car along the dusty road from Jos. And he brought with him a bag full of bread. They had not spoken, so there is no way he could have known.

"See?" Grandma told the children. "I told you Jesus would bring bread!" Caroline and Anna have not forgotten that story to this very day.

Bilhatu's Christian faith was so practical. You would never come to her house with lack and go out with nothing. It was simply not possible.

She was industrious and organized. She had land and buildings. People came to her to learn how to do things, and she taught them the Bible. She would get up early in the morning and always prepare ahead of anything and everybody. The strength I saw in my grandmother taught me to respect women. My father loved my grandmother: they were great friends. She was one of the reasons he married my mother.

Grandma Bilhatu lived in a modest house with a roof of thatch and floors that were either earth or cement. There was a parlour, a kitchen, and our rooms. As you entered, there was a pen for all her animals. She kept cows, sheep, goats and ducks. When that beautiful smell of animals greeted your nose, you knew you were home.

As a little boy, it was my job to rear the goats. Giving me any job was almost certainly a mistake: every single day was trouble. Some say nothing much has changed.

Our daily routine was simple. It was like this: you tolled the bell, then said your prayers. When I refused, they hit me on the head. "You go and toll the bell!" I would be crying. Then you took your animals out in the morning and didn't come back until evening. Every child did the same. They went out barefoot and happy in the heat.

For the first few days I protested, because I was used to wearing shoes and proper clothes. It was war between me and my grandma, a war I could never hope to win. She would say, "Did you see anybody wearing anything? Silly boy! You get out of here!" And when I did, I loved it. We wore nothing – not a stitch, apart from a rag to cover our private parts.

The wilderness was great. We took our goats and sticks and beat each other up. We could catch rabbits, eat mangoes and fruits of every kind. Up we went into the hills. And down we could come, sliding down the hillside on metal tins we had beaten flat. We would take our rags and tie them together into a ball to play soccer.

Then it was time to take the goats to drink water. The other children were wiser. They took their animals to places where they could keep an eye on them. Apart from me. My goats wandered off and I could never find them. And I just didn't care.

It was always a joy to go out. But coming back was another story. My goats were left to find their own way home. Often they would enter somebody's farm and help themselves to their produce. So to avoid a court case, about a quarter of a mile from home, I would start screaming and crying: "The goats have gone off!" And I would whine, "I don't know what they do!" But the goats were more sensible than me. Somehow, they always got home.

And eventually, I also went home to Mum and Dad. I bade farewell to Bilhatu, and civil war resumed in the Kwashi household.

It was my mother who fired the first shot, when she took it on herself to administer to me a teaspoon of cod liver oil every morning and evening. It was her fault, and she had only herself to blame.

For me, there was no escape. I tried my hardest to vomit it out, but my mother had a way of squeezing my mouth to make sure I would swallow it down. She stroked my throat like a cat while I spluttered and gagged. She said, "This is good for you. You take it!"

Parents didn't explain a thing in those days. If I refused to take it in the evenings, then she would just pour it over my rice – and that was terrible. Then in the morning, she would feed me sliced bread smothered in Marmite. I hated it (although I love it now)! But back then, I didn't have a choice.

Then every evening she would bathe me before I went to bed and rub mentholatum on my chest, back, and throat. It was more than a boy could bear. So I devised my own method of getting away from all this. While Mum was out on some errand, I would perch one stool upon another and climb the rickety structure until I could reach the cupboard where there were all these hated medications: the castor oil and the mentholatum. Then I would take them outside the house and throw them into the latrine. My mother didn't seem to catch on. She just thought she'd mislaid them. But she would always replace them. I didn't know why.

Today I know that cod liver oil is considered good for helping you to avoid malaria and Marmite is considered good for the eyes. Potiskum was dusty and at night it was very cold, and kids would be sneezing with runny noses, so mentholatum would help with the breathing. Much later, when I read up on all of these things I realized my parents really meant well for me. And later, when I got married, guess what? I did the same for my kids.

I would make sure whenever I came to England that I would buy giant-size packets of cod liver oil capsules and Marmite.

Many years later, when I became a bishop and I was packing up my children's room to move, I rolled up the carpet… and couldn't believe my eyes. I realized it was confession time.

Whom does a big, grown-up bishop confess to? His mama, of course.

I came from working in the office and saw her sitting on the ground with two of her grandchildren. She was wearing a light-grey blouse and wrapper and one of the girls was pretending to plait her hair. I said, "Hey, young lady, how you?"

She said, "Fine."

I said, "Mama, you look nice!"

Mama knew that tone of voice. And she didn't trust it.

"Why are you saying such good things today? What's the problem?"

She knew me too well. I said, "Honestly, Mama, I want to confess."

"Con-*what!* I'm not a priest! Why now?"

I said, "Do you remember the cod liver oil bottles that used to disappear?"

She said, "Yes."

"Mama, I used to throw them in the latrine. Did you lose your mentholatum?"

"Yes."

"Mama, I used to put them in the latrine. Do you remember losing your Marmite bottles?"

"Yes!"

I said, "I was the one, honestly."

She said, "Ben, it's over fifty years… why are you confessing now?"

I said, "Mama, you know we just moved house? When I was rolling up the children's carpet, I found all my cod liver oil capsules, hundreds of them."

Mama laughed. What goes around comes around.

§

My early memories are sweet. I was a lively chatterbox, who was liked and who was loved, but I was in trouble all the time, right until I went to senior school.

I climbed the fence. I fell out of a tree. I tattooed my body with oil from cashew nuts and ashes. (My mother was anxious when she saw the marks, and feared some strange parasite or disease, then was furious when she discovered I had made them. Mercifully, they faded.) I stuffed a peanut up my nose and kept it there for days until it began to germinate. I pelted the neighbour's guava tree with stones to bring down a juicy one onto their roof. (Unfortunately, the unripe ones came crashing down as well and made a thunderous racket on the zinc, which got me into trouble.

Still, I became a good shot with a stone.) I even managed to break open a young man's head. Not just any young man, mind: he was a prince.

The prince's name was Lawrence. His father was King Dimka of the Ngas people. We were both ten or eleven. And I must have done something to make Lawrence mad, because he grabbed a handful of stones and ran after me.

So I got a stone of my own and said, "If you don't stop, I'll throw this and you'll be dead!"

He said, "You can't do that!"

But I did – and I got him right in the forehead. When I was a full-blown bishop, Lawrence came up to me and pointed to the scar.

I should point out this is not the usual way the Kwashis treat their house guests, but young Benji always wanted to be in charge. There were parents in our town who didn't want to see me in their houses, because they feared I would mislead their children. I would! I would take them to the cinema from the age of ten. There was a wild side to this young Benjamin. I was convinced that, because of my family background, I could get away with anything. If I acted like royalty, it is because I was.

My family belonged to the Angas tribe. These were migrants from the Yemen, who in the eleventh and fourteenth centuries moved to Borno State, the place where the terrorists Boko Haram later made their base. Then, in the jihad of the eighteenth century, they became scattered. Many migrated to the hills of Plateau and settled there.

My father's family were princes. And on my mother's side my grandmother Bilhatu was the daughter of the ruler of the entire Angas kingdom. King Bewarang was converted to Christ in 1907 by the earliest missionaries who came to the country from Cambridge, and his conversion had a tremendous impact. It opened doors for more missionaries to come and bring the gospel.

But it meant my great-grandfather had to abdicate the throne. He had little choice: the tribe was animist, and it was the duty of the king to offer sacrifices to the gods. Some of these deities lived in trees, some in the air. Some controlled the harvest, while others controlled the winds. They demanded blood sacrifices, and these could be human beings, depending on the whim of the gods at any given time.

So my great-grandfather left his throne and his family rejected him, and he settled in his farmland, with his wives, children, and grandchildren, and his Christian faith.

All this means I have royal blood from both sides of my family. And this has its uses! It means I'm not easily looked down upon by either the state or our tribes. But it is also a terrible thing to be told you come from a special family. Young Benji was convinced that nothing could harm him. And that's not healthy for a headstrong young man who has yet to learn to control himself.

It wasn't that my father didn't try. He was a disciplinarian who made it very clear who was boss. But in my case, he woefully failed. He succeeded with everyone else, except me. And everybody in the family blamed him. They said it was his fault, because in my early years, he had spoiled me. Now I became the scapegoat, and they blamed me for every bad thing that happened. It broke my father's heart for at least ten years.

I was beginning to think it was my lot in life to never do anything right. But if that was my lot, then it would also be my liberation. If anyone asked me to do something, I would say, "Are you sure you want me to do it?"

They would think it over and quickly say, "No! No! No!" This gave me freedom from any responsibility.

As I learned later, from my own children, a young man or woman needs to be managed well. But all I got were complaints. So I made up my mind: "To hell with everything!"

I was angry. I felt the family expectations were far too high. My misfortune was that my older sisters from my father's first marriage had by now accomplished so much. Helen was married and at the foreign service. Mildred's husband was a major general. Margaret's husband was a permanent secretary in the civil service. My older brother, Isaac, was with KLM and Sarah was at university.

The entire bloodline was one of accomplishment and they expected me to do the same!

I hated even to think about it, so I chose to become a failure at everything. I failed my exams – deliberately. It was only when I became a Christian that I found that studying was the most joyful part of my life. Until then, I refused to try. I failed my GCEs along with my Military Academy exams and barely scraped a pass in half of the subjects I took.

They all used to scold me, "Benji, don't you know you're from this family? This is how you should behave! You must behave, you must succeed!" But none of this meant a thing. It just infuriated me. Instead of driving me to succeed, it did the opposite. I began drinking away my life.

I was a fashionable young man, into James Brown and Jimi Hendrix, and I was fed up with my dad picking me up on the way I dressed. He said, "You know, you're from a ruling house!" But it didn't mean a thing to me.

So I chose to walk in the opposite direction. I would leave home and become my own man. I would be free to see what the world was like, without people constantly chiding me that I was supposed to act like some prince.

My poor mother didn't know whether to hate me or love me, but I was her son. She taught me the meaning of gratitude. She was forever grateful. She would be grateful no matter how small the gift. Her last words in Hausa were "*Sai godiya*" – "Nothing but thanksgiving."

Towards the end of her life, she stayed in the US feasting on cake until she was no longer quite so petite. But when my mother eventually died, it was with all her own teeth, and thanksgiving on her lips.

YOU'RE IN THE ARMY NOW

For my next big step into senior school, my dad laid out a range of options before me. I chose military school.

It was the time of the Biafran civil war. I wanted to discover how brave I was, and what better place to prove my courage than in the army and on the battlefield?

Selection took two solid weeks and there was no guarantee of acceptance. I was stripped naked and checked for every complaint, including flat feet. Along with health exams came written exams and verbal exams. My one advantage was that I had been a Scout. Out of 1,000 boys, they accepted just ninety – including me.

My mum thought the army would teach me a lesson. She was worried about the fighting, but hoped the military would discipline me and turn out the kind of son she wanted.

"Just go!" she said. "Your troubles will be many. The army isn't a playground."

Although I was not yet in my teens, these were not child soldiers. There was no question of any of us going to war until I had graduated from secondary school.

The Nigerian Military School was a British idea. It was modelled on the Boys' Wing of the British army. It was an elite school, run by the Army Education Corps, whose teachers were graduates and officers. Many had Master's degrees, so we were all expected to come away with great grades in our O-levels. This would prepare us well for our A-levels, and after that officer training. Well, that was the theory.

Their aim was to produce top-notch educated soldiers who would provide leadership across the ranks of the Nigerian army. Some would be sergeant majors, while others would rise to second lieutenant or major general. All were certain to become leaders.

The raw recruits travelled by train to Zaria on a Nigerian army warrant. It was January, and it was cold. All of us arrived at the same time from all over the country on different trains. Military trucks were waiting and the sergeant was waiting too. He had a voice that would raise the dead.

"All of you coming to military school say, 'Yes, Sir!'"

The shouting and the screaming scared the hell out of me, just as intended.

"You boys coming from your father's house: we are going to show you, this is army!"

I found it hard to understand the sergeant's English, if it was English at all. For the first time in my life, I was frightened. They shook the brains out of us.

With all the other little boys, I hauled myself up on a rope and into the back of a huge, old khaki-coloured British Bedford.

At camp, the quartermaster handed us our blue PT shorts, brown canvas shoes, and jungle hats. And that was the last we'd see of our civilian clothes. From that day on, we had become government property. By now we were no longer human beings, we were numbers. And my number was 63NA/674.

Next, they lined us up for our haircuts in our PT shorts. Those clippers were a great leveller.

Buzz. "Next!" Buzz. "Next!"

Everything you did, you did while running. Talking was out of the question.

"You're not a human being, you're a number!"

"Yes, Sir!"

"Idiot!"

"Yes, Sir!"

"Bastards! Idiots!"

Every morning, once the bugle blasted reveille, the shouting began and we were out. The noise was terrible. Parade, and then back for more drill. When it came to mess, we were ravenous, but there was never enough time to finish your food. Everything was done at once, and on the double.

"Come on, you bastards!"

There was not a minute when you were not in trouble, and when the second-year students returned, it got even worse. These seniors were devils. They used to wait until we had a moment to spare for ourselves. Then they would call out: "Last boy!" All us juniors would come running.

One senior I will never forget. His name was Anthony. He picked on me to fill his plastic jerrican from a specific tap some distance away where the water was said to be sweeter.

My friend Herbert came with me to keep me company, and to have some mischief. He said: "I have a pair of dividers... Let's puncture his jerrican – and he will never call on you again."

We did. We turned his jerrican into a colander until there was water spurting out all over. I reported back: "Sir, look at your jerrican: something has gone wrong with it!"

He made me do frog jumps, where you squat down, hold your ears, then leap up. He had me doing these frog jumps for hours. Then he ordered me to roll on the wet floor for hours more.

It ruined my evening, but that was indeed the last time this senior sent for me to run his errands. I met him later when I was a bishop and he was the governor of Oyo State. We just laughed.

We were studying secondary school subjects along with our military training in the craft of warfare: geography, tactics, map-reading, vehicle maintenance, first aid, health, throwing grenades, and firing guns.

It was wild. And I loved every minute. It was a huge success.

And after year one, I became the senior yelling my head off at the others. Believe me, I didn't spare them.

Our rifles were ancient British Mark 4s. They weighed a ton and when you fired them, they would slam into your little boy's shoulder and hurl you to the ground. We would fall like ninepins, no matter how hard we tried to resist. And we would get up rubbing our bruises. But we got used to them.

By the third form I was a good shot – one of the best. Now we were firing AK-47s – Kalashnikovs. You would run and fire, run and fire, and when you were doing it all together, these weapons made their own music. As kids we would blast away at painted men on targets; we were trained to see and not be seen, to kill and not be killed. These were years of opportunity, and we loved them all.

By my third year I was appointed to the command block. I had risen to the rank of corporal provost and the army was my life. I fell in love with the army and I fell in love with this country that paid my school fees, taught me English and arithmetic, and was even paying me to play with rifles. And by forms four and five my pay had risen to £5 basic, with an extra five shillings for every rank. I could hardly believe it!

We were given British training, and that carried an air of responsibility and dignity, whether you were an officer or a private. The army was the hope of Nigeria.

On Sundays, we had to parade to church. If you didn't, you would be dead and buried.

"You registered in this squad as what?"

"As a Christian, Sir!"

"So you refuse to obey God today? Well, then you will receive hell from a man!"

That was training school. It didn't matter where you came from, that was the Nigeria I was trained to believe in, serve, and defend. I was bitterly disappointed when the civil war came to an end before I could join the fight.

My duties as a provost were to arrest criminals, prosecute them, and execute judgment. If you were absent from class, dirty on parade, or if your bed wasn't properly folded at the corners, you would be required to provide manual labour to serve the Nigerian nation. I would cut your leave while you would cut the grass, clear the gutters, and clean the toilets.

Never a second was wasted. And once you'd fallen behind with your duties you would be given more to do, so you would fall into even more trouble, God help you!

I graduated from military school after four-and-a-half years. And still at the age of seventeen, I announced I was going to join the regular army. Mama just threw up her hands and surrendered. She said, "Yes, yes, go and die!" She was fed up with me.

As a sportsman in the army, I played football, basketball, and hockey, and I ran. And if you played sports for your garrison, it meant you could avoid being regularly on parade. And that meant they would not inspect your hair. Providing you were clean-shaven and kept your hair firmly pressed down, you would be safe enough. But you had to make sure you didn't fall into trouble, because the first thing they would do at the guardhouse was level your hair with a razor.

So I looked like Mick Jagger. Off-duty, my hair was long and tied in a bandana. My chest was bare and I tottered about on platform shoes. That was what we did. I was caught up in the explosion of youth at that time.

Whatever James Brown wore, we wore. We had hot picks – electric combs to straighten our hair. When James Brown did a tour of Lagos, Philip Morris gave away cigarettes for free, so we all got hooked on those. I was a wild child. Not many families wanted me anywhere near their daughters. I wasn't actually that bad, but that was the image. And I was beginning to nurse the idea that I might go into music, which made matters worse for my mother.

And that was how we parted, with no good memory of my leaving. As far as my mother was concerned, I was gone. But as much as she was grateful I had left, so she could have some peace, she loved me and wanted me back.

She would run to her own mother and cry and cry and say, "Where's Benji?" And her mother would always say, "Benji is going to come back." My grandmother was not moved as much as an inch by the fear that I would be lost.

§

My dream was to go into the Nigerian Defence Academy and become an officer. For now, I was posted to Ojo Cantonment in Lagos and assigned to Supply and Transport.

The Biafran war had just ended, so there was a major reorganization, with many troops returning from the front. Ojo was a new cantonment. We were the forerunners and they had yet to organize inspections. It meant there was no one to go over my room in the barracks with a pair of white gloves. I was free! Free from my parents and free from school, and free from the demands of parade inspection.

Freed from external pressure, my self-discipline began to slip until it went into freefall.

I was biding my time before going to train as an officer. And to while away my spare time, I drank. We all did. That was the culture. I drank anything and everything: whisky, beer, brandy, Guinness. My favourite was Heineken. I had a glorious display of hangovers in the mornings, but somehow I still managed to get to work.

But when it came to my written exam, I had been drinking heavily before it and failed. My friends and colleagues went on to the Defence Academy ahead of me, while I went on to the clubs and discos to dance.

When we danced, we went into full display. Girls liked you for the way you moved or the way you dressed or your love of life. Lagos was full of young, misguided girls who wanted to like you. But I was careful, and I'll tell you why.

Once, during a trip home, my father said to me, "Ben, you are now a man." And he offered me a chicken meal – a whole chicken. I loved chicken. And only the elders ate chicken, so this was a meal with real significance, but when that significance became apparent to me, I rapidly lost my appetite.

While I was filling my mouth, my father said a second time, "Ben, you're a man."

I smiled.

A third time he said, "Ben, you're a man." Then he added, "And if any girl comes here to this house and says she's pregnant, you must marry her. Even if she says there were 100 men and your name is just one among them, you must marry her, even if it's not your child."

I pushed my chicken to one side. Fear gripped my stomach and there it remained. The fear of the Lord is the beginning of wisdom, but right then, the fear of John Amos Kwashi was far more real, and I was afraid of my father's authority to his grave.

The irony was that the other soldiers were more promiscuous than me by far, even though I was the leader and I was in charge of parties.

There were two good reasons for taking charge: I could hold my alcohol, and I was the one who could lay hold of a car. My older brother was in Lagos and most of his friends could drive. So I knew where to find a car, and I had grown up knowing how to drive. So no matter how drunk we all became, Ben Kwashi was the one who could take everybody home.

When it came to girls, there was a decency instilled in me that I knew not to have sex with a girl without being committed to her. I would not take advantage of her. I respected girls and I respected myself, though I was certainly not a saint!

Then the day came when every soldier was paid a backlog of arrears. At that time, the Nigerian Naira was equivalent to the British Pound. I received close to 2,000 Naira in war allowance and arrears. I had so much money that I didn't know what to do with it! I gave some to people, sent some to my sisters, lavished even more on expensive clothes, watches, and shoes. But mainly, I just drank my back pay away. It was a hell of a lot of drink!

STOPPED IN MY TRACKS

t was drawing to the end of 1975, and with it the end of my teenage years. I had time off from the barracks and was out on the streets of Lagos with my friends. We were heading for a hotel disco, and I was ready for action!

Psychedelic was my style. From top to toe, I was pimped, from my blue-frilled shirt to my black bell-bottoms. My shirt was wide open too, to reveal a silver chain that matched the rings on my fingers. My platform shoes took me all the way up to the stratosphere.

On one sole, I'd glued a matchbox cover, so when I wanted a light, I could just lift my shoe and scratch that match. Man, I was hot! People thought my shoes were on fire! They would say, "Ben, where did you get these shoes?" It was my party trick from Lagos to Jos. So we set out to hit the town. But the action we found was not what we'd expected.

There was this man speaking in the street, a soldier by the name of Dominic Oke. He was a corporal in his thirties, wearing pressed khaki shorts and a short-sleeved shirt – an out-and-out square. He was uneducated, an Anglican, and in the chaplaincy – and I just wanted to floor him. Poor misguided Christians, what did they know?

Dominic looked at me and said, "God loves you."

"You must be joking!" I shot straight back. "You don't know me! God doesn't love people like me. God loves good people."

My friends were going on ahead. I grinned and waved them on, "Don't worry, I'll join you."

I turned back to Dominic. "Mind if I smoke?"

No, he didn't mind. He was not judgmental in the least. He was a gentle, calm, and gracious human being. And within ten minutes he had me in tears.

I said, "My past is terrible, God couldn't love me. I've never heard anybody say anything positive about me."

And what they had said was right! I had broken somebody's head, attempted to take somebody's car, and got caught taking a motorcycle without a licence. Everything I'd done for eighteen years had been wrong. Even when I did my job in the army, it was only for the salary. In the army, you're told what to do. It was easy obeying orders. Everything was, "Yes, Sir, no, Sir."

But now I was an officer-in-waiting and living in a room on my own, and that was a different matter. It was my first real taste of freedom. But to think of anything good to do with that freedom was beyond me. And even when I tried, it didn't seem to work. So I had given up.

Now there was this man assuring me that somebody called God loved me, and that He would give me another life. I needed that other life desperately, but I had a dilemma. Of course, I'd heard this story before. I was a grandchild of a pastor. But for me, it was just that – a story. My father, my mother, and my grandparents were all Christians. But I had not seen any dramatic change in the lives of believers to show this story was real and it really worked. Where was the proof?

Dominic told me to believe it because this story of Jesus had really happened. It wasn't just a story. It was history – His story. Somehow, I had not heard that before: that Jesus actually did come to the earth and did die on the cross for people like me. It never came close until that day, until Dominic assured me that Jesus knew about me before I was born, that He died for people like me, and specifically for me.

Dominic said that today, if I accepted Him, He would begin to work in my life. If I took Jesus at His Word, I would see Him at work in my life too.

All I could say was, "Wow!"

He continued: not only would Jesus come into my life, but the Holy Spirit would come into my heart.

Now, that was more difficult, because I liked my life and didn't fancy the idea of some spirit setting up home there. The idea of spirits to me was some wildness, like somebody losing their mind. But Dominic said, "No, this is the Holy Spirit of God. He will help you live the life that God wants you to live. You will see Jesus actively at work through the Holy Spirit."

This was freaking me out, because I thought something weird was going to happen and I would go mental! But Dominic said, no, I should give this a chance.

I was rooted to the spot. I just couldn't move.

He asked if I wanted this change. I said, yes, I wanted this. I was tired of always wanting to do what was right, but finding it impossible. I said, "OK, let me give it a try. If it doesn't work after one week, then I'll go back to my old life."

So Dominic asked me to pray for Jesus to come into my life and to forgive me and to take me from now on.

The change was immediate. That was evident when we got back to my house and I opened the door.

I was angry with myself when I saw the room I had lived in for nearly a year. I say saw it – what I mean is, smelled it. The room was dirty and littered with used cigarettes and unwashed plates. The bed had not been made. I began to cry and then to wail. Tears rolled down my cheeks. Why was I crying? I felt, "God, if it's true and You forgive me, then I'm really sorry." My tears became uncontrollable.

I tore down all the posters, of Jimi Hendrix, James Brown, and Fela, a Lagos musician. I pulled them all down and burned them. I threw out the filthy dishes and pots that I hadn't washed for months, which had fungus growing on them that I hadn't even noticed. I even burned some of my bedsheets. The cleaning frenzy continued until 1 a.m. the following morning.

When Dominic came to check on me, later that day, I was so weak, I couldn't even go to work. He was very kind. He said there was a ship berthed at the docks called the *Logos* which was full of Christian materials. We bought so much – some by the Navigators, some by Campus Crusade, even Christian music! I didn't know there was any good Christian music. I scooped up armfuls of records and tapes.

Over the coming weeks, we did Bible studies together. I looked into the promises of God and the Holy Spirit confirmed each one. After one month had passed, I had cleared all my debts. I no longer owed anybody anything in the barracks. Until then, I'd been eating and drinking and buying cigarettes on credit. But now, I had paid off everyone. I had money to spend and to spare and I was clean.

Dominic was a quiet character who used to witness calmly to others, while I was noisy and lively, so Dominic used to drag me out and draw people together and say, "Ben, would you preach to them?" So I would preach – and to my amazement people would come to Christ. This was something else! It frightened me.

Until now, I had set my heart on becoming an army officer, but alcohol and exams had been a poor combination. While I was busy failing exams, some of my colleagues were on their way to Sandhurst.

Then I believe I heard God's voice asking me to leave. He wanted me to be an evangelist. That calling was confirmed in a number of ways. My preaching was having an effect. I had joined Dominic's church, St Paul's Protestant Barracks Church in Lagos, which held its meetings in the military hall.

The church recognized my calling too. I had become busy in the church after work hours. They put me on the preaching rota and let me help lead the youth and the choir.

§

By now, my army colleagues were getting worried. The other soldiers wanted to know whether it was frustration at failing my exams that was driving me to religion.

My senior, Samuel, had just come back from a break at the Academy.

"Ben, you don't have to go this far! Some of the juniors have gone ahead of you, but your turn will come: don't worry. Don't be frustrated, just keep trying. Being an officer is the key thing."

I said, "Sir, I'm not sure I'll even be in the army any more."

He said, "No! How can you say that? Just keep trying."

He couldn't understand. He had been commissioned as a second lieutenant. Others tried to reason with me: "Ben, the army is your life!"

They could see the change in me, and they didn't like it. When they arranged parties and I wouldn't come, they couldn't believe it. I lacked the confidence to tell them what really happened, but eventually Dominic said, "Tell them the truth."

So I did. I told them I preferred to go to Bible studies and choir practice. That went down well. One said, "Wow, Ben is going to be a Reverend Father. That's nice." It was mockery.

Another said, "Give it six months, but if you know you're going to disgrace God, then you'd better leave."

But my two army chaplains realized I was genuine. One, a colonel, did everything to get me to apply for my commission to the chaplaincy. But all ambition to be an officer had departed. In its place, I was fired up with a desire to accomplish a different task. That task was not yet clear to me, but I knew I had a mission to carry out.

I had been a lost kid, and there were so many other lost kids over so many generations that I needed to reach, who needed somebody like me to help them. And coming from the north of Nigeria, I knew how few of the people had been reached with the gospel. This became the focus of my ambition: to reach the whole world with the gospel.

§

When I had left home at seventeen, I looked like a rock star. Now, after almost two years, when I went home, my mother would have had to be blind not to notice the difference. My haircut, my shirt, my shoes, my whole demeanour had changed. It was sensible. And so was I. Mama could see the change the moment she saw me, but she wasn't sure what that change meant, or whether it was even a good thing.

Mama wondered whether I was up to my old tricks. Because when I had wanted something, I would pretend to do something good. Or it would be, "Mum, there's a Christian conference…" and she would give me money, but I wouldn't go. But now, I wasn't asking for a thing. Nobody was forcing me to do what was right. I was just doing it. I was even sweeping up around the house. And that's what made Mama nervous.

On Monday, when she heard me praying, she wasn't sure I was normal. I was remembering my past sins, and worrying whether God had truly wiped them away. I would cry and wail, and when Mama heard this, she was worried.

"Ben, are you OK?"

"I'm OK, I'm OK."

And this went on until one day I told her I was getting the idea of going into the preaching ministry. She said, "What!"

"Mama, I think God is calling me."

Mama put both hands on her head and said "What!" And when an African woman puts both hands on her head, it's because somebody has died or something terrible has happened: something so hard that no human can bear it.

She said, "Ben, please! It's OK that you're a Christian but please don't go into the ministry. That's for sensible people. I thank God He's worked in your life but please, the ministry is for people who are gentle!"

She knew me. I would slip back. Somebody would annoy me in church and I would go and break their head.

So I went to see my grandmother. By now, Bilhatu was in her seventies and needed a stick to walk. She stood there in her flowing white blouse and her multicoloured wrapper while I told her my experience. She was not at all surprised. Not at all. She just smiled and said, "Benji, that's no news. I always knew Benji would come back."

And she went into her room and brought out my inheritance. It was my grandfather's black leather Bible and his reading glasses, along with the *Book of Common Prayer* and a couple of other books. He had given her them to keep, so that when I was ready for ministry, she should give them to me.

She said, "This is your legacy."

"What?!"

"Yes."

Bilhatu told me that before I was born, when my mother came to deliver me, my grandfather had prayed to the Lord and asked for a male grandchild to take over his ministry. And so, when I was born, he asked my dad to give me those names, Benjamin Argak: The strength of my right hand, and One way to God.

So that's why, when my grandfather heard my mother calling for more meat, he slaughtered a second ram, because he knew that God had answered his prayer.

I still have that Bible, that Prayer Book, and those silver-framed reading glasses. The Bible is in Hausa and the *Book of Common Prayer* had been translated into Angas in 1921.

It felt as though I was being passed the mantle. And that bothered me. How could my grandfather have known? What kind of people could be so confident that somebody like me would never go missing but would come back?

So Bilhatu blessed me.

AT A CROSSROADS

It was an enormous sergeant who was the powerhouse at the barracks church. As acting pastor, Staff Sergeant Felix read the lessons, led the prayers, collected the offerings, and seemed to do everything, even though I couldn't be certain he knew the Lord.

For some reason, Sergeant Felix didn't object when Dominic asked me to help with the choir and lead some Bible studies, but he drew the line at letting me do anything on Sundays.

I had a pretty low opinion of clergymen at the time. Most clergy, back then, were old, retired civil servants whose messages had little appeal for a growing young man. They seemed miserable and their services were boring. No clapping your hands and no guitars. You could be happy outside the church, but as soon as you entered the doors, everything had to change.

At that time, there seemed to be no place for young people in the church. They only seemed to notice you at Harvest Festival or Christmas when they needed extra hands to decorate or clean the church. There was no attempt to get young people involved in the gospel ministry, and most of them thought the gospel was far-fetched. Once you had been confirmed, you would graduate from church. Back then, church seemed self-satisfied and complacent.

It was thanks to brother Dominic that I became engaged in church. He took this active young man, who never had a dull moment, out on the street and round the houses. He got me to share my faith, lead prayer meetings, and give devotional talks. He believed in me, invested in me, engaged with me, and set me to the task.

Not so with the acting pastor. I had a running battle with this sergeant. I would have preferred to talk to him in person, but he didn't seem approachable. So I put some thoughts in writing.

I produced a list of suggestions for the chairman of the church council, an army captain, and handed it to him in church. He read my note, frowned, and passed it across the chancel to the acting pastor. The sergeant read it, glared up at me, and pointed his finger. I was sitting at the keyboard at the time.

Then, as soon as the service ended, this big sergeant with his black-and-white cassock and surplice chased after me, his robes flowing behind him. They had to restrain him from giving me a beating.

Young people can be critical, and that's how he read my suggestions, even though I had intended them to be helpful. I simply pointed out that the church was growing and asked whether other confirmed church members could be allowed to do some of the readings. And as he was the one who was always preaching, I wondered if he could see his way to letting others preach too. But the clincher was probably when I asked if he would account for the tithes and offerings that he collected.

Come to think of it now, I can understand his objections. His response was to sack me from the church. I had been saved at the age of nineteen and excommunicated by twenty.

But that didn't stop me.

The Bible study had grown from thirty people to sixty every week. We moved it to my house, and along with it came much of the life of the church. With no Bible study and no one to lead the choir, St Paul's emptied.

After two months, the acting pastor turned up at the Bible study. I braced myself for the worst, but he was just coming to see for himself. Afterwards, he found it in himself to say, "Ben, you must come back to church." God was at work.

During those eight weeks I had one of my earliest experiences of hearing the Lord speak. I was praying, "Lord, what did I do wrong? Should I go and apologize to the acting pastor?"

But what I felt the Lord say was, "Go back to the church and serve My body as an evangelist. Go and repair it."

That call was to build the body and bring home people who are lost – not to leave and start another church. And that remains a key principle in my life today. I vowed that whenever I saw things being done in the church that I believed were wrong, I would never repeat that mistake.

When I returned to the church, the PCC discussed the points I had raised and put them into practice. Then in 1976, a proper ordained priest was sent to us, and he recruited me to be his assistant.

The Revd Dare Sila engaged me in putting microphones and speakers around the church and leading the youth. He drew me in. Then the chaplaincy gave me the opportunity to help teach English to the staff, to teach the women how to read and write in Hausa, and to give the children Bible classes after school. The barracks children were always seen as a bit of a nuisance. They gave me opportunities, and I got to work.

I was young and played music and basketball, which drew in other young people to the church. Dominic's young recruits also came along and brought others. St Paul's became like a youth church. The numbers doubled.

People trusted me. They trusted their children with me and invited me to pray in their homes.

Suddenly, my officers liked me. I had turned into a reasonable boy. Sergeant Lawrence was a big bearded nurse who had children of his own in the choir. As I was leading a song, I could see him shedding tears. Afterwards, I heard him say, "Do you notice something has happened to Ben? I think Ben could make a pastor."

I laughed and laughed! Conducting funerals was not for me!

Another sergeant wasn't so sure this leopard had changed his spots. Sergeant Samuel was in the Education Unit and he believed young Kwashi had gone too far. He asked me, "Did you know it was men who wrote the Bible?"

I said, "Yes," but quoted 2 Timothy 3:16–17: "All Scripture is God-breathed and is useful for teaching, rebuking, correcting and training in righteousness, so that the servant of God may be thoroughly equipped for every good work." It was as though Sergeant Samuel was seeing that part of Scripture for the first time.

I would preach at the top of my voice, urging people to turn to Jesus. And people believed it! Believe me, I was more surprised than they were! Through our ministry, attendance grew to more than 500 within a year.

Much credit for those increasing numbers must go to brother Dominic. He was a quiet evangelist, who would encourage people to come together and pray. They would gather and he would say, "This evening, brother Ben will give us the devotion." So from block to block, from Signals to Communications, people were coming. It was something of a revival.

It was all a confirmation of my growing calling, and it confirmed that what I believed in was true. The promises were coming true.

I had taken my time to process what I believed. I had said I would give the Christian faith a try. I was converted as a soldier, and for a soldier, trust is a serious issue. So my conversion laid hold of me in three distinct stages.

Firstly, I needed to believe that Jesus died and rose and is alive today.

Secondly, I needed to see God fulfilling His promises and proving true to His Word.

And then I needed this invisible, but real, presence of Him in the Spirit.

And after a year-and-a-half, at the age of twenty-two, I reached the point of conviction.

I was confident that Jesus had proved Himself. I had become reconciled to God and reconciled to myself. It was clear God was real and the visible difference in me had proved it.

How did I know? I was at peace. I didn't have to go out to drink and to discos. I didn't have to look the way the world said I should look. If God was happy with me, then I was OK. I was saving money, I was able to pay my tithes and still have enough left over to give to others genuinely from my heart.

So when I heard both from the church and from people that the call of God was on my life, I received it and believed it. At this point, it was not the church or the army, it was both.

I would finish my duties as a soldier, then play hockey, soccer, and do athletics for the unit. And then I would go to the church. I was all over the place, but seldom in an office. I have never been the office type.

But when I really came alive was when they engaged me in evangelism in the Delta region of Lagos. I found excitement in riding in boats, going to villages, preaching the gospel, and staying with the villagers overnight. I loved it! Rural evangelism had won my heart.

Gradually, I came to realize there was more to being a pastor than conducting funerals and giving communion. I was beginning to nurse the notion that I could do this.

But things came to a head when the vicar asked me to put my name up for the chaplaincy.

The military chaplaincy? I wanted something that would take me out to people, where I could be useful. But chaplains were office-based. They weren't active in rural evangelism, and come to think of it they weren't active in evangelism in the barracks, either. A chaplain's life seemed formal, dry, and dull, a world apart from my experience in the rural areas.

Out there, I found things I could help people to do to improve their lives, like simply boiling water before they drank it. No one had told them they could build their own toilets – instead of using the river. Nobody had ever explained these things to them. Teaching these things excited me.

Then a new chaplain arrived, a lieutenant colonel. He too asked me to join the chaplaincy, and I made it clear to him – respectfully – why I shouldn't. So he recommended me for theological training and said I could decide after that.

I had reached a crossroads. I was getting ready to sit for a short-service commission, which would lead to a career in the army. And now there was the option of sitting exams for the Higher Diploma in Theology at TCNN – the Theological College of Northern Nigeria.

Military or ministry? Or a ministry in the military as a chaplain?

Given my history of flunking exams, what followed was cream on the cake. I sat the entrance exam for TCNN in Bukuru and not only did I pass but I came top of all the candidates. What a turnaround.

Previously, I'd had so many conflicting threads running through my mind that I hadn't been able to concentrate on my exams. I was unhappy with the family situation, I was struggling to make sense of the contrast between wealth and poverty, and I was dissatisfied with family expectations that meant nothing to me. But now I was completely free from all that, because God had His own expectations of me, that I could embrace with joy.

But my options were still open. I still had an interview for officer training at the Military Academy in Kaduna. And it was there that I heard the unmistakable call of God on my life.

That night in Kaduna I was praying, "God, show me what You want me to do. Is it an army career or a call to the mission field?"

Early in the morning, the bugle blasted us up to parade. A sergeant and warrant officer were screaming, "Hey, you boys, get up, get out!"

Everybody was shouting, "Come out, you bastards! Idiots! You wannabe officers, come on, get out! Come quickly! Run out – run, run, run!"

For the first time, the noise, the insults, and the curses were an irritation. I had been doing this for five years in military school, but today everything inside me rose up against them. The conviction fell upon me: You don't belong here. *This is not my life*, I thought. *I can't be insulting people and cursing like this.* Overnight everything changed.

Instead of heading out on parade, I set about packing my things. I was completely calm. I knew the time had come to leave.

My decision was confirmed when that short-service commission was unexpectedly cancelled. But everybody said there would be another, and they tried to persuade me to wait and reconsider.

The company commandant sternly reminded me how much the Nigerian government had invested in my life and how the right thing to do would be to serve my nation.

The chaplain did his best to ignite some spark of enthusiasm for the chaplaincy.

And then a stronger temptation came.

I loved basketball. So did the commander, who had played for the national team. He saw me playing and set about arranging for me to be transferred to another brigade where I would be able to play basketball for the army.

But my feelings for the military had gone completely cold. I had made up my mind.

Before I could be transferred, I received my acceptance into TCNN. More than 100 applicants came forward for ordination training. Out of those, only five were selected. And of those, I was the only one sent to TCNN.

My military discharge was approved and the Bishop of Kaduna, the Rt Revd Titus Ogbonyomi, endorsed my application and accepted me as a member of his staff.

The Archdeacon of Jos was a local pastor who knew my father. The Venerable Timothy Adesola was over the moon. And when my father heard that I was going into the ministry, he rejoiced greatly. In 1930 he'd been selected for ordination training, but at that time, colonial officers were looking for staff. Dad was a trained teacher, so the CMS released him to the colonial government to help start schools.

It was Archdeacon Adesola who broke the news to my dad: "Well, something you didn't do, your son is now doing!"

My father clapped his hands for joy and – even better – he agreed to pay all my fees.

He was so excited. He was retired by now. Reclining on his sofa in his large sitting room in his chiefly gown, wearing his silver wristwatch, he looked at me through his black-framed glasses and said, "I want you to finish your studies and then go to Cambridge. That's the place to study – Cambridge!"

Everything with my dad was Cambridge, never Oxford.

The missionaries who had brought the gospel to us had come from Cambridge. He loved both their diction and their manners. He wanted me to speak English like a Cambridge man. And he added, "I would like you to go to Cambridge to learn how to teach. I want you to be a teacher."

When I protested that I was an evangelist and wanted to preach the gospel, he argued, "No, a good trained teacher will always make a pastor, but not all pastors make good teachers. I want you to teach theology."

At the time, I was convinced the Lord had other ideas. Eventually it became clear that some of my father's prayers must have got through to the Almighty, but that was a lot further down the line.

Later that same year, I went back to the barracks just to complete the paperwork. I couldn't wait to collect my discharge papers. I didn't even wait for my army gratuity. It would have been around £8,000, enough to pay my school fees and buy a car and maybe even a plot of land. But I felt it would be a complete distraction to chase that money. I just wanted to get going with the work God had given me.

And when I left St Paul's Church, they wished me well and sent me off for all the world as though I was one of their chaplain officers.

ON THE SHOULDERS OF GIANTS

The Theological College of Northern Nigeria was way out, on the outskirts of Bukuru. With neither taxis nor transport, the only way to get there was to walk. It was worth it.

TCNN was built on a huge parcel of land. On one side was a hill that reached more than 300 feet above sea level. From there, you could see over most of Jos. From a flagpole on a roundabout flew the green, white, and green Nigerian tricolour. And in the middle of the college was a stone-built chapel, in the American Reformed style, with a spire stretching up tall and straight.

Most of the school was built of mud and stone, plastered and painted cream, and around the campus were dotted pine trees, oranges, mangoes, guavas, and ornamental trees.

All the classrooms had chalkboards and smooth cement floors and could seat at least thirty people. There was a basketball court, which put a grin on my face, and areas for lawn tennis and volleyball. The design was mainly American, but the college was interdenominational, with missionaries who were CMS, Lutheran, American Lutheran, Christian Reformed, and Baptist.

Not everyone in the family was convinced I would last the course. Many thought I would never cope without my princely soldier's salary. My older brother, Isaac, turned up to encourage me, and my mother came, bristling with caution, to remind me of a distant relative who had started out in seminary some two years earlier, brimming with good intentions, but had quit to get a cushier job as a prison officer. "We hope after a year you will not run away!" The sheer reproach of it dogged my footsteps.

Well, I could see where they were coming from.

There I was, without any allowance, nothing whatsoever. If I went to work for a local church, I could earn sixty Naira a month.

But sixty Naira would buy you just twelve loaves of bread. And there were catechists down the road, with wives and children, who somehow had to manage on that. As for me, I lived on whatever people would give me out of kindness. Sometimes they brought grain or soup or a carton of milk or Ovaltine. Sometimes nothing. I just had to learn to live and be content.

And to everyone's astonishment, I was content. I had peace, I had joy, and I was happy. I had a room of my own with a wardrobe. There was a bathroom and toilet and a water heater, so I could even have a warm bath.

I was assigned to two churches in Vom, to the east of Jos, which kept me busy each weekend. And God blessed it, as He had blessed the work in Lagos. The people took me into their hearts. The older women felt sorry for this little 22-year-old boy. When I went into town at the weekends, they would give me packets of this and that, with a look that said, "Pity this boy who has gone into the ministry and is going to die. Let's look after him."

My younger sisters also took pity on me. Anna would shop for me each month and Caroline, who was already in school, would send money. And term after term, my anxious mother would dispatch parcels of foodstuffs, because whatever the school was feeding us would never be enough.

I learned a lot over those four years of how to manage with little. By my third year, I was able to buy a bicycle of my own – a splendid Raleigh. It cost me 45 Naira. Such abundance was made possible by the governor of Plateau State awarding a scholarship to every student of theology. That scholarship had been backdated, so I was able to refund my father's money and still have a little left over.

The scholarship also covered my books. How wonderful! My small room was stuffed with devotionals such as Oswald Chambers', but the books that had the greatest influence on my life were biographies. I loved to read about Billy Graham, John Wesley, Charles Spurgeon, Samuel Ajayi Crowther, and D.L. Moody. But although these books made an impact, I found myself wondering how such stories could really be true.

Of them all, Samuel Ajayi Crowther intrigued me the most. Three times he had been sold into slavery. The third time he was being transported to the Indies, when his ship was intercepted by the Royal Navy. Captain Henry Leeke had been leading the drive to capture slave boats on the high seas, following abolition.

Leeke was a Christian who witnessed to these ex-slaves and Crowther was one of those who made a serious commitment to Christ. He was taken to Freetown in Sierra Leone, where he became an outstanding student and disciple of the missionaries. Soon, he began to evangelize the slaves.

This was at a time when nobody thought that a black man could have the intellectual capacity to read, learn, or be creative. Our brains were considered so underdeveloped as to be less than human. Crowther became a leader among the slaves. He was a preacher and teacher and translated hymns into his mother tongue, Yoruba.

Henry Venn was an Anglican clergyman and reformer from the Clapham Sect, along with William Wilberforce. He invited Crowther to join his ordination class to see how he got on. Soon, Crowther was teaching the class himself. Wilberforce and the other freedom campaigners took Crowther's exam sheets to the Bishop of London and asked, "Do you have any reason not to ordain this black man?"

So in 1843, the newly ordained Crowther returned to Freetown on the staff of the CMS and was asked to lead the missions in Nigeria. His ministry even caught the ear of Queen Victoria, and some fifteen years down the road, he returned to England to give his testimony to the queen and her consort, Albert.

Crowther informed them, "You have stopped the slave trade on the seas, but the only thing that will stop the slave trade in the hinterland is the gospel, accompanied by agriculture, education, commerce, and health." That was Crowther's proposal, which Queen Victoria accepted. Over twenty years, Crowther planted more than 200 churches. In 1864, he was consecrated again in England, but this time as bishop to the Western Equatorial Territories beyond the queen's dominions.

I read such stories of these amazing exploits and, frankly, they dismayed me. Every day, I sat down and said, "Lord, I have a bicycle, I have security, I have peace. I have everything, but what am I doing? I have not done one-hundredth of what these people did!"

I read the story of Bishop Festo Kivengere, the Billy Graham of Africa. Whenever he preached, crowds would gather. I almost despaired when I read that. "Oh God! My life is wasted! When will these things happen, Lord?"

I read of Wesley who went by horseback throughout England. He would preach and get thrown out, get doused in cold water and pelted with stones, and he would just keep going.

I said, "Lord, when will this happen to me? I don't just want to be in the ministry and get a stipend and retire and then die. Lord, You have used these people, and You can use me too. I know my life has been terrible, but I know Your will is exciting and adventurous. When will it start?"

Given the troubles that lay ahead, it would start soon enough. Meanwhile, I still had a good deal to learn, if I was to be able to stand.

I made good friends. Among them was Obed. Obed, like me, was from Plateau State, and we were about the same age, but that's where the similarity ended. I was a city type, and Obed was a village boy, strong in stature and character. Obed would step out with dirty shoes, and I would call him back to brush them. He would go out without a jacket and I would lend him mine, or drag him back to make him iron his trousers. He knew no better. Obed was a simple guy, but an honest Christian man. I liked him because he understood me.

Our school was rather legalistic. People believed that a good Christian should be well dressed, well behaved, obedient, and quiet. Well, that ruled me out! I can't sit quietly, that's the problem. I turned up in jeans and was noisy and wouldn't hesitate to speak my mind. The rest of the class considered me flippant, frivolous, and not yet converted. But Obed could see beyond that.

In our very first week of college, we found ourselves in crisis. Our third-year students were holding a demonstration against the school authorities. They considered the faculty had acted unjustly in promoting a student from year two to year three.

The third-year students took exception. They refused to sit in class with this junior when they had had to study for an extra year. And they tried to recruit all the other classes to go on strike.

When they came to our class to explain their case, I raised my hand and said, "I understand the injustice. But my bishop sent me to this school, and when my father paid my school fees, he didn't tell me to come here to examine what the faculty does or does not do. He paid my fees so that I could come here and study.

"I sympathize, but I want to state very clearly that even if my whole class is going on strike, I will not join." And others, including Obed, followed suit.

Obed said, "Ben, you're saying the truth, that we need to follow God and guard our calling." That's how we formed a team, with Nash and Iyasco, who also opposed the strike. And together we scuppered the whole thing. Our class refused to join the demonstration.

Obed, Nash, Iyasco, and I became four praying friends. Together we stood firm for what we believed. And we paid a price.

The hatred I endured over the next two years was palpable. There were people in school who refused to talk to me, and I accepted that as my lot. Whenever I would say anything, they would say, "No, no, no!" It was especially obvious on the football field. Sometimes I would get roughly tackled, until the spectators would call out, "No, that's wicked!"

But I didn't mind. I had asked God to make me humble and He had asked me to humble myself and follow Him. That prayer became a daily prayer in school. God was preparing us for bigger things.

§

Not all of my friends were Christians. I made a Muslim friend who owned acres of land nearby, where he grew tomatoes, cabbages, bananas, and sugar cane. He supplied tons of tomatoes right the way down to the south of Nigeria. His name was Zaki.

Zaki was much older than me, but we were about the same height. He was a lean and cheerful man whose teeth had long since abandoned ship, and who wore a grubby kaftan, rubber shoes, and a small circular crocheted hat. From the look of him, you would never know he owned the place.

I went to preach to him, and that's how we became close friends.

I had learned from Dominic Oke, who brought me to Christ, that God had given me a gift that I was scarcely aware of. Dominic was a quiet, ascetic person, and given much to prayer. I tried my hardest to be like him. But after a few months I said, "Brother Dominic, I don't think I can be a Christian. I've tried to be quiet, but it's not working. I want to talk!"

He said, "Ben, quiet is how God made me. I've been admiring you and hoping that I had your gifts."

I said, "Really, I can still be a Christian and be noisy?"

He said, "Yes!"

I have always found it easy to engage people in conversation. Dominic said, "That's why God called you. You can make friends easily. You will win people to Christ."

I believed him, and it was true. When I met people, I didn't engage immediately with Bible talk. We talked about everything else, and covered so much ground there was no turning back. They had to listen to me now.

When I preach, I tell stories of who I am and where I come from so people can see I'm a real human being. Then when I present them with a true and authentic gospel story, they have to make a decision. That's how I preach.

My Muslim friend Zaki told me, "Some of you people

come here just to preach. But you want me to be your friend. I like you."

He told me he was originally from Kano.

I grinned and said, "That's your problem, you people from Kano are thieves and crooks. You're too clever for Nigeria. You put stones in your baskets instead of onions. You're all traders. I'm afraid you might even try to sell me!"

He said, "You must be from Zaria."

I said, "Yes."

"Oh, you guys are all slaves!"

So we would tease one another mercilessly about every sour aspect of our ancestral past. And we went on teasing each other until finally he accepted me praying for him.

That first week I got to know Zaki and he got to know me. And when I turned up the second time, I was screaming, "Where is that man from Kano? Come here!"

And he would say, "Where is that boy from Zaria? Come here!"

And when the other farmers saw us at ease, they would let me talk to them. That's how I win friends for the gospel, especially Muslim friends.

One of our teachers at TCNN was a scholar in Islam. Jeremy Hinds was an Anglican who had learned the Koran backwards and knew how to evangelize Muslims. He even looked like a Muslim imam, with his beard and djellaba.

This tall, gentle man was an inspiration. He incarnated the gospel among the Muslims. He made friends with them and lived among them and gained their trust. When they found he could interpret the Koran, they were shocked. They invited him as a speaker into mosques all over West Africa. He never hid the fact that Jesus was the only way to God.

Jeremy saw my zeal for evangelism and recruited me into the ministry. He would send me to pray with the Muslims and I would stay with them for days. They would read their Koran and ask me whether I had a word for them. I was looking for adventure and said, "Lord, send me." And He did. In the end,

I became addicted. There was not a weekend where I would do nothing. I would always finish my college assignments and head out to the Muslims or my local church.

I wanted the whole world to know Jesus. Jeremy showed me we should open our hearts to win everybody to Christ: white or black, male or female, young or old, anyone, anywhere. Jeremy taught me that you will never win Muslims unless you first befriend them. The Muslims appreciate love and kindness and they respect integrity.

Back in the 1980s I was spending a lot of time among Muslim communities. I found the Muslims had a zeal to cleanse the land of profanity, immorality, and perversity. They thought they were acting on behalf of God. The mistake they made was to equate Christianity with American adverts that depicted half-naked women. The Muslims thought these were Christians! You have to live and work among the Muslims and get into their hearts before you can understand why they do what they do.

I have found so-called Christians whose unbelief troubles me more. They hold a form of religion, but have never experienced the living Jesus. They have not experienced the fulfilment of His promises in His word or His Spirit guiding their lives. They are religious, but have been short-changed of every benefit of that religion by preachers of the gospel, pastors, and professionals.

First Dominic, then Jeremy taught me how to win friends for the gospel. But some theologians, it seems, are less interested in winning friends than in overthrowing enemies.

In my second year in college we were taught liberation theology by a softly spoken white man who explored the idea that Christians, especially black Christians, should overthrow their oppressors.

Our teacher was Timothy, a tall American with a beard and glasses. But he was no rabble-rouser. He taught dispassionately about this most passionate of subjects and had a hatred for bloodshed.

Coming from a Reformed background he may have been holding onto a little guilt for the way the church had encouraged apartheid. And although our teacher was always calm, some of his students warmed just a little too much to this incendiary subject.

Eventually, Timothy fell ill and left. His position was taken over by a Nigerian who was a little less tempered in his approach.

We studied books and heard stories from South Africa, Latin America, and the US, and phrases like this: "When I feed the poor, they call me a saint, but when I ask why the poor are hungry, they call me a communist."[1]

Stirring stuff, but I could never swallow whole the message of that theology. I agreed that people needed to be liberated and set free from the shackles of slavery. But then what? If the gospel is not the end of the story, then one man's liberation would simply lead to another man's enslavement.

What captured my imagination was the story of South African Steve Biko. The account of this anti-apartheid campaigner had been written up by journalist Donald Woods, who escaped to Lesotho and finally England. If a white man could be so incensed by apartheid as to risk his life to oppose it, then why should I hate the white man?

When it came to question time, I had running battles in the classroom. Some of my colleagues simply could not understand why I, a black African, was not on the side of liberation theology. But even in my twenties, I could see it could lead to violence, and I wondered how such violence could be justified, and where it would end.

I wondered out loud how we could be sure that violent opposition was not born out of envy or hatred. What I saw around me was a failure of humanity, and that only the gospel had the cure for poverty and hatred. I had seen it, believed it, and experienced it for myself. The gospel alone could cure these things. And unless we worked for that gospel, people would arise, and you would not be able to stop them.

I could see bitterness and hatred taking root in the hearts of some of the students. But I knew that if I embraced

---

1   Dom Helder Camara, Archbishop of Recife, Brazil.

the same, I would never be able to preach to the white man, and that mattered to me.

Opinions began to polarize, which led to a shouting match in the classroom.

I raised a question: "I can see liberation theology setting people free, but setting people free for what? When the gospel sets free, it sets free totally."

The other students would hit back: "No, no, no! Ben, you have been bought over by the white men. You're a bootlicker. You don't understand, you've been born into privilege!"

I said, "Excuse me. With the privilege my father had, he helped pull people up. I've seen that."

Whoa! Nobody understood me. We were reading from James Cone, whose idea was that every means should be used to overthrow the wicked. But I came from a military background. I know what "every means" can do. One bullet is all it takes. You never know who will fire the next.

The gospel itself has a power against the forces of evil that is beyond anything physical. The gospel has no need of violence. People wonder, how did Wilberforce accomplish so much? Or Martin Luther King or Nelson Mandela?

That gospel had proven its power for me. I was not prepared to trade this gospel for a thing. I didn't want my gospel to be tainted; I wanted it pure and transparent.

Some began to say in class that white teachers should have no place in the school. And by now, most of the other white teachers were heading for home. I suspected the principal interest of some of the agitators was in taking over their positions.

Then what I suspected actually happened. If we stand in the place of judgment, God will judge us. If we fail to do better than those we remove, then we ourselves will be held wanting. Before long, the flowers and the trees that had graced the college died and the place became dirty and fell into disrepair. "Is this," I wondered, "liberation?"

The issue at the heart of liberation theology was oppression, so often born out of racism, which regarded those whose skin was a different colour as somehow less than human. And it was in my father's beloved Cambridge, of all places, that I had a run-in with racist attitudes.

§

It was the summer of 1980 and I was in Cambridge on placement, much to my father's delight. I joined the International Students' Outreach at Henry Martyn Hall. The way he had spoken about Cambridge, I imagined it a huge city full of cars. But everybody was on a bicycle, even the professors. I thought, "This is what my father wants me to come and see? Bicycles?"

We did outreach in a barn for overseas students who'd come to study English. In the evening we played music and did fun things to get them relaxed to hear the gospel. I was playing keyboard and guitar.

Mine was the only black face among 500 young kids. On my first day I was wearing a Nigerian outfit, and somebody asked me, "Are these your pyjamas?" Later, I was serving food and one of the other students told me outright, "You're not welcome here." Another, who was part of the leadership, later confided, "Many people are not comfortable with your presence here."

But look, racism is excess baggage that I can do without. Racism is the other person's problem. I choose not to allow it to be mine. There were too many other things to do. I was playing football and guitar, and in the drama group. The secretary in charge of outreach lent me a bicycle, so I was all over the place, volunteering for anything and everything.

One American girl, called Molly, asked, "Ben, don't you have culture shock?" She was petite, with dark hair and kept herself to herself. I had never heard of this thing. She had to explain it. I said, "Molly, my Father owns the whole world, and I have come to one part of my Father's world. Why would I have culture shock?"

My dad had raised us up with confidence and contentment and I never heard him resent a soul. The only thing my father resented was when you lied or were wicked to another person. That, he would rise up against. He would take us to the poorest of the poor in the village; he raised us to know that human beings were precious and did not choose their conditions.

When I was a child, he took me to meet a relative with leprosy. When I hung back, he pushed me: "Go and hug her!" I started to cry. I was afraid. Her hands had all gone and she hugged me and said, "My dear, I was a fine woman until I had leprosy." My father brought me up to have an accepting heart, and I treasure that.

He was especially respectful of the missionaries, more so than the colonials. He had been brought to Christ in the 1920s by the first missionaries in Zaria city. My mother was named Elsie after a wonderful missionary who came to stay with us.

But while all my parents' children had English first names, they all had Angas middle names. I chose to put my Angas name before my English name. So my classmates at TCNN knew me as Argak, rather than Benjamin.

By the time I went into the ministry I had come to realize that Benjamin was not actually an English name, but a biblical name, given by a father who loved his son, so I agreed to be called by the name he had given me.

§

One teacher who had a profound influence on my life at TCNN was Revd Harvey Kickover. He was a Christian Reformed pastor who taught us how to preach. He also repaired every technical thing in school, from the borehole to the basketball courts, and carried out most of the carpentry and electrical repairs. And he did all this while he looked after a wife who was paralysed, and their two children.

He would take his children to school, cook for his wife, and wheel her to chapel in her wheelchair. He never missed a class and he was never late for a thing – and he somehow always managed to return our scripts the day after he had collected them, properly marked. I will never forget his strength, his sacrifice, and his service.

It took a quarrel to make us friends. I liked to preach as

the Spirit led me, and I failed his class, because Revd Kickover insisted I should write everything down. That was what he taught, and I refused. I thought when he saw the power of the Spirit, he would be convinced. I was mistaken!

I wrote my sermon, then abandoned my written notes and preached from the heart.

He reprimanded me in front of the class. "Ben, you will have to do this again." He couldn't seem to appreciate that I was hot, that people liked my shouting!

"But, Sir, I've been preaching, and people have been crying and turning to Christ, so why are you asking me to do this?"

He said with a smile in a voice that was gentle but firm, "That's why you are in school. You've got to learn to do it well."

"Excuse me, the Spirit asked…"

"No," he said with a chuckle, "the Spirit didn't ask you to do that, Ben; you've got to do it this way…"

And when he'd finished, I followed him out of the class, still protesting. But he was insistent.

And he was right. It was a good learning process for me. The spirit that was within me must obey authority; it must obey school rules; it must follow the pattern of learning.

By the third year, I had realized that if you can't say it in ten minutes, you will never say it in thirty. And after half an hour, you will still be beating about the bush.

I am grateful to God today for what Revd Kickover taught me. Later I would encounter from their writings great preachers such as John Stott, Michael Green, David Watson, and David Pytches. And today, I both write and read my sermons and the Spirit still leads me. Although there are some sermons that are now written indelibly in my mind so I can get up and speak without having to write a thing.

§

It was at TCNN that my calling to active evangelism and rural ministry was confirmed. I joined the outreach and evangelism team and the Fellowship of Christian Students, and was assigned to two different churches. I helped my friends Nash and Obed in outreach for their COCIN church (Church of Christ in Nigeria), and they helped me with outreach for the Anglican church. And to cap it all, there was basketball and football. God is good!

Not only was life exciting, but wherever I went, people became Christians. And the lives of those who were already Christians were lit up with a fire and enthusiasm for the faith.

The schools outreach assigned me to secondary schools around Jos, and I found I could engage with these young students and communicate easily. I played my little guitar and preached and the fellowships were growing.

One of our staff called me to one side and said, "Ben, you have gifts in evangelism but you also have a gift for teaching." I wrote it down in my journal and remembered what my dad had said about becoming a teacher. He might just have been right…

Today, I still keep a journal of what God says to me. Going over my journals confirms whether my dreams are just fantasies or God speaking and giving direction to my life.

When I read back some of these entries, I just laugh. "This is silly; this didn't work; but this one – this was God." After many years, I can see where the Lord has led me, and where I am on track. I can hold on to that.

As I read, I see passages of Scripture that keep coming back, such as Matthew 6:33, which God first highlighted to me in 1978: "Seek first the kingdom of God and His righteousness, and all these things shall be added to you" (NKJV). From seminary to this day, that portion of Scripture has kept reappearing.

At times, getting guidance can be like panning for gold. You need to sift the dirt and the stones to get any nuggets. You need to be patient and persistent. But in it all, my calling was starting to emerge. I had a heart for God and the desire to evangelize, and that had been crystallized by the recognition of others.

By my third year in seminary, classmates were coming to my room and looking to me for counsel and direction. And I was learning to take care neither to mislead nor to misguide them.

THAT VILLAGE GIRL!

By my second year at college, in 1979, I became convinced that I needed a wife. The last thing I wanted was to begin my ministry wifeless. I didn't want to have to put on a clerical collar and start running around after a woman. My friends Nash and Obed had the same problem.

So, we went to the mountain near the theological college to find a place where we could shout to the Lord without troubling a soul. I bellowed, "Lord God! Please, Lord! I want a wife who will help me with the ministry. Oh God, give me a wife! Please help me!"

I needed a father's wisdom, so I went to spend some time with my dad. To my surprise, he raised the subject before I could open my mouth. He said: "I want you to swear to God that you will never beat your wife."

I laughed, "Dad, I don't even have a girlfriend! What's your problem?"

But he was determined to put me on oath, so I had to swear that I would never, ever beat my wife.

When I went back to the seminary, I talked this over with some of my closest friends. If I had important things to share, then I would go to Obed. When I told him about the conversation, Obed's eyes widened, and he said, "Wow! Why did your father say that?"

I really didn't know. But I began to wonder.

Another weekend, I travelled to where my mother was working and tentatively asked her if my dad had ever beaten her.

"Whoa!" she said.

My mother had been an only child. For many years she had been treated like a queen in her parents' house. She was hard-working and capable, so everyone respected her. She was not accustomed to being ill-treated. But she had left my father for a time, to stay with her mother, while I remained with my father.

I went back and told my friend. "Obed, this is what I discovered."

And Obed said to me, "Your dad must be a good man. He doesn't want you to repeat his mistake."

Subsequently, there were many things my dad shared with me as a warning, so that I could learn from his experience and be spared from repeating his mistakes. By now my father was older and more relaxed. He had lost some of his sternness. I called him Baba.

Baba used to love boiled chicken soup, with onions, carrots, potatoes, and, of course, very hot peppers. We would eat the soup with a spoon and tear at the tough, wild chicken with our fingers and then wipe them on our napkins. And we would relax and talk about the events of the day.

As we were eating one day, my father put on his teacher's face and said to me, "Ben, be careful with women, be careful with alcohol, and be careful with church money."

I said, "Baba, I'm born again!"

He said, "Yes I know, but you're going into the ministry. And when you visit homes, if they know what you like, then that is what they will give you. If they know that you like a bottle of beer, they will bring you two. And if you take the two and visit another house and take two more, then in that third house you will divulge information that you really shouldn't, and you will have betrayed the trust of the people."

He continued, "The church is a trap. The moment you betray the trust of anybody who has poured out information in confidence, then your ministry is dead and buried. You may never recover, because the story of what you did will go ahead of you until you die."

I wasn't expecting this conversation. I went cold. I couldn't eat. And Baba continued.

"As for money," he said, "you will see a lot of money, and there's no man who's not been tempted with money. So if you make up your mind early not to be interested in church money, then you will save yourself and your ministry.

"If you are not interested in money, then you will be able to check those who want to take church money. If you attain the position of always checking them, they will respect you. Don't show interest in money. It will ruin your preaching."

Sometimes I just came to see what Baba would say on a subject, and he would always give me wise words.

"As for women," he said, "you are younger. You will love women, but more women will love you than the ones you love. If you're not clever, your ministry might end in no time at all with women."

"No," I said, "I left that in the world, and the Lord will save me."

But Baba shook his head. "Yes, but you are in the world where women are, and they have not left you! And in the church, there are 100 people with 200 eyes. You don't know what they're thinking, you don't know what they're saying, so be careful. Always be careful with women."

I shared that counsel with my friends at seminary and they said, "Your dad is a great man. We wish we had dads who would counsel us with words of wisdom."

So I learned to value my father's advice and enjoy my visits to listen to him.

One day, he decided to find a wife for me.

He showed me two girls at different times. Both were beautiful, but they were not for me. I said, "No, Baba." And now they are married to my friends!

Baba was worried for me until I brought him Gloria. He loved Gloria at first sight. But as for me, I was just indifferent.

I was in my third year at college when Gloria turned up. Gloria was one of only two girl students so, inevitably, she became the centre of attention, though she seldom welcomed the fact. She was certainly not the centre of my attention. She was not my type. Gloria was a typical country girl who really didn't want to be noticed, a simple village girl who was so naive she didn't even know how to make herself up. At least theological college ought to be a safe place for a country girl like this.

Gloria introduced herself to the class and said she was from Numan in Adamawa State and the Lord had called her to work with women and children. I wasn't really listening. Instead, I made fun of her. "So you're this village girl? What brings you here? How many women and children will you find in this place?"

But Gloria gave as good as she got. She would turn to my friend Obed, a village boy himself, and say, "Look at this Lagos chap! He's dressed for a party!"

She took the teasing well. She would laugh and laugh. Gloria didn't smile with many men. She was a country girl. Mess with Gloria at your peril.

The only other girl was Anna, who was in my class. Anna trusted me and we became friends. She, Obed, and Nash had been classmates in secondary school. Anna and Nash were in my singing group. Nash played the guitar while Anna would sing.

Anna was small, trim, bright, black, and gifted, and seemed older than her age. She was a sharp talker, completely unlike Gloria. Naturally, Anna and Gloria shared quarters and became firm friends.

Then Nash fell in love with Anna. Nash was a six-foot-tall basketball player, neat and sleek and very handsome. Even today, when my own hair is fleeing the scene, Nash still has his Afro. He never came out without his shoes polished and his shirt ironed. He was very particular, which he got from his father, a schoolteacher. Nash was like an English gentleman. He would take his time, study, and choose his words carefully. He was meticulous.

But right now, this careful man was looking for help in choosing his words. Nash needed the assistance of a smart city boy to show him what to say. So I coached Nash in how to court Anna.

"If you like her, go and tell her. Take her out!"

"Really?"

"Honestly, Anna is a pretty girl. She's very intelligent. If you marry her, I will be very happy.

"Anna is a beautiful girl, truly," I continued, "but that's not what you're looking for. Tell her you have prayed and that you're certainly not in the business of just making boyfriend and girlfriend. Tell her that you love the Lord and you're looking for somebody with whom you can share this ministry. Tell her you believe that she's the right person for you. Tell her the truth."

My dad had warned me, "Never say to a girl, 'I love you,' unless you mean it. Never tell a girl a lie, because you might end up marrying a lie."

However, just to ease the process a little, I suggested Nash take Anna out in his father's car and head for a scenic location to make his proposal. He should definitely go and propose by the dam.

But Nash, who never acted in haste, took his time. It took him a couple of months of careful coaching and encouragement by me to get round to it. That was OK. It gave me time to prepare Anna too.

When I saw other fellows showing an interest, I would say to Anna, "I notice this man coming around you, I'm not happy about that one."

I made sure that I discouraged every single guy she was thinking about. Anna trusted me and began to feel secure enough with Nash to let him take her out. And when he came back, he announced, "Ben, I did it! She agreed! And we prayed."

Nash asked Obed and me to be his best men at the wedding in the college. But Nash was stupid enough to tell Anna that I had coached him into courting her.

Anna raged. She said, "You crook! You old crook! You city boy! You Lagos boy!" It took her a while to calm down.

I arranged the dance at the wedding reception. There was only one problem. For many of these Christian types, dancing was a sin. Gloria was upset with me. She told Anna, "This guy is not a Christian!"

But Anna put her right. "Believe me, Ben is a committed Christian. Don't believe what you are seeing."

Now they were trying to fix me up. But there was only one girl left and I made it clear to everyone that I was just not interested. "Gloria might throw a kitchen pot at me one day. You never can tell with these country girls."

Gloria got stuck into everything. She was in the Fellowship of Christian Students, the choir, the drama group, my musical group, and also the hospital outreach. I was coordinator of missions, so I got to see her often. But the question of interest didn't even arise, because I had a girlfriend at Jos University who visited me often. Her name was Deborah. And when Deborah jilted me, I fell in love with another girl, Taaziyi. I introduced Taaziyi to everybody, and they got to like her. These girls were far more stylish than Gloria and, believe me, they were nice Christian girls.

I brought one of these girls to meet my grandmother. I told Bilhatu, "We have prayed, and I want to get married."

Bilhatu said nothing, but she went into her bedroom and prayed, and then she called me in. She said, "Ben, that's not your wife."

When I came out, I didn't say a thing to the girl. We drove back to Jos. Three months later, she jilted me.

Two nice Christian girls and both of them walk out on me! It could mean one thing and one thing only. God was calling me to celibacy. I would be a priest who would never marry. That was clearly God's plan and purpose.

So I started writing to the schools of celibacy. They sent me a form, and I kept it on my table. I planned to take it to the bishop and tell him I was convinced marriage was not for me, and I would need his blessing to go and train to be a celibate and come back for his ordination.

One day, Obed and I were having a heart to heart about marriage. His heart had just been broken, and after we prayed, he informed me, "I think Gloria would make a good wife for you."

I couldn't believe my ears. "Are you stupid?! You think the girl is foolish? She knows all my girlfriends and she knows I am a city boy, and she is not interested in any city boy and she wouldn't agree. Any case, she's too local for me. She wouldn't fit in."

And that was that.

And then I was paying a visit to the married hostels and a little girl, aged about five, came running over. She was Gloria's neighbour, so Gloria was there too, and this little girl said, "Uncle Ben, when you marry Gloria, I will be your flower girl!"

Gloria wasn't happy. She walked away. Everybody else fell about laughing. I said to the little girl, "Why did you say that?"

She said, "I just know." That's all she said. She was in Gloria's class at Sunday school.

A member of my tribe, who was a student pastor at the church where my mother worshipped, came to my room and said, "Gloria is your wife."

I wasn't best pleased. I said, "Where do you people get these ideas? You're stupid. Don't push me into something that will end in disgrace."

Does that sound harsh? You won't think so when I tell you what I had just witnessed. One of our schoolmates had recently proposed to Gloria, and Gloria took great offence. The whole world bore witness to that offence!

The unfortunate student proposed to her at night after she had been to the library and was walking to her room in the dark. She put him right, marched home, dropped off her books, then marched back all the way from her single person's hostel, in search of this boy. And when she found him, she double-underlined her message, so this wretched boy could be left in no doubt, no doubt at all. It was civil war that night. Gloria shouted the place down: "Where is he? I will teach you a lesson today!"

All of this was close to my room, so when I heard this shouting, I drew my curtain and turned off my light. I didn't want anybody calling on me to come and settle the issue.

Gloria was raising a hullabaloo. She was yelling at the top of her voice, "Come and fight me! I'm gonna fight today! I'm going to teach you a lesson. I'm going to show you how! You're going to see the hell out of me! Who do you think you are? Do you think I've come here to look for a husband? What do you think of yourself?" And all of this was in public at nine o'clock at night. Eventually some people calmed her down sufficiently to escort her well away.

And I laughed it all off with Obed. "Look at the wild creature you're asking me to fall in love with! She might beat me up one day! See what I told you about country girls? Village girls will fight you in the middle of the market and they don't care. Civilization is not part of their kettle of fish. They will tear your clothes off and you will be the one in the wrong. I don't want this kind of thing."

Some of us boys are too vain to learn the lessons that wisdom tries patiently to teach us. When another boy got too affectionate, Gloria wiped him off, right then and there in the street. She had no guile. She said, "Look at you, with your reading glasses. You can't even see properly! Go and look for a wife elsewhere."

Propose to Gloria and the shockwave would shatter every window around the campus.

§

Our drama team was in the final day of rehearsal for a home-grown play that we would be presenting to the university. It was a cautionary tale about a Christian brother who backslid, left the faith, and went off with women and drink, who left his wife pregnant before his life ended badly. This was the kind of entertainment we used to put on in those days.

Gloria was the wife in question. In our play, she fell in love with a Christian brother who sang in the choir, while she was in the women's Sunday school. It was an hour-long presentation; it was Thursday night and we were set to perform on Saturday, when Gloria sat herself down and declared she was pulling out.

I said, "Come on, you're the lead actor: why would you say that?"

But she wouldn't say. Not a word. For two long hours of us trying to wheedle it out of her, Gloria would not explain why. We had booked the hall at the university, laid on a bus, and got everything ready. But all Gloria would say was, "I'm not going to do it."

Everybody pleaded with her. I said nothing, but inside, I was fuming. *This girl is an absolute disgrace. These rural girls have no respect, no civilization. She is a disgrace to the whole college, a disgrace even to me!* But I didn't say a word.

I was the elected Students' Union president. It was a few months before my ordination and I didn't want so much as a whiff of scandal around me, so I sat there burning inside. *Who did she think she was?*

Well, her father was the Crown Prince of the town of Rugange in Adamawa. His own father had been the first colonially installed king in 1946. That meant Gloria was a princess, who thought she could say whatever she liked.

Eventually, the drama president shrugged and said, "Well, we'll have to tell the university the drama is off." And that is how we closed the meeting.

I was boiling. I went and sat down and wrote Gloria a stinking letter. When I'm angry, my English is good. The vocabulary was well chosen: "You village princess, you think you are above yourself, you're holding us all to ransom. I'm also a prince, but look at how I present myself to the school. You can't humble yourself, you have forced the drama to a standstill. You're no good for anything!" I went on for two long pages and made sure Gloria got the letter by giving it to someone who dropped it round to her that same night.

So Gloria went to Anna and showed her the letter. And both of them sat down and cried.

It was the following morning and not yet 6 a.m., and I was in the middle of my quiet time. College had taught me to be an early riser. My room was just big enough for a bed and a wardrobe, my reading desk, and a little sofa. On the wall was a poster, "I can do all things through Christ who strengthens me." This was one of those days when that would come in handy.

I was still in my pyjamas when there was a rap at the door. It was Anna. Her headgear was roughly tied. I could tell at a glance she had come to fight. She was a determined lady. I'm sure her husband, Nash, had tried to discourage her, but Anna was in no mood to listen. Ordinarily, Nash himself would have come to say, "Ben, I think you've got this wrong." But Anna's face said it all. She was raging.

She pressed in.

"Who do you think you are? What do you think of yourself? You made us cry last night. How can you write such a nasty letter? You're not even a Christian! I used to think you were a Christian…" She went on.

I said, "Anna, cool down!"

"I will not cool down! How can you describe my friend like that? Why do you say these kinds of things?"

I protested that the letter hadn't been intended for Anna, but she would have none of that.

"She showed me! We're friends." Gloria had been chief bridesmaid at Anna's wedding. They shared a lot.

"Ben, you don't understand this girl. Do you think she's mad? You've misjudged her. You're wrong, you're wrong!"

So Anna went on until I considered she had cooled down. But I misjudged that too. I said, "Anna, OK, I'm very sorry." I tried to hug her.

She said, "Don't touch me, *don't* touch me! You've done a terrible thing, you're a disgrace!"

Anna was so convinced. Even though she offered no plausible explanation for Gloria's behaviour, she managed to persuade me that I was badly in the wrong. She said, "You don't know what Gloria is going through." But whatever that was, she wouldn't say.

All Anna would say was, "You had better ask her!"

Perhaps if I went in private, Gloria would explain… "OK, I'll go and apologize. Let me follow you now."

But Anna cut me down: Gloria was going to the market. Besides, she *really* wasn't ready to see me.

When Anna had gone and I had recovered my composure, I began to prepare what I would say.

It was then the uncomfortable truth dawned on me.

It came as a shock.

Deep down, there was something I knew, if only I would face it and admit it.

The truth is, everything I wanted in the woman I was going to marry, was already there in Gloria. Everybody else could see it. The only reason I kept pushing that away was the sheer terror that Gloria would do to me what she had done to others, and I would get thrown out of school and then I would be dead and buried – no ordination, no career, all of it ended because of a girl.

I was more afraid of her reaction than of the truth that was dawning in my heart.

The truth was, I loved that girl! That very morning I had been dragged kicking and screaming to face the truth.

But how was I to tell her how I felt without igniting a civil war, if her feelings weren't the same towards me?

I had every reason to be afraid.

In 1979 I had been posted to Numan for teacher training. This was Gloria's home town, and I had to walk past her older sister's house to the church where I served. As was my way, I made friends with everybody in the street; every family knew me. I would take my guitar and the children would follow me and sing and dance. The children of Gloria's oldest sister became close to me.

A couple of years later I got to know her family. Gloria was away at the time on postings in Denmark and Germany for her Lutheran church. We travelled back to school together, but I was careful with this crazy girl, because I had seen her temper on full display. Even in the taxi, she had scared me. She had bought some roasted meat that she didn't like. She was so angry that she had thrown it at the seller because she thought he had cheated her. I pretended not to see it.

I found out something that caused me great alarm. You see, Gloria's nickname was Petrol. *Petrol.* Her older brother called her Petrol, and she even answered to that. If you want to burn and utterly destroy a thing – and fast – you use petrol. She was named for her hot temper and short fuse and her ability to flame out any human being – except her mother.

Gloria would stand up for her rights, and the rights of everyone in the house. You couldn't cheat anybody when Gloria was around. She would face up to anyone. Fear was not something Gloria possessed. She was always with her mother, looking after her business, and she would never let anyone cheat her. Her father, being a prince, had married other women. So Gloria fought her mother's battles with her dad.

Her mother had helped raise this firestorm. She had told her, "You're this black, ugly girl!" So Gloria could never believe she was pretty, and if you told her she was, she would not believe you. Gloria grew up ready to stand alone by herself because nobody else in the world would stand up for her. She was ready to fight the world and she was ready to fight you too!

What was I letting myself in for?

§

I finally had to admit to myself that when I wrote that letter to Gloria, I was actually writing it to myself. I was trying to persuade myself by any means possible that Gloria was not the one.

So what on earth should I do?

I might have done an outstanding job advising Nash on the affairs of the heart, but what I did next betrayed every sign of desperation.

That evening, I gave it the full peacock. I wore a flowing, bright blue, brand-new shirt, blue jeans, and a pair of black polished leather-soled sandals I had bought in England. I was clean-shaven and liberally aftershaved, and I crowned the look with my silver chain and necklace. Eat your heart out, James Brown.

When I turned up, Gloria was reading. Her room was neat and tidy, as ever, and she was wearing a long yellow dress with short sleeves and well-plaited hair.

I tried to make small talk; I came close and said, "What are you reading?" But I wasn't even listening to her answer. After a couple of minutes, she pulled her chair back and got up and walked into her bedroom. I stepped back, ready to make a run for it. She came out with the letter: "Why did you write this to me?"

I had to play for time. I stepped forward and said, "Let me see, did I write this?" I flicked the first and second pages and saw my name and said, "Yes, yes, I did."

I needed to get myself together; I didn't know where this was heading. This felt like a court case without a jury, just me, Gloria, and God. As for God, His mercies never fail, but Gloria was primed ready to explode. So I put my hands in my pockets, affecting nonchalance, and took a step back.

What came out of Gloria's mouth was not what I'd expected. "Why did you think of me this way to write this letter?" I fell quiet. I had wanted to ask her why she had pulled out of the play and then, when she'd given a reasonable explanation, to make my apology. But nothing was going as planned.

I quickly said a prayer and cut to the chase. "I need to tell you the truth. I wrote it because I love you."

She said, "*What!*"

I took another step back. She turned around again and went into her room, searching no doubt for some blunt instrument to use as a weapon. I opened the front door and ran for dear life.

§

Maybe she would come out and start screaming, and I would be held responsible, because I had been in her room. I certainly didn't want to be found in my own room. So I ran all the way to Obed's and said, "Quickly, switch off your light just in case this mad woman comes after me."

"Which mad woman?"

"Gloria."

"What did you do?"

"I told her I love her."

"Are you *sure*?"

"Yes."

"But she's ruined our drama, she has damaged everything!"

Obed stroked his chin and said, "OK, let's make tea and drink it and I won't turn on the light." Sensible man.

I stayed in Obed's room until 1:30 a.m. All the time, I was waiting for Gloria to turn up and start yelling, but I was spared, at least for that evening.

§

The following morning the inevitable happened. Gloria sent over a note saying she wanted to see me. Quickly, I needed to find some excuse to hold off this confrontation, so I decided I would have to look like a mad man when I saw Gloria.

I had a Boys' Brigade meeting. That was it! That was my straw and I grasped it. I made the snap announcement that today we were going to paint all our equipment.

I planned it all in my mind. I would have paint all over me. I would not give Gloria a moment to say a thing. I would go to her and ask her for soap to help me wash. Then I would scrub and scrub. But as soap alone would not wash off the paint, I would ask her for some kerosene. Then when I was trying my hardest to scrub myself clean, I would request a cup of tea. That would keep her busy for a few moments more. So I would scrub and drink, scrub and drink, and then I would tell her I would see her later in the evening, and then I would run away. That was how I would put off the inevitable.

And for some reason known only to Him, God honoured my plans.

I said to Gloria, "How are you today? I saw your note. What are you doing later in the morning?"

I didn't give her time to say a word. "This paint! It's terrible! It's not washing off. You have some soap? Oh, it's still not washing. Do you have some kerosene from the stove? Can I have a cup of tea, please?" And I gulped down the tea and left.

Whatever Gloria was going to say, I was just not ready to listen. I was so sure she was going to say no.

Later in the evening, I came again. This time with a different plan. Gloria was reading again at her desk. I came close to her to see what she was reading, then a little closer, until she could feel me leaning over her. I told myself, "If this girl is saying no, then she will push back." But she did not do a thing so I arranged to come and see her again after the Sunday service. Then I quickly kissed her on her cheek and ran away.

Not a word. Oh, was I encouraged! I had played for time and it had paid off. She didn't slap me, she didn't say no, she didn't fight, and I had come out of it alive!

But still, I couldn't take a thing for granted. So I didn't go back to my room, just in case she decided this boy who had given her a peck on the cheek should be brought down a peg or two! So I hid out in Obed's room that evening. And I told him all about it.

"Do you know, I gave her a kiss on the cheek and she didn't say anything! She didn't say no!"

It was too much for Obed. "You're lying!"

So we hatched a plot to try to prevent the very real possibility of open warfare breaking out. Obed and I agreed to go together to her room at mealtime. And we roped in Iyasco as both our excuse and our reinforcement.

Iyasco and Gloria had studied Hebrew together, so that would be our diversionary tactic. The Hebrew conversation went well. There was still no sign of pending hostilities. So I made some jokes and, to my surprise, Gloria even laughed. Inwardly, I was beginning to buzz. I was saying, *Thank You, Lord; thank You, Lord; thank You, Lord! I truly am loving this girl now. Father, please help me!*

Eventually we said we would have to be leaving and Gloria turned to me and asked, "Are you leaving too?" That was my cue! And that was how it began.

When I visited Gloria again in her house, with Nash and Anna in tow as bodyguards, she was comfortable and at ease. So I started to tell my friends, who encouraged the relationship.

By now Gloria hadn't said no, and she hadn't said yes to being my girlfriend. But she had let me come close and let me hold her hand, and she had let me introduce her to my friends.

But when it came to preparing for my graduation and ordination, I made a diplomatic blunder. Shortly before I left for the ordination, I walked her round the football field and asked her to marry me. Almost. Well, it was a hint – a strong hint. I said, "I'd like to introduce you to my father."

Well, that could mean only one thing!

She didn't respond, so I continued. (Obviously, I had to spell it out to this village girl.) "I want to marry you. Would you marry me?"

Would you believe it? She walked away.

When it came to my ordination, I didn't know whether Gloria would come at all. And I wasn't about to ask her. I'm telling you, you didn't handle Gloria with kid gloves, you needed asbestos gloves.

Anyway, I almost didn't make my ordination myself. I would have missed it, had it not been for the intervention of Bishop Titus Ogbonyomi.

Bishop Titus was even smaller than me, but he made up for it in demeanour. He was a retired lieutenant-colonel, and a director-general of the chaplaincy of the Nigerian army.

He was brisk and firm and barked his orders. He had no time for time-wasters. But amazingly, he had time for me. I was one of the few people who could make him laugh. I like to laugh, and when I laughed, he laughed too. He had been following my annual reports from the college and was satisfied with my progress.

It was the bishop who set the date and venue for the ordination retreat. He made an exception to fit me in even while I was still finishing my exams.

I signed off my last paper on a Friday and took a taxi to the ordination retreat, turning up at the door at 7 p.m.

"Have you finished your exams?" he asked.

"Yes, Sir."

"Good. I've told them not to take any photographs until you arrive."

Favour from the bishop, and favour from Gloria too, and way beyond any favour I could expect! On her own and all by herself, Gloria had made cookies for my ordination. She showed up with them at the reception outside the church.

Despite this miraculous signal from on high, Gloria refused to have her picture taken with me. Everyone else was taking photographs with me, but not her. Gloria didn't care for photographs. She wasn't that type and I knew better than to push it. She kept her distance and served other people.

But when we were coming back from the ordination, she gave me another clue. Instead of taking public transport, she returned with me in my friend's car. I escorted her to her hostel and she seemed happy and pleased. So I thought I'd stretch my luck – not too far, just a little. She had conceded this walk, so we discussed many things. And I was left with… hints, just hints. I grabbed on to each like a drowning man to driftwood.

What was her fear? I don't know.

What did Gloria see in me? I couldn't be sure, but she had led me to believe it was something. She later told me she considered me to be intelligent and liked my sense of humour. That made me feel good, because I had never considered myself that way. She said I was loving and caring. And she told me that even before I had made up my mind to fall in love with her.

That was in her first year, when she had a motorbike accident. Gloria had bruised her knee and was limping. She couldn't go to class because she couldn't sit still for any length of time. I went during the break to see her. She was trying to make tea, had boiled some eggs, and was limping from her room to the parlour. I said, "No, no, no! You sit down. I'll do that for you." So I got her the boiled egg and the tea and made sure she was comfortable.

She said, "Your wife will enjoy you serving her!" This was way before I had any feelings for her. She told me I had a good heart.

Gloria had never had a boyfriend. She wasn't naturally affectionate or romantic, but as you got close to her, she would open up a little. But if she ever wanted a hug, she really didn't know how to show it.

What I liked about her was that she was a definite girl. She had stood up to all thirty members of the drama group. I liked that. I said, "This girl is tough!"

I admired her and I still do. She was straight. She would never tell a lie. What you see is what you get.

§

Graduation followed ordination in quick succession. My graduation in 1982 was a huge occasion. I was in a gown and black mortar board, but we were far too religious to throw them in the air. My close friends came, along with my family, and of course my mum and dad.

My father was dressed like a king, in a brand-new, flowing white gown. It was embroidered front and back, with a matching kaftan. These things were expensive! He was given a front seat and sat there beaming. My mother was gaily dressed, with matching headgear and wrapper of shiny silver, oxblood, and blue. Her blouse was white, shiny, and dotted with stones. And to set off the ensemble, she wore fine white shoes.

But beneath that gay apparel, my mama carried her worries, because graduation meant her Benji would have to go out to work.

She was asking: "Do you know the people you are going to work with?"

"Mama, I don't know."

"Benji, at the church you are going to meet different people, you be careful now! Are you sure?"

"Mama, I'm sure. I survived school for four years; I'm going to do this."

"You sure you want to go into the church? You could go to school and teach young people."

"Mama!"

"Ben, you're not even married!"

Well, it wasn't for want of trying.

I was still waiting for Gloria's answer.

At my graduation too, Gloria made more cookies – plenty this time to serve to my guests. She even sent some to my room. But still she wouldn't meet my mother and father. My parents had heard from different sources that I was trying to woo this girl, but they didn't know for sure, because I hadn't officially told them. They must have been as bewildered as I was.

This woman was keeping us all waiting. And that wait continued. Meanwhile, although she hadn't said yes to me, she had said yes to another. And that gave me hope. Let me explain.

My grandmother, Bilhatu, had fallen ill with cancer. The students were visiting patients in the hospital. We were all boys, with one exception. My grandmother looked at the only girl in our group and asked, "Are you also in the pastor's school?"

She said, "Yes."

Bilhatu asked, "What's your name?"

"Gloria," the girl replied.

And my grandmother, who had never seen this girl before, said these words: "Will you marry us?" I heard it with my own ears. And so did my schoolmates who were visiting the hospital.

And Gloria said, "Yes."

My grandmother frightened me. When she prayed, God answered. If only Gloria would answer me too.

Graduation did tie up a few loose ends. The hostility some of the other students had shown from those early days when I had defied their call to strike had simmered on to the end. But they were in a minority. Whatever I did in school, I threw myself into it wholeheartedly. I pursued excellence and was popular. I was the driver, the one operating the grass-cutting machine, and a star at football and basketball. I had contested student elections and won, and somehow still managed to come top in the exams.

At graduation, some of the students came over and said, "Ben, I want to ask your forgiveness. I hated you for years." But all this helped prepare me for what was to follow. By the time I finished school, I was twenty-six. A man was being made. I had learned to stand alone with my head clear about what I believed and my heart free from bitterness. It is still my joy to do that.

Today, my friend Obed is the vice president of the Church of Christ in Nigeria and has a doctorate. Nash is in Arizona, and a senior counselling manager at a university.

Iyasco was killed at his church in Kaduna by rioting Muslims. They murdered him and burned his church.

That fire consumed everything, except his Bible, which he held onto right till the end. Although the edges were scorched, Iyasco's Bible remained intact. My friend had died in his early fifties, and I remember thinking at the time, "It's coming close."

BREAKING THE MOULD

Along with my ordination came my first rejection. Bishop Titus Ogbonyomi intended to post me to a large church in Gusau, in the north-west. I was twenty-six and the church made it clear to the bishop in no uncertain terms that to send them this inexperienced boy would be nothing less than an insult. I got my letter of appointment on the Saturday morning, and the news that the church had rejected me that same afternoon.

It was a bit of a shock. I was determined to go anyway and give them the chance to get to know me.

But the bishop and the provost scratched their heads overnight and came up with a better plan.

There was a young man who had just been posted to St Andrew's Church in Zaria who was having second thoughts about God's calling. He had left the ministry entirely. That meant there was a vacancy, but not necessarily for me.

St Andrew's was looking for a traditional vicar from England, so the bishop asked them whether they would put up with me for a while, until they could find the proper vicar they were seeking.

I was dispatched to St Andrew's on a sale-or-return basis in 1982.

St Andrew's, Zaria, had once been a small colonial brick courthouse that would seat about 100. It was no longer big enough to dispense justice, but it was big enough for a church. The town had outgrown it. The courthouse had plenty of land, which was donated to the church in exchange for a more modern courthouse to be built on another site on the same road.

What marked out this former place of law as a place of grace was its thick coat of white paint and two crosses outside and within.

The congregation of St Andrew's was almost as white as its brickwork. One white vicar had left and they had been trying to recruit another for nearly three-and-a-half years. I was to be their first black pastor, a stopgap, until they could find the right person, and then I would be moved on.

Every registered member of the church was older than me. Zaria was an academic city, boasting a university, polytechnic, aviation school, teaching hospital, veterinary research institute, and the military school where I had trained. More than half the congregation were professors.

I shared my testimony and preached the gospel. I brought in my guitar, which raised a few eyebrows, held concerts at Harvest Festival, and led a youth ministry. Family was the key. We looked after children and young people, so parents could be assured they had found the right place to bring their families. We used James Dobson's "Focus on the Family" videos for teaching.

We reached out to the poor, the orphans, and the sick, and before long, the congregation had grown in numbers until the cosy courthouse was straining at the seams. We were having to think about building a new church. Life was bubbling!

§

Not everyone was overjoyed at the change. There were some who felt the church had become rowdy. They grumbled that the sermon was dragging on beyond fifteen minutes, and that the service had been stretched out to an unendurable hour and a half.

But we were gaining young families! I was doing baptisms and confirmation classes and the Bible studies had grown so large we had to break into groups.

In the first five months, our numbers went up by about forty per cent. This excited the church – at least some of them. After my six months' probation was up, they went back to the bishop and said, "We think we've found our vicar."

After a year and a half the church had doubled from eighty to 160, exceeding its capacity. And it continued to grow, so that by the second year, the old courthouse was choked with people. When we reached 200, we had to build benches outside for the overflow. By now, more Nigerians were coming to the services. Along with them came even more academics from the university.

Somehow, by God's grace, senior members who were older than me submitted to my leadership and were putting themselves forward for training for the ministry.

Numbers just kept on growing. And nobody was more surprised than me. I had been fine as a boy soldier, leading younger boys, but I never thought older people would look up to me for leadership. I was afraid. Fear fell on me every day, as these people came to me to say, "Vicar, what should we do about this?" I lived in constant fear as I offered my counsel. I was unsure about my own advice, and unnerved when I found people were actually following it.

What I feared the most was misleading them. I was always begging God, "Please assure me, please tell me if I'm doing the right thing!" And He never would!

It was afterwards, when events showed we had made the right decision, that I would say, "Thank You, Lord!" God was leading me more by reassurance, than by assurance in advance. I felt Him laughing at me and saying, "You're on track. You're doing the right thing."

Among my church members were commandants, colonels, and the Commissioner of Police. Many of the elite were coming to St Andrew's and I needed to find a way to speak into these people that would transform them.

If these movers and shakers became Christians and could be persuaded to work for justice, then how many poor people would get saved? If these leaders could be persuaded for God, then the influence of the gospel would flow throughout the land.

So I got persuading, and somehow, God helped me to motivate them. I believed what this church needed was teaching from the Scriptures, so I went back to my lessons at TCNN and reworked my teaching notes.

It was music to my ears when some of the white church members, especially the British teachers and professors, developed an interest in rural evangelism. Rural outreach had been part of the colonial tradition of the European missionaries and they embraced it anew.

I challenged the church to become a springboard to the community. We had so many doctors and nurses: I dared them to offer one day a week to outreach. They came with their medications, spent hours with people, and found it fulfilling.

There was joy in the giving. The congregation rose to it, even though their vicar was dragging on their pockets to build clinics and establish schools.

We reached out to the villages and built new churches and vicarages. We furnished them with things from our churches and homes that we no longer needed.

Church members would come to me and ask, "Vicar, would they need this one? I'm not doing anything with it in my house…"

"Sure!"

More and more people were coming forward to train for the ministry, so I chose to establish St Andrew's as a teaching centre, which my father would have loved. That same year, I was invited by Canon Josiah Fearon to design the curriculum for St Francis Theological College in Zaria.

My dad had wanted me to be a teacher, and I had refused. But now I was doing all that I had assured my father I would not.

It was important for new leadership to emerge, to spread the load and harness the life of the church. And emerge it did, from among the same members who had been sitting there for years, underused. They would come forward and say, "Vicar, I want to help!"

Many had been involved with Campus Crusade for Christ (the outreach and discipleship organization, now known as Cru). Our church became the major hub for CCC in the whole of Zaria, across the denominations.

As a result, many church organizations asked me to become their chair. When the bishop asked me to be chairman of Gedege

District Church Council in Ikara, the first thing I did was travel the vastness of this Hausa-speaking local government area to see the need for myself.

They were a forgotten people, ignored by government, with a desperate need for education and health. So huge were the cultural differences that the people had felt at war with their own bishop. For nearly four years, they had nothing to do with him. They had poor relationships with their deacons and archdeacons, who came from outside and could not speak Hausa.

On my first day, they drove me out. They said, in Hausa, which they were convinced I wouldn't be able to understand, "Kwashi, *ka kwashe kayanyka, ka tafi.*" "Kwashi – pack your load and go back!" And they threw back my letter of posting from the bishop.

But I wouldn't go back. Instead, I went to the next village, Rafin Tabo. I had preached there previously at a St Andrew's outreach and had a friend there. I asked him privately, "Is it true this district doesn't want me?"

"Who said so?"

And I explained.

"No, no, no. I've got a home here: you can stay here!"

So I called a meeting and I told them what I was going to do.

I asked every church to give me two leaders each, for two weeks. They were lay leaders and farmers. Some were illiterate. They barely knew how to take morning and evening services according to the prayer book or conduct weddings. We taught them everything, and showed them that the church existed as a vehicle for evangelism for the kingdom of God.

Then I called for another six people, two from each of the parishes, that I could train at St Luke's Hospital in Wusasa as medical auxiliaries. This would allow us to open a clinic for basic medical care. The next major town was fourteen miles away, and many sick people died before they could reach the hospital.

They gave me four names to start with. And when the parish that had thrown me out got to hear about the clinic, they softened and sent me the final two.

Meanwhile, I started a programme of church building in Bazana and Rafin Tabo, as well as a school project. We coupled the gospel with development that would raise the living standards of the people. And as the story spread, so did the work.

The people of Saulawa had started their own primary school and I was able to help it grow. There was palpable joy in the air. To finance the work I appealed to my well-heeled parishioners at St Andrew's and they gladly gave.

We set about the construction in the style of the Church Mission Society, which I loved. "Folks, the mud is here, the stones are here. We will do the building and I will look for somebody to roof it for us. We will build it ourselves. That way we can afford it."

When some of them got sniffy about building with mud and made the case for cement blocks, I challenged them over how they would finance such a grand construction. They said, "We will sell our farm produce, we will do a harvest." And more often than not, their contribution was healthier than anything I managed to bring in from outside.

This self-motivation brought the district churches back to life. We would do our part and invite others to meet us halfway. That's how we were able to build clinics, churches, and vicarages.

These clear and visible results fired up the younger generation, and some three months later, the same Gedege church that had driven me away invited me back. They had refurbished the vicarage and asked me to move in.

I refused.

"Why? Haven't you forgiven us?"

"Yes, I have forgiven you. But in my mind, this is where the clinic will be."

They shouted with joy! And that was where the clinic was.

St Luke's Hospital supplied us with medications and, by the time our health workers had graduated, the clinic had taken off.

The St Andrew's congregation grew from sixty to more than 400 in four-and-a-half years. We planted forty leaders in the rural areas and transformed that one church into more than seventy congregations.

I hadn't even finished visiting all of them before the bishop posted me again. After I had gone, the work continued. They planted so many churches I lost count of them.

Oh, and did I tell you, on the way I found a wife?

GLORIA GIVES HER ANSWER

I called my second-hand Mazda panel-van Brown Girl. She had tinted windows and air conditioning and was my pride and joy.

I was in the Mazda now, having my ear bent by my friend, Sule Bassi, who was an assistant lecturer at the university and a member of the church. "Ben, you're a liar! You're a Lagos boy, but Lagos hasn't left you. You're a city boy and a crook!"

I had taken him to meet Gloria at her home, a round trip of five solid hours' driving.

We came in the evening and found Gloria sweeping up outside. She greeted us, sat us down in her parlour, then disappeared in her bedroom and didn't emerge for the next forty minutes. My friend was mad at me!

"This girl wouldn't even talk to us!"

As I drove the two-and-a-half hours back to Zaria, he worked me over. "I thought you were a real Christian! I know you are my pastor, yes, but look, that is not how to get a wife! If she is really your wife, why didn't she want to meet us?"

She just said, "Welcome, welcome," and then she went. Queer creatures, these women.

And that was that. Until many months had passed. And then, one fine Sunday morning, I was preaching in my church in Zaria and there she was. Gloria had come from out of nowhere and travelled early in the morning to pay a visit.

After the service she produced some documents and handed them to me. There were two friendship cards. And a letter.

The friendship cards were from the leader of our drama team at TCNN and told a story. Apparently, the night before the final rehearsal of our ill-fated play, he had proposed to her and she had refused him. And that made him mad. But Gloria got even madder back. Her mother had taught her to stand up for herself. So she did. That was why Gloria refused to do the drama and why she shouted down the entire hostel.

The letter was a different matter. It showed Gloria had been hauled before the diocesan board of her church and threatened with dismissal from school. The story was all over her church and cathedral, right up to the bishop.

Rumour had it that Gloria had fallen in love and betrayed the trust of her Lutheran diocese, who were training her for ordination. It was said she had run off with an Anglican man, who was unreliable, a fake, and who was deceiving her. This rascal had girlfriends in Jos and Zaria but had promised to marry her, and she had foolishly agreed.

The bishop asked who this scoundrel was. It turned out this scoundrel was me!

But Gloria had not even responded to my proposal of courtship, let alone marriage.

Her elderly bishop, Akila Todi, a fine, godly man, decided to investigate the matter himself.

He said, "Aren't you the young lady who went to Denmark and Germany and received good reports about your work? Has this young man proposed to marry you?"

Gloria said, "Yes."

"What did you say?"

Gloria replied, "I've not said anything."

"Well, do you want to marry him?"

And Gloria said, "Yes."

So she'd answered everybody! She'd answered my grandmother, she'd answered her bishop... but she still hadn't answered me!

Her indirect response was a confirmation and I felt great! But it was more than my life was worth to show it!

Gloria needed to get back to school. On the way to get her taxi, I could bear it no longer and asked, "OK, so will you marry me?"

Again, she didn't answer. She just looked at me and smiled and laughed and said nothing. I said, "Talk to me, Gloria, please!"

She said, "But I told the bishop I would marry you."

"But that's not me! You've told everyone, including your church council, except for me!" And she switched to another subject.

So, with jangling nerves, I put her in her taxi and sent her back to school.

And then I started pumping out card after card and letter after letter to her. No reply followed no reply. In hot pursuit they came.

I couldn't make it to her graduation because I was a priest and had to work. And it dragged on this way until my birthday. By then, I had had enough. It was 1983. I wanted a wife in place before the dawn of a new millennium or the return of our beloved Saviour. I was not a patient man. I didn't have the luxury of time. I was engaged fully in the parish as a priest. Many churches needed me and I wasn't about to put on a clerical collar and go around chasing women.

I said, "Lord, this is going on for too long! Maybe the wife You want me to marry is someone else."

So I prayed.

I gave God a list of names. There was one girl, Stella, who was a nurse. She brought food to me and checked to see how I was. She was kind; somebody kind would be nice. There was Margaret, an agricultural officer, and there was Gloria.

So I prayed to the Lord: "Gloria has not answered me. She's refused to respond to my letters and cards, and I have begged You, since I saw Gloria. I didn't process those celibacy forms and now I am in this dilemma. Should I really go back on those forms and consider being celibate? I'm ordained already. But please, whatever You do, don't give me a wife who will not serve You, who would be a heartache to this ministry and to me. I couldn't bear it. I would break down. I would fail. I can lay down my life for You to use me as you choose, but with a wife like that, everything I do would be a failure.

"I have told every young man I know to hold on to the Lord and take this adventure with You. I will recruit as many young people as will dare to take this trip of faith. Lord, let me take this trip, but I want a wife to take this trip with me. I don't know where, I don't care, but I'll go wherever You send me; whatever You say, I will do. I will not fear, I will trust You and obey You. Lord, take me."

I sang "Take My Hand, Lead Me, Lord". I sang "Be Thou My Vision". I sang all those hymns. And I meant them.

Now it was crunch time. I had to know. I said, "Lord, is it Margaret?" He said, "No." It was like an audible voice. In my mind it said, "You would choose Margaret because you're thinking of her resources; you'll get financial resources, but you will not get a wife."

I said, "What about Stella?" He said, "You have chosen Stella because you think she's your wife. She's not your wife; she will be somebody else's wife."

And then I said, "What about Gloria? She has not replied to my letters or anything."

And the voice went silent. I had heard enough. I didn't need anyone to tell me. This was about 10.30 at night. I got up, grabbed a bath bag and an extra shirt, leaped into my Mazda, and headed straight to Numan.

Gloria was God's choice for me. In my walk with God, I had reached the conclusion that when God went silent, I should get up and act. This has happened to me a few times. God's silence means He wants action. I just said, "Lord, I'm gone!"

§

I was hauling up a hill on the outskirts of Jos, travelling fast, when I thought I saw a figure up in front of me. I hit the main beam and saw I was heading towards the back of a trailer that was struggling up the hill without rear lights.

I swerved to overtake it on the bend, and as I did so, I saw bright lights coming towards me. It was a tanker. I went to slam on my brakes, but realized that if I hit them too hard I might veer beneath the trailer in front of me. So I tore off the road and into the bush.

By God's grace there were no rocks, stones, or side barriers on the hill. So I tore out from the bush to overtake the trailer and continue on my journey.

Had I hit that tanker nobody on earth would have known about it. Nobody knew where I was. It was the middle of the night. What had happened to me would have been a public question without an answer.

I had left after 11 p.m. I would get into Jos about 2:30 a.m. From Jos to Numan was another six hours.

I kept my foot down and myself awake by listening to Gabonese dance music on the radio. I knew that by the time my tank ran out I would be in Numan and the petrol stations would be open, so I could head back on a full tank.

If I left Numan at about 9 a.m. or 10 a.m., I would get back to Zaria in the early hours of the morning and into the church before the service.

My army supply and transport training came into play. I had water, and some coffee if I felt a little weak. I could stop the car, sluice my face, pour some water over my head, and then continue.

I figured I could drive for eight-and-a-half hours to Gloria, pop the question, drive eight-and-a-half hours back, and still be in time for church. I didn't need long with Gloria, just long enough for her to tell me whether she would marry me or not.

These were the days before phones. Phones could only be found in the major cities, and even then you would need God's help to get a dial tone.

I made it into Numan at 8:30 a.m., exactly as planned. My military logistics training had stood me in good stead.

Gloria was the first to welcome me, not that it was much of a welcome. There was no, "Ben, it's great to see you!" She just asked me, "What brings you?" And then she disappeared.

Gloria's younger sister, Bridget, seemed more excited than Gloria to see me. She took me to a guest room, gave me water to clean up, and prepared some breakfast. But where was Gloria?

I didn't want a showdown, I didn't want to start anything, I didn't say anything. But she had just disappeared. No kiss, not even a handshake. And after breakfast I was sitting alone. What I didn't know at the time was that Gloria had arrived just before me. She had just driven back from visiting her uncle in Yola. But it wasn't tiredness that had driven her away, it was this awkward, unfathomable shyness that I was beginning to recognize. It was Gloria being Gloria.

It was 10 a.m. before Gloria resurfaced. And she said I should escort her: to where, I didn't know. She jumped into the car and gave me directions. We were driving away to some place where I would not be able to speak the language.

All the women came out to see me, and there was I sitting like a teddy bear, not understanding what was going on. Everybody was polite and greeted me and offered me drinks. Apparently, Gloria was introducing me to her relatives.

From there we went to another house, where I understood nothing beyond the greetings. Then we got to another place where finally the wife of one of her relations spoke my language. She listened to Gloria and told me, "So you are the one who is going to be our in-law!"

And I said, "Wow, now I get it!"

Gloria had told them all, but she had still not told me.

That afternoon, she took me to meet one of her uncles in the village. To get there, we had to cross a river, but there was no bridge. Gloria said she knew a way. Great if you were on foot, but my exhaust hit a rock and split. It made a terrible noise.

I said, "No problem, no problem. I can fix it."

"Sorry, Ben."

"No, that's fine. That's OK." She was guilty. I was gracious. I decided to push it. "So you've been introducing me?"

"Yes," she confessed.

When we arrived at the village, we went to see her aunties and all the key people that mattered, those who needed to see me and find out who I was. She introduced me appropriately, and I was welcomed and received the same way.

On the way back, I had my exhaust welded and repaired and we had dinner with Gloria's older sister, Sarah. Afterwards, I said to Gloria, "I have to go back."

She said, "No! You can't go back!" There was still so much to do, so many to see.

This woman was a mystery. She had kept me at arm's length and now she wanted me.

I said, "Gloria, I sent you fifteen letters and twenty cards of all sizes – the most expensive cards I could find. Didn't you get them?"

"I got them."

"But you didn't reply! So tell me now, please, so that I don't lose my senses or look at any other girl. I'm so sure, Gloria. Will you marry me?"

"Ben, you can't go back tonight, you just can't!"

"Gloria! Nobody knows I am here! Not my father, not my mother, not my church – only God knows I am here. I have to go back tomorrow to give people communion and to preach. I can't phone and I can't tell anybody to stand in my place. If I'm absent and they tell the bishop, I will be in trouble."

We argued back and forth and she started crying. She didn't want me to go. So for the first time, I held her. And she didn't resist. I kissed her and said, "I have to go."

"Ben, please!"

"Honestly, I have to go."

Then, I said, "Gloria, I am planning the marriage. Could we do it in October?" It was already September. "Please?"

She said, "No! We have not done everything. I still have to tell everybody!"

Finally, she had come out of herself and our conversation was lively, healthy, and good. But she had uncles to see and others to tell. She wanted to put everybody on high alert. She said the time was too short.

"It's not too short," I argued. "In a couple of weeks, we will be married. I'm ready. Tell me your size?" I asked. This was to make bridal clothes for her. Though I didn't need her to tell me.

I had already looked her up and down and sized her up. We city boys, we knew our stuff.

But the time had come to leave. It was 10 p.m., I had a long drive ahead of me and I couldn't be late for church.

"I have to go, Gloria, I have to go now."

She reluctantly told her sisters, but they thought I was making my excuses. They told me to leave in the morning.

Reluctantly, I left.

She was tearing at the Mazda's taillights as I drove off, thankful to God and excited.

I'd had two days and two nights without sleep, but I got back to Zaria on time. I have no idea what I preached about. All I know is that somehow I didn't fall asleep in my own sermon. It was pure adrenaline. Nobody knew and none was the wiser. Then I rested on Monday morning and caught up with my life once again.

A couple of weeks later, I drove to Numan again, this time for two whole days. I wanted this wedding to hit the road quickly. I saw Gloria's father for the second time. Back in April, I had asked him formally if I could marry his daughter, but he was a prince, so he said nothing. I had expected that, but I still needed to show him my face.

This time, I observed the proper protocols. I brought a few gifts and a little money to buy mats. The tradition is, you bring mats to your father-in-law, and if he accepts them, he is committed. He did, and that was done. The dowry was just 200 Naira.

There were also expectations of what you should do for your wife, but I was ready for that. Ahead of time, I had bought her wedding rings and clothes, feminine things that would make a young girl happy. I bought her a watch and had her bridesmaids' clothes made. And my older sister bought the wedding gown.

Nevertheless, there was still a diplomatic incident, which Gloria's father graciously overlooked, when he offered me a chair and I foolishly sat down on it. I was supposed to decline and to sit on the ground. We had a chuckle about this Lagos boy's lack of good manners.

Finally, we agreed a date in December. Their family and my family agreed. Now all that remained was to tell the bishop that I had found the girl I wanted to marry. I told Bishop Titus she was a graduate of TCNN.

"Are you joking?"

"No, Sir."

The bishop scratched out a note and told me to take it to Numan. No problem, it was another excuse to visit Gloria. The note informed her she had been offered a job, to teach at a new theological college the bishop had started, St Francis of Assisi, in Wusasa, Zaria. Gloria was to teach Old Testament and African traditional religions.

Things were moving quickly. We were married on 3 December 1983.

PART TWO

FIRST DROPS OF BLOOD

When I came to St Andrew's in 1982, I received a wonderful present. At least I thought it was wonderful. Gloria wasn't so sure. The church sexton presented me with a beautiful brown Labrador puppy. I named him Cracker.

Cracker followed me to Bible studies and prayer meetings. Every member of the church got to know him. Cracker would sit peacefully at the back until the benediction. And as soon as he heard the sung amen, he would jump up and trot outside to greet the departing church members with me.

Cracker was not always a great respecter of the faith. Back in his training days, before Gloria, Cracker took a liking to my small leather-bound Bible. He found it to his taste and gave it a good chewing. And after that, he tore it to pieces. I almost killed him.

Gloria would not have been surprised. Where she had come from, dogs were only good for barking and you kept them outside. Why would you want to keep a guard dog indoors? You fed them and they went around barking. That was the deal.

My dad had trained me to look after dogs from about the age of five. Cracker had lived in my room from the beginning; he was my constant companion

Cracker travelled with me to most places. He was an excellent guard dog, but he knew my closest friends, and he would never bark at them. The first time Gloria came to visit, Cracker never barked. That was a good sign. Though Gloria often felt like barking at him.

But Cracker was my dog, from well before Gloria entered my life, and things were staying that way.

After our wedding at St Paul's, Pankshin (which was full to bursting), I needed to drive back to look after St Andrew's Church. I was taking treatment for malaria and feeling drowsy, so Gloria packed our things in the body of the panel van, while I took a nap.

When I woke up, Gloria had spread all her pots across the back seat. They were arranged carefully across the full width of the seat, so they wouldn't bang against each other and break.

I said to Gloria, "Where's Cracker going to sleep?"

She hadn't given him a thought, which was a mistake. When I went travelling with my friend Cracker, his place was always on the back seat. So I rearranged Gloria's pots and gave pride of place to my beloved Labrador. And to make it clear to Gloria that she could never come between a man and his dog, Cracker leaned forward and put his head on my shoulder while I was driving.

Gloria has a sensitive nose and hated the smell of dog. It was beyond her how I could let a dog cuddle up so close. She said, "Ben! He is breathing, he's breathing!"

Well, what did she expect a Labrador to do, hold his breath?

But sweet reason did nothing to ease Gloria's deeply offended sense of smell. She waved her hand in front of her nose and put her head by the window for fresh air. Dogs, she kept reminding me, were just for barking.

Gloria's sense of smell soon grew even more acute after she became pregnant. The very smell of Cracker made her sick. So she built him a little doghouse and moved him out, along with all his belongings.

Cracker went reluctantly, and showed his displeasure by refusing to eat Gloria's food. When she served him his dinner, he just walked away.

Gloria and Cracker never got along, until she had our first baby, Hannatu. When Hannatu arrived in 1984, Cracker was excited and happy. When baby Hannatu was on the floor, learning to crawl, Cracker would be there, watching her every move.

Hannatu was a chubby little baby. She was always hungry and a messy eater too, which was greatly to Cracker's advantage. He would patiently wait for the crumbs to fall, and there would be plenty. But when Hannatu grew teeth and we could serve her shredded meat, that stretched Cracker's endurance beyond breaking point. He could no longer be content with just the leftovers.

Hannatu watched her meat disappear with mounting fury. She grabbed Cracker round the neck and sank all of her baby teeth into him and refused to let go.

I said, "What is this?"

"He ate my meat! He ate my meat!"

Cracker loved Hannatu, and when he wasn't helping himself to her meat, Hannatu grew to love him. I'm not sure I could ever say quite the same of Gloria.

St Andrew's was excited to see Gloria. They held a beautiful reception for us and plied Gloria with gifts. We lived in the newly built vicarage, which had two bedrooms and was rendered cream on the outside and painted a fashionable shade of orange within.

And with a wife to help me, the work went from strength to strength. The more St Andrew's got stuck into rural evangelism, the more we saw. And everywhere we looked, there was need.

§

But by now I had a need of my own. Shortly after we had Hannatu, I began to see small drops of blood when I passed water. By the Christmas services, I was beginning to feel pain at the back of my right hip. I went to the hospital and they decided to conduct some tests.

They concluded that I had a urinary tract infection. They plied me with medications, but it didn't get better. Some days I would feel OK, but others I would not. I couldn't eat much, and in the evenings I was cold and shivering.

After further tests, they found my kidney was infected with tuberculosis. I was losing weight and most evenings I would have headaches and fever. Yet another test, by Professor Bello who was in my church, confirmed the diagnosis.

As it dragged on, I couldn't eat and became sure I was going to die. I sat Gloria down and told her that she should brace herself for hard times ahead. She was still young, in her twenties, and she should arrange to move out of the vicarage and begin a new life. I wrote my will, told Gloria what I wanted done, and showed her all that I had.

I informed my immediate boss, Josiah Fearon, and we discussed sending me to the UK for treatment. My church prayed for me and some of the priests also came to pray. Back then, problems like this could be life-threatening.

Then a professor of urology at Ahmadu Bello University in Kaduna conducted yet more tests. And after a month I went to see him.

Professor Garg sat me down and said, "Reverend?"

"Sir?"

He said, "You must be near God."

"How so, Sir?"

"The result shows no trace of any infection."

I was shocked. I said, "How can this be?"

He asked me about pains. I said no, the pain had subsided substantially a week ago. By now I could even drive myself again. I was feeling better – even that morning.

He said, "I'm sure you're near God."

I said, "Sir, you can be near God too."

He asked how. So I explained to this Indian professor how Jesus had saved me. I gave him my story and told him it could be his story too, if he took the same steps as me: to accept Jesus as the saviour of the world and his own saviour and to repent of his sins.

He was aware of those sins, but he didn't know how to turn from them. I explained that he should humble himself and pray for Jesus to take over his life. And right there, in his office, he prayed and accepted Jesus and repented of his sins.

It was all a mystery, but two weeks earlier I had had a dream.

Now, I don't put too much stock in dreams. Gloria has many dreams, and I've often poured cold water on them. Sometimes, you dream if you eat too much. And if you are in pain, you can dream. That was what I suspected about this particular dream.

In my dream, I saw a fair girl who was a member of my church. She was a nurse and she was crying. Nobody knew why. People were trying to console her.

I asked what the problem was, but she wouldn't tell me. She was crying uncontrollably. So I said to her, "OK, I don't need to know what your problem is, but I know someone who will solve your problem. Come with me."

We walked along the footpath across the polo field to St Andrew's. I opened the church and she followed me in. I took her to the chancel, where there was a black wooden cross nailed to the wall. I pointed to it and said, "See, He will solve your problems. Jesus will." And I walked away, and then I woke up. That was my dream.

Now, I understood from that dream that Jesus had solved not only the girl's problem, but my problem too. It is Jesus who will solve every problem.

When I told Professor Bello about my healing, he shouted, "Hallelujah! We praise the Lord!" He rejoiced that God had worked a miracle, and he testified in church the following Sunday. Professor Garg also came to church that Sunday and has continued to do so ever since.

There's been no trace of the problem from that moment.

Thank God. I had work to do. There were many other people with needs.

The roots of their problem went way back.

GATHERING STORM CLOUDS

Historically, the Hausa-speaking people of Kaduna Diocese had been conquered and persecuted more than a century beforehand. In the early 1800s, radical Islamic reformer Usman dan Fodio led his Fulani army against the Hausa kingdoms of the north. He ravaged their lands, forcing them to convert or be killed, and then installed emirs from among his own relations to rule over them.

Many of today's jihadis take their inspiration from dan Fodio, the founder of the Sokoto caliphate, which conquered land spanning parts of current-day Cameroon to the edge of Burkina Faso, incorporating most of the present north of Nigeria and a chunk of the Niger Republic. Dan Fodio only faltered in his stride when he approached the Plateau and Middle Belt region.

British influence in Nigeria had been growing, and the might of the British Empire quickly overcame the Sokoto caliphate. Britain incorporated their sultans and emirs into its colonial class. These Muslim leaders were opposed to the spread of Christianity, so the Colonial Office of Lord Lugard banned evangelism and missionary work in the northern cities.

There was only one place you could escape those strictures and that was the wilderness. Out in the bush, the indigenous Hausa people were unseen, unknown and unwanted. They were a people without official rights or existence. And there they remained undiscovered until they were reached by the gospel.

Unsurprisingly, these outcasts embraced what they heard. The inclusive gospel message of liberty and personal value swept through the bush like wildfire. Today the descendants of these people are educated. They are in the army, serving as pilots, and all over the country in various fields of endeavour.

But while those who embraced the gospel prospered, the long shadow of jihad continued to spread across the land. The legacy of Usman dan Fodio continues.

§

As I criss-crossed these rural areas, I could see much that was wrong. Much of it was ignorance – a lack of education that nobody seemed willing to address. I discovered as a young missionary that it was impossible to do evangelism and preach the gospel, if the gospel did not enable those who heard it to lead better lives. The gospel had to be practical. People needed to experience the greatness and the goodness of God in their communities.

These people had land, but they didn't know what to do with it. So I would encourage them: "Register your lands, get certificates of occupancy, build schools, build clinics, then get more land. With your agricultural products, I can link you with people in town, so you can avoid the middlemen and make more profit."

I found myself engaged in commerce, education, and healthcare. This was the gospel. The people loved it. They became confident. They could make things happen! They discovered they didn't have to be poor. For the rural poor to be lifted up, they simply had to be taught how to manage their economy.

The principle I'd learned early on, that works and which I still operate today, is that God will never punish an honest, righteous man. Therefore, I taught that we need to show righteousness and honesty in all our dealings, with finances and with people.

I also learned that all dishonest gain and cheating are cursed by God and will never be blessed. So, if you want to be rich and to see good days, avoid cheating. Avoid dishonesty completely, and God will bless you. Then add to your honesty hard work, faith in God, and the fear of the Lord. It will lead to prosperity, both physically and spiritually.

People beyond the community of faith liked people like that, because they were people they could trust. Being honest, hard-working, and having faith is good business, and I love that.

I found excitement in seeing the power of the gospel at work. Those rural communities have become great contributors to the development of Nigeria, in the church and society as a whole.

The more I got involved in active gospel ministry, the more God placed a burden on me to care for the poor and the needy, the widows and the children. It was a burden that I carried joyfully, and rural evangelism became a pursuit of my life to this day.

In all this, my calling was evolving. It came down to Christ first, then education and community building.

§

In evangelizing the poor rural people, I was exposed to their predicaments and their plights, to their injustice and oppression. I found that politicians were taking advantage of them, and I began to speak up on their behalf. I became a voice for these people.

Nigeria was under a military regime at the time and that regime was perpetuating injustice against Christians in the north, so I began to speak out about this in church.

From its pages, the Bible speaks directly into issues of injustice in society, and this formed part of my teaching series from the pulpit.

It was about this time that General Babangida took Nigeria into the Organisation of Islamic Cooperation (OIC). Yet Nigeria was a secular state, guaranteed by its constitution. According to Section 10: "The Government of the Federation or of a State shall not adopt any religion as State Religion."[2] So the arguments for going into the OIC were not plausible, but Islamic socialism had its appeal for some in the military and Babangida in particular. That's how Libya and Egypt had developed politically, and the general saw it as a route to remaining in power. He would get the backing of Islamic countries, led by Saudi Arabia.

---

2   Constitution of the Federal Republic of Nigeria, 1999, Chapter I, Part II, Section 10: http://www.nigeria-law.org/ConstitutionOfTheFederalRepublicOfNigeria. htm#Powers_of_Federal_Republic_of_Nigeria

Babangida had already begun to polarize the army on religious grounds and was retiring Christian officers ahead of time. He was opposed by his chief of general staff, Commodore Okoh Ukiwe, a Christian from the east of Nigeria. Ukiwe argued, "Nigeria, as a country, should not be a member of a religious organization." Religious affiliation, he insisted, was for individuals, rather than nations. He lost his job as a result.[3]

All this sent a signal that Nigeria could be Islamized by military might. This was polarizing the country and I feared for the future of my children in northern Nigeria where we Christians were already in a minority. If Nigeria were to become Islamic, then our children would have no future, because the fundamentalists recognize nobody outside of Islam. Their future would be one of persecution, segregation, dehumanization, and even extermination.

Does that sound extreme? In most Sharia states in Nigeria now, Christians have second-class status. Christian towns and villages have been wiped out. Villagers are being killed. All over the world, Islamic authorities turn a blind eye to abuses against Christians. This opens the door to criminality and lends legitimacy to radicals and extremists.

So I began a teaching series in church with my influential congregation, urging them to be wary of military regimes that dabbled in religion. And as my teaching began to impact some of these high fliers in Zaria, the story began to spread that I was a revolutionary preaching against the leadership of the country.

Radical teachings were gaining traction in the mosques, including those of Ahmad Deedat in South Africa. He was an Islamic theologian who denied that Jesus was the Son of God. If you were a true Christian who believed in Jesus then, he said, you should drink poison to prove it, because Mark 16:18 said, "when they drink deadly poison, it will not hurt them at all".

Deedat's own poisonous theology had spread to Kano, which was next to Zaria. Students at the university there were

---

3   "Ukiwe: A Life of Courage, Consistency", by Charles Kumolo, *Vanguard*, 1 January 2018: www.vanguardngr.com/2018/01/ukiwe-life-courage-consistency/

now screaming "Islam only". Intolerance towards Christians and the Christian faith was heating up in Zaria too.

I cast my mind back to what I had seen in Zaria when I first arrived in 1982. On billboards and walls, in bold letters, were those same words "Islam only". At the time, I didn't take that seriously, but that was before Babangida took Nigeria into the OIC.

What I had seen in Pakistan, Egypt, Bangladesh, Iran and Saudi Arabia, I could see happening in Nigeria in front of my own eyes. The writing was literally on the wall.

People began to send me materials that confirmed my concerns. Ahmadu Bello University in Zaria was a hotbed of intellectual Islam. The Muslim Brotherhood in Egypt was also spreading its materials. I was receiving unsolicited tapes outlining Islamic strategy and pointing to its unmitigated success in Iran.

While the Shah of Iran was still in power, Ayatollah Khomeini was in exile in Paris, producing tapes calling for the Shah's downfall. The theological schools had listened to his teaching and spread his gospel of revolution, until the Ayatollah himself was ushered in as the nation's messiah.

Now the teachings of Ayatollah Khomeini were flowing into Zaria and Kano, where Shia Islam was gaining a foothold. And along with these came recordings reviving the jihad teachings of Usman dan Fodio.

I began to teach the church to stand strong in the gospel and brace up for persecution. I didn't realize that persecution would appear so quickly from around the corner, and that it would begin with me.

At St Andrew's I thought if I could educate these top military men, police, and professors, they would see the coming danger and speak up about it. But St Andrew's had two weaknesses. It was an expatriate church, where most of the members were white. And most of the Nigerian leaders in the congregation were professionals from the south where the issue just seemed too remote.

They were convinced I was exaggerating the risk. They would say, "Ben, do you really think this could happen in Nigeria? Please don't raise this kind of alarm!"

But I had listened to the teachings coming into Nigeria. And I had already seen this teaching played out in Iran. Shia or Sunni, the theology was much the same. It was anti-Saudi, anti-US, and anti-Western. And it was identical in its call to persecute Christians.

Very few in the church could see what I was saying and even fewer agreed with me, including those from the north. But all the signs were there.

§

Inevitably, at St Andrew's, I developed enemies and allies. When you press for change and speak out against injustice, that's what happens. Mercifully, my greatest ally was my bishop, Titus Ogbonyomi. He had a tremendous respect for his family and his dependants, whom he raised for the Lord. All of his children are now in ministry. Bishop Titus was a model for me.

At the beginning, I had felt intimidated by this stern ex-army officer, who wore a cross of nails, but that changed when I started working with him more closely, as I've said.

There was a debate at Synod concerning an investigation into a district, and the motion was about to be passed. I was convinced the problem was nothing more than a misunderstanding between people of different languages. I wasn't happy and raised my hand. Bishop Titus asked me to bring my contribution.

I said I felt sure that there were still those who needed to be listened to. I believed the motion should be suspended until a fuller report had been given. The bishop agreed. He said, "The suggestion of this young man – fine – let us do it this way." The motion was reversed.

But that upset many others and they told me so. During the break, two senior clergy took me out and tore me to pieces. They told me I should never do that. "Once the bishop has decided on a voting pattern, nobody changes it," they said. "You are disgracing the bishop. You must go and apologize."

I went immediately to see the bishop, who was sitting at his table.

"Sir, I want to see you."

"Yes, yes, come!"

When you greet the bishop you bow, one hand in front, one behind. It's the ecclesiastical version of the military salute.

I bowed down and said, "Sir, I am deeply sorry. I didn't know that I shouldn't have said what I said, and that as a result the motion has been..."

"Who told you that?"

"No, Sir, I just felt that maybe I have offended you..."

He cut me off with a tut: "Silly! Get out of here. That is nothing! You did the right thing, Ben!"

I couldn't believe it.

When we came back after the break, there was an interpretation from English into Hausa in another of the motions. I raised my hand and he acknowledged me again.

"What is it?"

"Sir, this translation is wrong." I explained what it meant.

He said, "Look, young man, would you come to the Secretariat right now? Move! Go!"

I thought I was in trouble again. He continued: "You are now deputy assistant secretary: help us with this translation immediately."

So in 1983 I found myself in the Secretariat. The bishop was an honest man, who was looking for honest people. He hated lies, and too many people were trying to deceive him. He wanted frank discussions with those who were bold enough to disagree with him.

As my influence grew, so did the opposition towards me. Some of my senior colleagues began to accuse me of courting popularity, because I stood up for the poor. There were those who hated me, disliked my gifts, and spoke no good of me anywhere. They would tell me to my face that I was trying to make myself more popular than the bishop, and they would belittle me in public.

Then the churches in Zaria got together across the various denominations to elect me regional chairman of the Christian Association of Nigeria (CAN), which was highlighting the risks of joining the OIC.

One of my archdeacons complained to Bishop Titus, "My Lord Bishop, do you realize he is chairman of St Andrew's?"

The bishop said, "Yes."

"Do you realize he is teaching at St Francis?"

"Yes."

"Do you realize you're also making him the district chairman in Ikara?"

Of course the bishop realized. "Yes."

"Do you realize he is also the chairman of the Zaria Christian Association?"

"Yes, Ben will do all four."

In Ikara, where I was district chairman, the number of churches doubled. And attendance was booming at St Francis and St Andrew's.

Whenever you make an impact your critics will misread your motives and accuse you, and others will laud you and try to put you on a pedestal. While some gathered round to accuse, others gathered to whisper, "Ben, you should start your own church."

There were Christians in Zaria who wanted me to move out of the Anglican Church. They said, "The Anglican Church is of no use to you. They don't understand who you are or appreciate what you have."

But all of this would be blown away by the storm that was about to break in Zaria.

§

The meeting at the polo field was the climax of a week of prayer. The church had been praying from the Sunday, and Christians had congregated at interdenominational prayer meetings in different groups throughout the city from the Monday onwards.

At that time, we didn't know the crisis was coming but I had been warning the church about the Islamization that was threatening Nigeria. We knew this was not a battle of flesh and blood, so we called on the church to pray that this strategy would not succeed.

For the final Saturday meeting, the only place large enough to take all the Christians was the polo field.

It was early February 1987. Some 15,000 gathered there for prayer under a clear blue sky. We prayed from 3 p.m. to 5 p.m. A pleasant breeze kept our bodies cool, but the people were charged up for God. They were excited. For two hours, there were loud amens to prayers that were punctuated by music.

A plump Baptist teacher came up to take the microphone. I will never forget her. Mrs Dorcas Ajani stood there in her multicoloured wrapper and her light-blue blouse, and she prayed – how she prayed! "Lord, whatever they are planning against Christians in Nigeria, wherever they are, send confusion in their midst. May their plans backfire against them. May they disagree and scatter!" It was from the heart.

Then after two hours of prayer, it was my turn to speak. I had fifteen minutes to close the meeting. This was not a time for ecclesiastical robes. I mounted the podium in my jeans and checked shirt. I had never spoken to so many people before and I was afraid. Throughout it, I was praying: "Lord, help me say what You want me to say to these people."

I had taken an oath when I was ordained that I would preach, teach, warn, and rebuke. When I spoke out at the polo field, it was in fulfilment of this calling. I was preaching to warn the people. If I had kept silent, I would not have been at peace with myself.

The charge given to me at my ordination was from Jeremiah 37:6, that you must have a word from the Lord. There was never a single sermon that I just got up to speak spontaneously without first giving adequate study and thinking it through, without first considering its lessons and application.

So today on the polo field, if I was being charged with giving a warning, then a warning was what I had to deliver, whatever anybody might say.

§

I gave my sermon in Pidgin English. Most of the ordinary people could understand Pidgin. When I began to speak to them, they cheered.

I said, "Hallelujah!"

They shouted, "Amen!"

"Praise the Lord!"

And 15,000 bellowed, "Amen!"

And I began my message. It was taken from Exodus 14:13: "Make wuna tanda put, make wuna see wetin God go do…" Which means, "Stand still and see the salvation of the Lord."

I read, "The Egyptians you see today you will never see again!" And they screamed, "Amen!"

Then I closed my Bible and gave the explanation.

My message that day was we should get up and do something about what was happening in society before matters got out of hand. I was telling people to get up and be a Wilberforce. These were people whom God had put into society to call a halt to evil, and I was calling on them to shine their moral light in society.

My message then was the same I would give to anyone today: "Stand up for what is right. Stand up against evil and ill in society. The standing up itself is your authority, because you know what is correct.

"Don't wait for someone to listen to you before you do what is right. Do what is right, because it is right to do. We must get up and stand on our convictions. We must do the right thing and be willing to pay the price."

The message I gave on the polo field was that we know evil will never win, not in this life nor in eternity. We had no reason to fear evil or surrender to evil because Satan was already a defeated foe. To submit now would be to submit to a lesser authority, an authority that had already been defeated. And that would be senseless.

Even if they killed me and burned my house, they would be the losers today, and they would be the losers tomorrow, in eternity. So, to fear them would be useless, and to fail to confront them would be cowardice.

Secondly, I said that, although they might burn our churches and our houses, we would rebuild them. We might lose our clothes and possessions, but we would get them back. In fact, we would get better ones. Even if we lost our lives, we would get them back, and better, because Christ never lies. Either way, we had nothing to lose.

And if we did nothing and allowed evil to survive, we would have no guarantee that our lives would be good. The best life would be one lived out confronting evil. Live or die, you would lose nothing. Philippians 1:21, "For to me, to live is Christ and to die is gain." If I live, I serve the Lord. If I die, I go to be with the Lord. Either way, I'm in business.

This was the first sermon many of them would have heard in Pidgin. They were jumping and they were shouting. They left encouraged and highly charged. But some of my own church members were shocked to hear me preach in Pidgin.

I felt the constant reminder that, unlike these leaders, professors, and commanders, I had never achieved the rank of army officer. I was a private before God called me to the ministry. Of myself, I had no authority to speak to such people – except that God was speaking through me.

Until my dying day, I will always remind myself that the only reason I am standing here is because Jesus saved me, Jesus called me, Jesus ordained me, and Jesus sent me. I was under that single authority, and I hold on to that all the time. So those who accused me of seeking fame or renown, or some measure of influence, simply didn't know me.

What kept me going was the verse that had set me running as a student and had followed me throughout, Philippians 4:13: "I can do all things through Christ who strengthens me" (NKJV).

That one sermon established my leadership and introduced me to the public in Zaria. Sermons have a way of travelling. Tapes were circulated and those who were not there heard all about it.

That sermon proved to be timely. If I had not preached that message, I would have had no authority later, when I had to tell the people to stand still. In little more than a month, we had need of such a message.

THE BURNINGS

I f the writing was already on the wall, few were willing to read it. Until 10 March 1987.

The day before, some of our students and young people came to me and said, "Sir, some of the Muslim kids are saying they will kill us, and that they are going to kill you too!"

I said, "Are you serious?"

They said, "Yes!"

On 6 March 1987, a young Christian was preaching in Kafanchan, some three hours' drive away, at an open meeting at the College of Education. A young Muslim girl was passing and accused the Christian of making some reference to the Koran.

She shouted, "Allahu Akbar!" and accused this Christian preacher of desecrating the Koran and insulting the Prophet. So a fight began that night. This was 170 miles away, further from us than Sheffield is from London.

By 9 March, the tension had reached Zaria and Katsina. It was difficult for me to believe that something so remote could affect us – unless it was part of a plan.

I went in person to the Commissioner of Police and told him I'd heard that Christians would be killed that night.

He was a Muslim. He said, "No, no, there's no such thing. If there is, I'll let you know."

I went to check with the divisional police officer, who was a member of my church. He too assured me that nothing of that nature would happen here.

But it did.

The following day, in the afternoon, they started burning churches and destroying property belonging to Christians. And the rioting went on for seventy-two hours.

It began with a phone call: "We think one of the churches is on fire."

"Where?"

"Sabon Gari."

That was close to the army barracks, just three miles away. "Are you sure?"

"Yes."

I tried to get through to the police, but the phone just kept ringing. Nobody was picking it up.

Before I went to prayer that evening, a police officer who was a member of my church came by and said, "Ben, can I take you away from here?"

I said no. I was home alone with my daughter, Hannatu, who was two-and-a-half years old. That morning Gloria had travelled back to her home town, Numan, where her uncle had died. She had taken our baby, Rinji, who was just six months old. Thank God they were both away and that Gloria knew nothing about what was happening.

There were signs that things were getting out of hand. The phones were buzzing with other reports of burning churches. The military commandant, who attended my church, advised the police to make sure I was kept alive. If anything happened to me, there could be a backlash. I was the restraining factor to prevent the Christians fighting back.

I agreed to move in with Dr Bitrus Ikilama-Gani, a member of my church. Dr Gani was a blind physiotherapist, who had trained in England and was influential and respected around the country. He was a handsome man in his mid-forties, a little taller than me, and he had completely lost his sight in his early childhood.

People came, bearing news that grew worse by the hour. Some said they had seen churches on fire in Samaru, a short drive down the main road.

Then a professor from the university said he could see fires everywhere. He suspected many churches were being burned.

Word came that the chapel at the university had been set ablaze. That was even closer. The professor was visibly angry. He and others had tried to get through to the police, but couldn't. So I tried to raise the police commissioner. I couldn't get through. Then the divisional police officer. It was impossible.

By now the phone was constantly ringing and a steady stream of worried people were turning up at the door. We had to abandon our plans for a prayer meeting.

People were telling me, "A Baptist church has been burned."

I said, "Where?"

Then another Baptist church. Then an Anglican church, and then another, from all over town. What had begun hundreds of miles away was at our door.

What I kept hearing was, "I don't believe it, it's just not true. This cannot be happening in Nigeria."

As more people discovered where I was, leaders of different Christian denominations arrived, asking, "What should we do?" I was barely into my thirties and some of these professors and doctors were old enough to be my parents. They were senior in every way. But they were waiting for my order or a word. And they were ready to retaliate or commit revenge.

Before long there were thirty of them, crammed into that parlour, all shouting, "This is wrong! Ben, tell us, what shall we do? We are ready to take these people on. We're going to fight! We must defend ourselves! We must take up arms! We can't let them burn our churches and our homes."

I said, "No, you can't talk like that. We can only do what the Lord asks us to do."

But what was the Lord asking?

As more kept coming, along with their demands, I knew I had to find out. I excused myself, went to a guest room in Dr Gani's house, locked myself in, and prayed.

Still the people kept coming. They were asking Dr Gani, "Where's Ben, where is our chairman?"

And Dr Gani would say, "He's praying."

As the good doctor was fending off the steady stream of people knocking on his door, demanding to know what should be done, I was pacing my room alone, with the same question: "Lord, what should I do? The people are asking me. What should I say to them? What will happen?"

I was afraid. The whole world seemed to be waiting on me. But I had no word for them. "Lord, please, give me a word." I prayed that again and again until I got tired of begging for the same thing. I would pace, get on my knees, then pace again. At times I was flat on the floor, prostrate. This went on for two hours.

And then I realized, when God goes quiet, it is often because He has already spoken.

When I finally emerged at 3 a.m. the crowd had almost doubled. I knew what I had to say would fail to please those who were waiting.

I wrote something down on a piece of paper, handed it to one of the CAN officials, and said, "Go and type this up, and I will sign it."

It said, "Dear Christians, this letter is from me. The Lord says, 'Do nothing.'" And I signed it. As simple as that.

§

They were saying, "What?!"

"That's what the Lord said."

The sermon I had preached at the polo field only a few weeks earlier had come back to me in a flash. Exodus 14:13–14: "Do not be afraid. Stand firm and you will see the deliverance the Lord will bring you today... The Lord will fight for you; you need only to be still."

I knew this was God. It might not have been what anyone wanted to hear, but I was sure it was what God wanted us to do. "Stand still and do nothing." In the midst of my prayers, the confirmation came.

I asked one of our men to make copies. We rolled out several hundred and distributed them to all the churches in Zaria that night and the following day.

I was well aware in writing those words that I could have been ordering people to surrender to their deaths. In fact, that's what some said. Some couldn't believe I had written this. They recognized my signature, but thought I'd given it under duress. Some even thought the government had bribed me to say this.

But the amazing thing is the people believed me. They believed me and they trusted me.

After I signed the letter I went back to prayer, begging God, "Let there be no bloodshed, let there be no killing."

Yes, there were a few deaths. Some were injured and some pastors were beaten, but it could have been much, much worse.

It quickly became clear that what the militants had hoped for was not happening. The intention behind these attacks was to provoke Christians to retaliate, resist, or take revenge. The extremists were hoping we would provide them with the excuse and justification for more violence.

If Christians had acted with revenge, that would have resulted in the widespread arrest of church leaders. The government would have declared martial law. But that opportunity was lost to the extremists because our response was to obey God and do nothing. Instead the attacks became an embarrassment to the extremists.

§

The following day, the same professor who had raised the alarm went to see the burning churches and saw crowds of young Muslim men. They were gathering in their hundreds.

Reports of attacks were coming from two different parts of the city, Samaru and Kongo. Even at Sabon Gari, close to the army barracks, churches and houses were being burned. We heard that Muslims were threatening to go on the rampage in Katsina, 120 miles away, but the police there had stopped it. Why couldn't they have done the same in Zaria?

It still wasn't safe to go out, so we hunkered down in the doctor's house. By now we had been informed that my name was on a kill list, and mine was not the only one. The university chaplain had been targeted, along with several others. Dr Bitrus Gani, who had given me safe haven, was also on that list. The military commander had no choice but to evacuate us.

The military planned to escort us to a safe house in town that was well protected and surrounded by soldiers. But first they had to get us there. It was Wednesday afternoon, the third day of the troubles.

I grabbed my Bible and we headed out in convoy. Had I known what lay ahead, I would have packed a good deal more. I was confident nothing would happen to my house because our neighbours included a high-ranking official in the federal government, the chief magistrate of the Zaria Court, and the local government chairman. To cap it all there were government offices all around. It was an unlikely trouble spot.

A Land Rover swept ahead of our military bus, where I sat with Dr Gani and Hannatu, who was too innocent to be afraid. She sat beside me in her little blue dress with her hair pulled tightly into plaits.

On the way to the guesthouse, we passed hundreds of young people, mainly rough-looking teenagers with cutlasses, clubs, and machetes. They were shouting, "Allahu Akbar!"

There were two mercies for which we were grateful. First, they didn't know we were in the convoy. When they saw the military vehicles, they just parted to let us through. And in those days, they didn't have guns, otherwise many more would have been killed.

Hannatu stared at this mob and said, "Daddy, what did you do?"

I said, "Nothing."

"Why do they want to kill you?"

"I don't know."

We passed through one barricade and then another.

President Babangida made a broadcast to the nation saying the church burnings amounted to war, and those who had carried them out would be lined up in front of a firing squad.

It was bluster. Although the state governor had some men arrested, not a single prosecution was made and they were all released. It looked as though the extremists could get away with anything.

Abubakar Bako, the poor preacher in Kafanchan whose alleged blasphemy was seized upon as the excuse to riot, was declared a wanted man. Abubakar, a convert to Christianity, had to flee the country and run for his life – even though no shred of evidence was ever produced against him. Nevertheless, the radicals called for Bako to be brought forward, tried, and killed under Islamic law. All of this was the sign for us that what we feared had begun to happen.

In seventy-two hours, the militants had killed and wounded and destroyed more than 100 churches, along with Christian homes and businesses. Throughout those hours of chaos, not a single police officer made an appearance.

Those attacks had been well orchestrated. They were organized and deliberate. And the rallying cry for the violence was that allegation of blasphemy in Kafanchan. But what had Kafanchan to do with Zaria?

I believe the militants had planned this long ago. Their plan was to drive Christians out or to kill them. These things were already happening in Sudan and parts of North Africa, and inflammatory teachings were calling for the same thing right here in Zaria. And from Zaria, it would have spread all over.

§

By Friday, things had calmed down enough for me to drive to St Andrew's Church, what was left of it. The former courthouse had been burned down. Only a few days ago, the once white-painted church had been surrounded by ornamental trees and Queen of the Night that filled the air with their fragrance. Now the overwhelming stench hanging in the air was that of an incinerator. Everything inside was destroyed. Only the walls remained. The mob had poured in kerosene and set it ablaze.

My own house next door had fared even worse.

It had been blown up, we believe. People who lived nearby described a big bang, indicative of a gas cylinder thrown into the flames to blast the house apart. Though the walls remained, they were badly cracked. The burning rafters had caved in, plunging the corrugated iron roof to the ground, where it now lay in charred and twisted strips. Some had melted in the heat.

Had Hannatu and I been inside…

After three days the smoke had died down but the dust had whipped up the ashes and scattered them over hundreds of feet in every direction.

There was nothing in these ruins that could be salvaged. I gave up looking for possessions: everything was destroyed. Instead, I started to look for a witness. I took photographs and collected ashes from the church and the vicarage, from my bedroom and the children's room. Then I found my communion chalice. The flames had burned away the base, leaving only the silver-plated rim.

On the floor of the living room, still attached to a fragment of wall, I found a beautiful gold cross that had been given to Gloria in Germany. The fire had spared it. It was almost unmarked.

Today I still have the ashes of my house in Zaria. I keep them in my living room in a mock coffin to remind me that I died on 12 March 1987. They remind me and my children that every day that I live is a bonus. I am living on extra time. We will never forget.

§

Gloria was still away, and I was bracing myself to be soundly blamed for what had happened.

She had left for Numan the day the trouble began. Communications were poor, and Gloria never listened to the news, so it was a shock when the news caught up with her. After two days, someone came by from the Women's Fellowship to inform her that Christians had been attacked in Zaria.

"We've just been praying for them," she told Gloria. "They killed one of the Christian leaders as he was preaching. They said he was from Plateau State. He was not a very tall person, and they stabbed him with a knife…"

Gloria immediately grabbed baby Rinji, informed her sister she was going home, and hailed a taxi to take her more than 280 miles to Jos. She was convinced I had been murdered in the pulpit.

When Gloria arrived in Jos, she contacted my older sister Mildred to say she was going on to Zaria, another 150-mile journey. I'd managed to get through to Mildred to reassure her we were still alive, and she managed to restrain Gloria for a further ten days in Jos where she would be safe. Eventually, Gloria could bear it no longer and jumped in a taxi.

She arrived unannounced about a fortnight after our church and our home had been burned to the ground. She ran to me and we hugged and held each other. Then she took Hannatu while I took Rinji and we went together to sift through the remains.

Gloria is a thrifty woman and she had squirrelled away suitcases of brand-new belongings in a storeroom, cases full of things I had brought from a trip to America, all our wedding gifts, a pressure cooker, everything and anything that might come in useful one day. Apart from that, I knew there was nothing left, just a couple of changes of baby clothes and the one spare wrapper Gloria had taken to Numan. Beyond that, not a shred. I steeled myself for a tongue-lashing.

Gloria looked at the ruins and she looked at me. "Here it comes," I thought. And she said, "Ben, you're a preacher."

"Yes."

"You do preach that heaven and earth will pass away."

"Yes."

"Then it has to start with you, otherwise people will not believe it. Material things are gone, so what? Let's go."

I couldn't believe my ears. This was not just a woman, but the woman God had sent to strengthen me. I loved her all the more. She was still only in her twenties, but her wisdom was beyond her age.

She didn't blame the Muslims and she didn't blame me: she didn't blame anybody. She simply said, "Ben, heaven and earth will pass away, so why should we worry?"

From that moment, Gloria continued to live as normal – without a thing to her name, and without a single word of complaint.

UNDER SUSPICION

At St Andrew's, we resumed our services but in the open air. In time, we would rebuild the church and make it bigger. It had already been straining at the seams. We had the land, and now we had the opportunity.

People began to give us food, clothing, and utensils and Gloria, Hannatu, Rinji, and I were invited to move into a flat nearby belonging to the prominent former vice chancellor, Ishaya Audu.

It was about this time that I started to come under suspicion. It seems that in some circles I was getting a reputation as a firebrand preacher. Apparently, some saw me as a turbulent priest.

I had my own suspicions that members of the security forces had begun checking out the church. I discovered that a member of the Woman's Fellowship was a senior police officer. And a young man and a member of the choir were employees of the National Security Agency. It couldn't be a coincidence.

All this began to emerge after the crisis.

I was growing in influence and in the eyes of the military regime I had some dangerous friends. The Department of Social Sciences at the University of Zaria was considered a hotbed of radicals, whether of Islam or the left. These were fellows who wanted to change the world. And I liked some of them a lot.

I used to play squash at the polo club opposite the church. Whenever I saw these guys gathering for a beer, they would call, "Pastor... Reverend..." and I would join them. They would pass me papers that I would read and get excited about. I hate oppression and I hate corruption and we all had a common dislike of military regimes. Some of this must have found its way into my sermons. And that must have made the Babangida regime just a little nervous.

After the church burnings, I was asked to make a presentation about the riots to the Judicial Commission of Inquiry. Some Christian professors at the university helped with the research and on behalf of the Christians of Zaria, we wrote up everything we could. I took the opportunity to say some of what I had been saying from the pulpit.

But before I could make my presentation to the panel itself, a top security official from Lagos came to see me. He was a strong-looking man in his forties, with a military bearing, dressed in a brown suit, white shirt, and black tie. He said he was on assignment from the National Security Agency and asked me to tell him everything I knew about the situation and what I thought might be the solution.

Oh, the Lord gave me an opportunity! I was able to tell him all my fears about the theology of jihad and how it was a threat to Christians in northern Nigeria. I said everything! I spoke for hours. But my interrogator did not appear to be taking notes.

After we finished, he said to me, "Ben, I feel convicted… I must tell you… Everything you have said is in this briefcase. It has been recorded. Is there anything under God you feel you want me to erase?"

I said, "No. Please take it to the president – everything I've said."

While I was walking out, I said to him, "I have my coffin ready, so don't worry about me. I'm ready to die." We shook hands and he left. I never saw him again.

Even today, there is still a chance my phones may be tapped. The way I look at it, if they're interested in me, they will get their information. So I will make it easy for them – I've got nothing to hide.

Shortly after my brush with this agent, I made my representation to the Judicial Commission. From the way I was interrogated, I thought I was going to be shot.

I was representing the Christian Association of Nigeria. It was the first time we had sat before a panel of judges, police, security, and senior civil servants.

They fired question after question at me. When I responded, they would demand, "How do you know?" I could point to the relevant section and say, "Here, on such and such a date, appendix this or that…" It took an hour and a half. At times they tried to cut me short, but I would say, "No, I have to represent the Christians. We are the aggrieved, my lord."

Our evidence became a book: *And it Came to Pass…*[4]

§

Some in the church were also starting to have their suspicions about me. Once again, it was linked to my concerns about the military regime.

As well as a Shia revival that was calling for jihad, there was jihadi revival among the Sunni Muslims too. An Islamic scholar in Kaduna, Abubakar Gumi, had formed a movement called the Izala Society. They were a revivalist elite, and it was thought President Babangida himself had been tutored under this man who had said many terrible things against Christians.

In the army there was a new cadre, known as the Babangida Boys. These were young Muslim officers who were being fast-tracked to money and power beyond their seniors.

As a Christian leader, I had spoken out against injustice, along with the failure of the Nigerian economy. The profligacy of Babangida's government was clear to all. The Naira had plunged from two to twenty against the dollar, and he had dragged us to the IMF and the World Bank to take out unnecessary loans. And at every step, the general was bolstering his own succession. His overture to the Organisation of Islamic Cooperation (OIC) was part of that.

As a pastor in such a poor district, I could see that Nigeria was becoming trapped in slavery to debt from which we might never emerge. The Christians would suffer, and the Christians in the north would suffer the most.

---

4   Subtitled: *The Sordid Story of the Bombing of 113 Churches by Muslim Rioters within 20 Hours in March 1987*, Christian Association of Nigeria, Zaria, 1987.

So I had spoken out. But some believed I had overstated the problem. Babangida was not like that, they said: he was a good man, a nice guy, and his chief of defence and chief of general staff were Christians.

Some of my senior priests could barely contain their anger at my outspokenness. James in particular, let's call him that, was furious. He was older than me. Most of them were. He said, "You want to make yourself popular, don't you?"

"No, Sir..." I tried to explain.

"That's what you're looking for. You just want to be popular."

"No."

"Shut up!"

"Excuse me, Sir. Just let me explain..."

And all this came after the burning of the churches. Some people had come to me to say, "Ben, you were right." But at the same time, I could hear whispering from others. Some were muttering whether maybe it was me who had brought down this calamity upon the churches. Some looked at me in a way that seemed to say, "This is all your fault."

And with our churches in ruins, I began to wonder if they were right. I fell into moments of self-pity and self-accusation.

But I had one clear advantage. It was Lent, a time of prayer and fasting. So over this period, it was difficult for the devil to get through. Self-doubt was quickly defeated.

This was my prayer: "Lord, You saved me in Lagos. Your promises are true, and You have never failed in Your promises in my life. You brought me to Zaria. From a small number, we have grown. Your gospel is true. People are being saved. I have seen an army colonel, doctors, and PhDs come forward to pray the same prayer I prayed to receive Jesus Christ. I have seen churches born and multiply and grow. I cannot doubt You now."

I had learned to go privately into my place of prayer. This was one of God's greatest gifts: "your Father, who sees what is done in secret, will reward you" (Matthew 6:4). So I simply stopped defending myself. Every time there was an accusation, I would go into the closet and pray. This has become a lesson of life: go into the closet, examine myself, and ask for God's judgment and His mercy. Lay it all before God and walk away.

And in my prayer closet on this occasion, I received His encouragement.

Was I doing this to collect people's money? No. Was I doing it for popularity? No. Would I allow wolves to devour the flock of Jesus Christ? No.

Had I provoked the crisis in Zaria? No. It would have happened anyway. And it had started in Kafanchan, many miles away, which had no connection with Zaria.

Zaria was a high place of Islamic learning where the poisonous teaching of jihad was spreading like a stain. It had been Islamic scholar Abubakar Gumi himself who said that because of the sin of one man in Kafanchan (this hapless preacher accused of desecrating the Koran), Muslims should rise in jihad against Christians all over the country.

So I came out of my prayer closet with courage and confidence, not in myself, but in the calling that God had given me to His gospel.

The burning of churches in Zaria in 1987 had been a wake-up call for Christians. But it had been a wake-up call for Muslims too. Suddenly, ordinary older Muslims found themselves facing unfamiliar and troubling strands of Islamic practice.

You cannot separate Islam from politics. It is a mistake to try. Islam is about control. Its very name means submission. Traditionally, in northern Nigeria, Muslims accepted Christians living around them, going out about their business, even doing evangelism, providing those Christians did not aspire to dominate them. And Christians had grown used to a status quo that had existed since the colonial era, and had learned not to struggle for control in these areas.

But this change in mood and theology ushered in a new intolerance. We had already seen it in Sudan. Christians were being made to convert, be enslaved, or leave the country. The world powers were aware, but with one eye on oil, they continued to court Sudan. The black Africans were left without mercy in this world.

When the crisis came home, I learned how to live my life by faith and deal with my accusers. That crisis brought out my leadership style and qualities, but it also drew envy from those who were disinclined to follow such a young and inexperienced boy.

With the hindsight of half a lifetime, I can look back and say I am absolutely certain that I was raised for such a time as that.

And soon after that troubled time, the bishop announced I was to be posted to Zonkwa, south of Kaduna. He said he was moving me for my own safety.

In those days, the postings of clergy were done by archdeacons in counsel with the bishop. On my way to take up my new post, I ran into one of the senior clergy. He asked me, "What did you do to offend your seniors?"

"What?" I asked. It seems there had been quite some discussion before I was posted.

"Apparently the bishop was uncomfortable with you. They said you should be moved."

I didn't know what he was talking about, and he was not inclined to expand. He said, "OK, God bless you."

It was puzzling, because my letter of appointment was a clear promotion. It said I had been sent to Zonkwa as the district chairman, in charge of all forty-five churches over nine parishes. In those days, district chairmen were like local bishops, with the power of hire and fire. I was excited.

§

When we arrived in Zonkwa, it was in my beloved brown panel van. But my little Mazda set us off on the wrong foot. In our street, there lived a senator and a local government chairman. These were the only people with the wherewithal to own a car. Nobody else in the entire village had a vehicle, nor in the whole of our rural church.

Even though our house and all our possessions had been destroyed, for the villagers, this humble van was a symbol of unattainable wealth, and they resented it. It meant nobody was willing to support me financially. Whenever I asked to have something done in the church, they said, "We don't have any money. You have the money."

They also resented Gloria. In the village, people believed that if they opened up about their failings, they would be disgracing the community. But Gloria was not the kind of person to take things at face value. She would investigate everything. That was how we found out about the children who were drinking, smoking, getting pregnant, and stealing.

Their families thought that if we knew about their troubles, we would look down on them and condemn them. Because that was the kind of preaching they had heard in the village. All they needed was a little more acceptance, and that led to a little more honesty.

So, within the first six months of our ministry, the church changed. It grew exponentially from fewer than 300 people to some 700.

What won over the hearts of the women was Gloria's life. It began when a primary schoolgirl came to Zonkwa on a school visit. She fainted from sunstroke and a touch of malaria. But all the children were convinced she was troubled by a demon and had died. They fled back to their homes screaming. Gloria heard the commotion and came out and picked up this little girl.

In our communities, there was often a shortage of medicine. So I had brought more than enough pills and potions with me to go round. The little girl was boiling to the touch. So I sponged her down for half an hour and gave her paracetamol. After about an hour I administered chloroquine, two teaspoonfuls. I kept sponging her with tepid water, and about three hours later, her temperature had gone down. By this time it was 5 p.m.

Her parents had to come from distant farmlands, and when they finally arrived, they feared they were coming to fetch a corpse. That's what they had been told. They were distraught.

To their amazement, when I brought out their daughter, not only was she alive, but she managed to eat a little porridge. I asked them to wait for an hour before I could give her more chloroquine. Then her grateful parents took her home.

I had learned from CMS missionaries that you don't give medicines to the people to administer. They were not well enough educated to know how to do that. Instead, you asked them to come and take the medicine from you in person. And that was good, because it gave us the opportunity to witness.

Gloria was our nurse. No, she was our matron. She would deliver babies, help people keep their homes clean, and fight with them over hygiene. "Clean your toilet, bathe your children!" She was like a nosy old woman, always checking on people's houses and interfering with their businesses. "Look at your shop! You can't serve people that!" So, when they saw her coming, they would scurry into action.

"Quickly, tidy up, Mama Church is coming!"

Gloria was young, but they treated her with great respect. I would administer the medication and we would get talking.

The farmer whose daughter we had been treating for sunstroke came for some more medicine. He was a polygamist. Along with his two wives he had a guilty conscience. "I've failed God," he wailed. He believed his second wife was the end of his salvation, so he wouldn't go to church.

"That's a bad reason for not going to church," I told him. "Where did you read that?"

"That's what they said."

"Did you read that in the Bible?" I pressed him.

"No."

"So, are you believing in what people say, or are you believing the Bible?"

We became friends. The next time he came for medicine for his girl, he said, "Sir, can I come to your church? Can I bring my two wives?"

I said, "Bring everybody!"

Gloria grew the church for me. She interfered. She went

to the market. If she saw somebody with red hair, which was a sign of malnutrition, she would say, "No, she is sick! Bring her to our home."

She would feed them, and we would talk to them. Gloria helped them a lot. She taught them personal female hygiene. She taught them how to sit and walk like ladies. The girls loved her, but their mothers hated her, because their own children were now looking tidier, cleaner, and more presentable than them. Gloria won the hearts of the girls across all the denominations. They all came to Gloria for counselling.

There were two girls' secondary schools in the area and the principals loved Gloria too. When two schools came together to listen to Gloria at a one-day conference, 2,000 girls turned up. She would go weekly, one week to one school, one week to the other, and teach for free. And she ran her own Girls' Fellowship. Girls deserted their own churches to come to hear Gloria.

Now the mothers really did take exception. Their children were opening up. These girls were telling Gloria things their mothers wouldn't want Gloria to know. But for all those who took offence at Gloria, there were many others who took encouragement.

Gloria organized a women's conference that drew in 5,000 people. We followed that with a youth conference for upwards of 1,000. And I began a basketball team and started a league in Kaduna.

§

There were changes in the hearts of the people, and there were changes in the church too.

We asked the Lord to repeat what He had done through us in Zaria over the past four years. We had seen evangelism, churches growing, and schools and clinics built and staffed by locals. Believing for the same, we opened up the district for mission. And because we had made friends in the area, there was not a week when people didn't come to support the mission. Enthusiasm for what God could do began to take hold.

In my first month, I organized a weekday prayer meeting in Zonkwa town hall. After the church burnings, it was a call to watch and pray to prevent this evil from spreading. Everybody came. Nobody went to work. Thousands poured into my prayer meeting. The city came to a standstill. Police were all over the place, running around to keep order. Word went up to the governor. Change was in the air. We began to build up a head of steam.

Every church in the diocese had to raise its own funds, from which we paid our salaries. In previous years, the cathedral had been forced to subsidize the diocese. Money was so short, the district chairman had been unable to pay the salaries of his staff. They were owed several months' pay. But within the first four months, the Lord had helped us to inspire the people to raise everything we needed for an entire year.

We were able to clear all our debts and pay our diocesan contributions ahead of any other district. This had never happened before. We even managed to overpay. It was all done with full accountability and the books were made available for all.

Zonkwa was exciting for me, because while the people prospered, I also prospered. Gloria started a piggery, then set up businesses with guinea pigs, rabbits, chickens, and goats. There was no electricity, so we had neither freezer nor fridge. Whatever we cooked, we had to eat immediately. Even so, within twelve months, we were prospering.

Then God blessed two villages where we had started churches with bees. I helped the villagers establish honey farms. I had so many drums of honey that I was giving them away.

We planted cash crops of potato and corn on church fields to generate an extra income. Then we went on to the real business of planting churches, following the principles we had learned in Zaria. In twelve months we had planted eleven churches. And then we started another big financial drive to begin a school.

It was among the girls that Gloria was having the most influence. Some of the mothers resented it at the time, but even they came round later, when they realized that, before their eyes, their girls were turning into fine young ladies.

For the most dramatic turnaround, we had to wait a number of years. The one woman who disliked Gloria and me the most, who had led the charge against us, eventually had a total change of heart.

This influential businesswoman was in her fifties and held all the other women in her sway. Gloria had a run-in with her after she gave her an out-of-pocket allowance to attend a conference. So far so good. But then Gloria called her to account for how these funds had been spent. Accountability? That was unheard of! She was outraged.

From that time on, this woman spread evil stories against Gloria and set herself up in opposition to me.

But then her eldest son gave his life to Christ and was on fire for God. Years after we had left Zonkwa, he wanted to come to the Christian Institute in Jos, but had nobody to pay his fees. We were in Jos by then, so I awarded him a scholarship.

His mother came to see us and brought along three friends for moral support. But as soon as the woman clapped eyes on us, she started crying. She couldn't string together a single sentence. All evening, all she could say was, "Forgive me, forgive me."

We said, "If we hadn't forgiven you, we wouldn't have paid your son's fees." That son is now a canon with a Master's degree and a very proud mother. What we had planted took root over time.

We had one rascally girl in our care whose parents had given up on her. When she needed an education, Gloria took her to a public school. The principal was less than pleased. He said, "Mama, the last time you brought a girl to us she ran away, and we had to go and find her and bring her back to the centre. Now you're bringing another one. They all run away. Don't you ever get tired?"

Patiently watching this exchange was a woman who was obviously pregnant. She cut in, "Mrs Kwashi, please don't get tired. I am one of those girls. Mama, I was in Zonkwa. It was you who taught me to wash my pants and how to behave like a girl. Look at me now. A bank manager has married me! If you hadn't told me these things, why would this man have even looked at me long enough to marry me?"

Gloria just never gives up.

Good job too. After twelve months, the bishop moved us again.

It was time to fight the battle for Kaduna Polytechnic.

BATTLE FOR THE CHAPEL

Kaduna Polytechnic was jointly owned by all the states of northern Nigeria. They wanted to build a chapel and they needed a chaplain. The Polytechnic Christian Council had gone to the bishop and asked for me by name. So we set off for Kaduna.

Kaduna is not far from Zaria. I had made many friends there and not a few enemies. Some of the Muslims at the polytechnic knew of me by reputation and were wary. Some had me down as a troublemaker because of that huge prayer meeting in Zonkwa.

The Christian Council showed me the land where they wanted to build. It was July and the rains had stopped, so I said, "Why don't we get started?" We pulled in the student architects and engineers and they designed it.

I went to the provost, who was a Muslim, and said we were going to start building the chapel. And then I got a security call. The provost's office had received letters from the Muslim Students' Association saying there would be no chapel built on the grounds of the polytechnic. If any such thing happened, there would be civil war.

The provost asked me to suspend the building while he pacified the students. I told him, "No, Sir, there will be no pacifying, there will be no suspension. I am here for this purpose and this is what I'm going to do."

I got the students and we started preparing the foundations. The Muslim students were true to their word. They threatened to riot. Crowds began to build and there was a shouting match. Muslims and Christians faced up to one another in the open air and there was a stand-off.

The Muslims insisted, "You will not build!"

The Christians retorted, "We are going to build!" Both sides were equally determined.

The police were called in and, before matters could get out of hand, the provost closed the school. It was a sensible move and helped us enormously. While the school was closed, I told my student helpers to turn up with their tools each day and get to work. So, while the gates were locked to the rioters, we continued to lay out the foundations.

§

Persecution and opposition were one thing, but rats were quite another.

Gloria and I were put into accommodation at the Catholic Social Centre before being shifted somewhere more permanent. A year had passed since our house was burned down, so we didn't have many clothes. Whenever our friends gave us anything new, we packed it away neatly in a grey leather suitcase, along with clothes we were keeping for the children. We lifted that treasured case for safekeeping onto the top of the wardrobe.

The day came when Mr Afolayan, the chairman of the chapel, wanted to meet us with our family, so we decided to look our smartest. I hauled the suitcase down from the wardrobe and saw that rats had eaten a hole in the centre of it. And when I opened the case, I discovered they had chewed right the way through it, along with its entire contents.

I couldn't believe my eyes. It was too much. First our church and our home, now this. This one leather suitcase was all we had left.

As I picked out the remains of our clothes, I just started crying. My daughter's brand-new shirt and skirt and pants and sandals – all eaten through. Along with my shirt and Gloria's new outfits. It was the last straw. I began to wail. I cried so loudly that Gloria ran in.

"What is it?"

"I understand Muslim persecution, but I don't understand this. Look! Why would God do this to me? What have I done?"

Gloria took a look at the tattered remnants and she began to cry too. I was paralysed.

These rats were more than I could handle. Who had sent them? Why would God do this to me?

I said, "God, now what? Do You expect me to walk around in rags? That even rats should persecute me, and You will not help?" I had lost my perspective. Of course God doesn't send His children rats.

All this time, the chairman had been waiting for us to come to the meeting which was being held in our honour. Finally, when we didn't show up, the chairman came over to us.

I said, "I'm not doing this work any more. I'm done."

He said, "Why?"

"Look. My house has been burned down. I understand that, but look at this."

He looked at the suitcase and laughed. He said, "Ben!"

I said, "It's no laughing matter for me, Sir."

We had tears in our eyes. He calmed us down and said, "Just come as you are." So, we did. And as soon as I saw the people, the life came flowing back into me and I was healed. They showed me my office and the young men and women I would be working with, and I could see immediately where we were going and what we should be doing. I knew just what to do. I forgot my problems. I was excited.

When I came back home to that chewed-up suitcase and our belongings, I could see the funny side. The devil just wanted to break me down. He's a loser and my laughter proved he had just lost again.

With hindsight, I think God wanted me to release my tears. I had not cried up to this point. The man in me was strong and confident, but for some reason, this thing hit me terribly hard.

There was a need for me to be a child of God all over again and I returned to Him with joy. He wanted me to be human again, to feel what people were feeling.

As for Gloria… she was fine. She said, "You know, there are

people who don't have a thing. So why are we crying over this? Forget it."

But she wouldn't let me throw the clothes away. The following morning, she set about mending and patching them. We had no sewing machine, so she made do with a needle and thread. Gloria mended our clothes; in fact, she mended enough to give some away. She was totally undefeated.

§

While all this was going on, I was invited to preach at the cathedral in Kaduna. After I had spoken, the Diocese Education Secretary came to see me and asked for a copy of my notes. He was a retired principal and had been a classmate of the bishop.

I handed my script to him and he asked, "Have you done your Master's yet?"

I said, "Sir, I haven't even done my first degree in divinity yet."

He gave me a look and went straight to the bishop to tell him off for squandering his resources by refusing to train his staff. The message sank in.

The bishop asked for space to be set aside at the Theological College of Northern Nigeria in Bukuru, where I could train to get a Bachelor of Divinity. At least, that was the plan. But by now the school was already full. There was no room for me.

In the meantime, I was gallivanting around the wilderness preaching. When I returned I found three messages from the bishop. He had come to my hotel room in person on each occasion to deliver them.

I said, "Gloria, we are done for! There must be a problem. Why would the bishop come here to see me himself?"

So, we rushed off early in the morning to see Bishop Titus, the gruff former lieutenant-colonel. As soon as I got there, he ordered, "Ben, sit down! Write a resignation letter."

I was bewildered: "From where?"

"From the polytechnic. Write it quick!"

I couldn't believe it. "No, Sir!" I'd been in the place barely three months. "Sir, I can't write my resignation. I have to give them salary in lieu of notice."

"How much is it?"

"Four hundred Naira." The bishop motioned for one of his clergy who gave me the money and said, "Pack your bags. You're going to TCNN." Space had become available.

"But, Sir, I didn't apply to the school."

"You will write the application there and fill in your form there. You have your records?"

"No, Sir, all my certificates have been burned."

"Your records are there and they will give you admission."

It was all moving too fast. I said, "Sir, what about my wife?"

I'm not sure he had figured on Gloria, who was standing there beside me, looking even more bewildered than the bishop. I don't think he'd given her a thought. He looked doubtful: "Well, I don't know…"

I was taken aback. "So what will happen to her?"

"Mmm…" he scratched his chin. "She'll continue to teach at St Francis."

Gloria, who was by my side, piped up, "No, Baba [daddy], you know me, Sir! I will follow my husband, even if it is to cook for him morning and evening."

The bishop laughed and asked, "They have married quarters?"

"Yes, Sir."

"OK Gloria, you follow him and go and cook for him."

But Gloria ended up doing rather more than the bishop had in mind. Not one, but two places had become available at TCNN. And according to the school policy, if a student's wife was sufficiently qualified, then she could study there as well.

A month later I caught up with the bishop again at a service, clutching Gloria's papers.

When he clapped eyes on me, he demanded, "What are you doing here?"

"Sir, Gloria has got admission."

"Really?"

"Yes!"

"Bring it. Let me sign."

So he signed it. And then he drew back. "Oh! School fees!"

I said, "Don't worry, Sir. I will look for how to pay the school fees."

"God bless you, my son! Go back to school! Go back, go back!"

And the bishop arranged for me to be put on a stipend as though I was still working in the diocese. It was a great help.

I would like to have completed the polytechnic chapel before I left. But that chapel is there today, built on our foundations. They found a novel way to overcome the confrontation. The chapel would have stood right at the gate of the polytechnic. It would have been the first thing you saw when you entered. The Muslims didn't like that. So, the solution was to build the chapel, right there, and to move the gate. It worked.

By that time, we had moved back to TCNN.

§

They gave us a great welcome. They already knew us, of course. They were using our story as a case study for the students, so it felt like a hero's return. We arrived late in the day, and by then the hostels were full, so they housed us in quarters reserved for their junior staff. This was an elevation! Although I was there only to study, they appointed me chapel secretary.

Those two years at TCNN were a great time of rest and recuperation. The Lord said, "Come aside and rest in Me." And He blessed our work. I became one of the top students. It was good news for Gloria too.

Although neither I nor Gloria had actually applied to the college, we found ourselves sitting in the same classroom, training together for our Bachelors of Divinity.

We spent two years there with Hannatu and Rinji, leading an exciting life. They would go down to the nursery school in the morning and Gloria would teach them in the afternoon when we came back from class. And that was to prepare her for homeschooling, which is a later story.

Every weekend I would run away to preach to earn my keep. It meant we had enough to pay Gloria's school fees.

Her results were very good, and after two years we graduated.

§

It was now 1990, and the church was shifting its focus towards mission. My experience in Zaria had stood me in good stead, and I was invited to be principal of St Francis of Assisi Theological College in Wusasa. The principal's house was not yet ready, so we shared a hostel with the students.

In the whole school, there were only about forty-five students. I told Bishop Titus, who was chairman of the board, that this small number could never be enough to service the whole of northern Nigeria. What we had to do was recruit local indigenous students whom we would train and send back to their own people. "That's the way to do mission," I said, "because that's how Paul did it." Everywhere Paul went, he raised local leaders.

Bishop Titus could see my point, but he was doubtful. The finances were not good, he explained.

I said, "Sir, I will take responsibility if you will allow me. I can sort out the funding and the accommodation. Just give me permission."

He raised his eyebrows. "Ben, are you serious?"

"Sir, just say 'Yes.'"

He did. But he made it clear that he would hold me fully responsible.

I told Gloria that our first job, as soon as school resumed, would be to close the place down. We would start moulding mud bricks to build more classrooms, more toilets, and a vice principal's house. Gloria would organize the staff wives and other women and make provision for food.

Wherever I went, people raised support for the school, but we all had to buy in to the project ourselves. The Anglicans supported the students and gave them pocket money each week. So, I cancelled that along with the staff allowances and pooled all that money with the funds I was raising, because we were going to build.

There was rebellion in the air. But I told them, "Fine, there's the gate. It is very simple for me: I'm not looking for a job. You're the ones who are looking for a certificate. If there is any act of rebellion, I will dismiss you. I'm ready for you. The choice is yours."

At that, the students backed down. I told them, "You now have a mission," and the student numbers grew from forty-five to 107. Together we moulded more bricks and lined the foundations.

Up until then, St Francis had an elitist edge to it. One or two British missionaries who were with me didn't understand what I was doing. They felt I had changed the school ethos, that I was lowering academic standards and turning the college into a bush school. The rumbling grew into a campaign, which erupted like a thunderclap in one of the morning prayers.

One of the students, a Nigerian, was leading. He said, "Let us pray." We kneeled. He continued, "Let's pray for our missionaries who have left so much in England. They are here and they are suffering. Pray that God will reward them and help them and give them fortitude. Lord, in Your mercy, hear our prayer."

He continued: "Let's pray for these white missionaries…"

I saw red. I got up from my seat at the back of the chapel. I said, "Folks, this prayer is over. Sit down! If you have something to say, tell it. These white missionaries, they've got insurance, they've got mortgages. They've got furnished houses and a car!" And I pointed out how much they were earning.

I said, "My salary is less than theirs, with a wife and two children. I have no house. I'm sleeping on the floor with you. I have no insurance, I have nothing. Who is the missionary? I am my missionary here! These will go back to their houses. I have had my house burned. You're telling me the missionaries are suffering? Who is suffering? Get it right into your heads; everybody say, 'We are our missionaries.'"

"We are our missionaries!"

"Get up and go to your class!" I was mad.

Three months down the line, the bricks, which we had made with mud, hay, and straw, had dried properly. And we used them to construct our classrooms and hostels and the vice principal's house. These new students built their own accommodation, and together we built our new college.

To begin with, it was a strange time for me. Once I had completed chapel at eight or nine in the morning and the students had gone off to their assignments, I was left with nothing. I would sit down on a Sunday morning and say to Gloria, "I've done church. Now what?" I needed people.

Gloria thoughtfully brought me a cup of tea and said, "Ben, you're unhappy."

"You're right, Gloria."

She frowned. "I've been thinking. In 1982, you conducted a baptism under a tree not far from Wusasa. Is that church still there?"

I said, "You're right! Why don't we go there?"

We took the school bus, a blue fourteen-seater Peugeot, and drove to Karaukarau, nine miles away. By now they had built a big church and it was full to overflowing. When the people outside saw me stepping out of the bus, they screamed, "Rev. Kwashi has come!" The whole church ran out. "Rev. Kwashi! See, I'm one of those you baptized under the tree!"

We started a whole new service. I preached and came back rejoicing. I was so excited! And from that day on, when the students finished chapel, we knew it was time to get started. We went to the village and our lives came back to us again.

§

During our second year at TCNN, a professor came over from Minnesota and was teaching my class. Then it was my turn to preach. He came over after the service. "Ben, we need you in the US. This kind of preaching is what we need."

He offered me a scholarship in the Anglican department in his Lutheran seminary after I graduated.

True to his word, he sent no fewer than six admission letters, all addressed to me. He must have reasoned that six ought to be enough to overcome the vagaries of the Nigerian postal system.

When these letters arrived, I waited two days before telling Gloria. I was torn. We were putting the school straight on the mission path and the students were enthusiastic. But somehow, underneath it all, I was getting tired of the persecution and tired of the trouble, so when this letter came, I felt, "Lord. Let me go to America and have peace."

I was also feeling a little weary with the opposition I had encountered from some quarters in the Anglican Church. This invitation presented an opportunity that spoke directly to the way I was feeling. I thought I might as well go.

Gloria and I said, "Lord, if only You would repeat in America the ten years of ministry we have enjoyed in Nigeria, it will glorify You, Lord." I didn't see this as a temptation, far from it: I looked on it as an opportunity.

Everything had fallen into place. The scholarship had been paid. Three years for Gloria and for me – $66,000 – fully paid. It was too good to be true. I didn't even need to pray about it. Gloria was pregnant at the time with our third, Arbet, and when I told her, she was in favour. "That will be great! We will have our baby there."

That was it, case closed. I took the letter to Bishop Titus who said he would have a meeting to discuss it and give me his answer.

Meanwhile, as principal, I was invited to give a report on the school. Some bishops were happy with the progress I was making, others were not. Those opposed felt I had lowered the standard of education and cheapened the qualification. Some even seemed convinced I was set on destroying St Francis. They argued that no sensible bishop should send his students there.

I had argued it through with my chairman, my bishop, who trusted me. I said, "Sir, we are training people to go to England to study. We don't need that. We should train people who will work in Nigeria. We need to change our curriculum. In any case, the pastors in England are killing the church. The number of churchgoers is steadily declining. So, we will only be sending them to England to learn how to kill the church!"

Bishop Titus laughed, "Ben, you're crazy!"

"No, Sir, it's the truth. If we send them to England, they will learn how to be neither English nor Nigerians."

He said, "You're right!" The bishop came up with his own examples of priests who had gone to England. "They return and look down on us," he said. "They come back and inform me they should have light and water in their vicarages!"

I said, "We should train people to work with what they've got."

I realized we needed to train people who would address the particular needs of our suffering situation in Nigeria. They were living every day with bombs and gunshots, their houses and churches were being burned, and they were having to run for their lives. Our priests had to learn how to live the gospel in that context. That is how we needed to train them.

Opinions on my approach remained divided. But Bishop Titus later said it was the consensus of the bishops that my scholarship to the US should be deferred for a year so I could continue to develop the work. He wrote to the seminary on my behalf and, amazingly, they agreed to hold the scholarship over.

It was a lonely walk for Gloria and me, but God kept us focused and away from diversions, gossip, and time-wasting meetings. And over time, my approach to training was vindicated. Eventually, six of our graduates were appointed bishops.

God turned the story around.

Then everything became rather complicated.

§

It was now 1992. I had just returned from a trip to the Middle East. Gloria picked me up from Kano airport and told me Bishop Titus was asking to see me. She didn't know why, but he needed to see me immediately. I had done something wrong, but I didn't know what. What I knew full well was I couldn't face the boss in my jeans and T-shirt, so I went home to put on a cassock.

Bishop Titus prayed and handed me a letter. I tore it open. It was from the Primate of Nigeria, Joseph Adetiloye. I had been elected to the See of Jos. I was to be made a bishop! And I was to reply in writing within a week.

In one hand I had that letter. In the other, I held my deferred scholarship to study in America. Which was it to be?

Gloria was concerned. The way she put it was like this: we were not yet ready to be bishop, let alone Bishop of Jos. We knew the place too well.

Jos was my home diocese. It had been mismanaged. People had invented crises that were beyond repair. Christians were taking one another to court and there were secret societies. People hated each other and the church had emptied. In all its twelve years as a diocese, they had managed to plant just one church. There had been no good news from Jos for more than a decade. And Gloria and I had had enough of crisis, persecution, and danger. Why should we go to Jos?

I took all this to a prayer meeting with my friend Dr Bitrus Gani. While we were deep in prayer, the doctor said, "Thus says the Lord, 'Ben, America is the window, but Jos is the door. Jesus said, "I am the door."'"

No! I refused to believe it. But I didn't say so. I went back that evening and told Gloria. She said, "Ben, we are not going to Jos."

We needed to pray. But God seemed to be silent.

Sometimes people ask me, "What should I do when God is silent?" I have learned that if God has already given an assignment, He may be silent because your question is simply stupid. You have already been told what to do! Go and get started, and God will back you.

In my case, it was clear what was needed. Within two days I was ready to give my reply to the Primate of Nigeria. God had changed my mind.

The call that God had given me in Lagos had come back to me: "Go and repair my church." God was never, ever going to call me to comfort, but to His business. There was work to be done. It was not about what America could offer, but the work God had for me. God had already given me my assignment.

Gloria and I were in agreement. We prayed, "Lord, You did it in Zonkwa; You did it in St Andrew's Church; You did it in Ikara; You did it at the polytechnic; and now in St Francis You have done it. Please repeat all these years in Jos. We will go."

We went back to the bishop and collected our letter of appointment. He was very happy. He prayed for us and blessed us. Now we had to keep the matter to ourselves and wait.

In the meantime, I went to play guitar at a Christian concert in Lagos. During an intermission, a friend came over to me and said, "Hey, my Lord Bishop!"

I was astonished. It had not been announced yet. Until the primate says so you are on oath to keep silent. I said, "Hey, don't get me into trouble. How do you know?"

He said, "It's in the papers!" And he brought out the Nigerian *Sunday Times* and there it was, on the front page.

So I dressed properly and went to see Primate Adetiloye, a godly man, who was a disciple of Samuel Ajayi Crowther, with a heart for mission. He was based in Lagos. I said, "Sir, I saw my name."

He said, "Yes, God has called you. The House of Bishops has selected you."

I said, "But, Sir, I'm an evangelist."

He said, "Yes, we are looking for evangelists." He prayed for me.[5]

We started making arrangements to move to Jos for me to be consecrated on 9 February 1992.

---

5   Interview with Ben Kwashi on Clayton TV from Word Alive '11: https://www.clayton.tv/new/0i0/690

And so our term in St Francis ended. But not before Gloria had started a Girl's Guild in Wusasa. The girls in the leadership all went on to marry pastors. One of them was my younger brother. We also left behind the buildings at St Francis that I had designed and we had built with our own hands. The work was finished within five months.

The work in Jos would take longer.

THE WILD WIND

Jos is one of the most beautiful places on God's good earth. It combines mountains, hills, flatlands, and valleys, and that landscape is always changing. Geographers say it was probably volcanic. The soil is so rich that anything you plant there will grow and whatever you can grow in Europe will grow well in Jos. It's the only place in Nigeria where the British were able to plant Irish potatoes, which we now export across the land and beyond.

Jos is set on Plateau State, so-called because the entire land rises for miles around to 5,000 feet above sea level. Because of the height, the climate is temperate all year round. It can reach 32°C in April and May, but only for a few hours in the afternoon. Just occasionally, it will touch freezing point where there is snow on the hills. Many marathon winners have come from Plateau or have trained there.

Most of the people are agrarian farmers, descended from the earliest settlers who were animists. The people tend to be strong but gentle.

Plateau is mining country. There is tin, columbite, and precious stones, including topaz and amethyst – much of it lying almost on the surface, just waiting to be dug out.

It was the British colonialists who discovered tin and moved in to make the most of it. Jos was one of the earliest cities to be developed by the Europeans. It was here that Cornish miners established Africa's first hydroelectric plant in the 1920s. Over the years, those mineral resources have made Jos a magnet for the Chinese, Germans and Lebanese.

They have conquered with commerce what Islam could not conquer with the sword. The Fulani empire held sway over most of northern Nigeria. They came on horseback with their swords, but faltered at Plateau. The people fought them in the hills and the mountains and sent them packing back to the Ottoman Empire.

Jos grew famous for both its mining and its missionaries. Most of the missionaries arrived in 1906 and 1907, paving the way for many international Christian movements, especially from the US and the UK.

Where Islam failed to penetrate, Christian mission prospered. For these and many reasons, Jos became a target.

§

By now I thought I had seen the worst, but all that had gone before, including the burning of my home, was mild turbulence in comparison with what was to come. And it started in Jos.

The Anglican Diocese of Jos was embroiled in tribal infighting. The church clearly had problems. It was torn by division and accusation. Loyalties were divided between two tribes: the Igbos and the Yoruba. They were at loggerheads over who would control the diocese.

That rivalry surfaced in the 1980s when a new provost was installed. He was neither Yoruba nor Igbo. An offering was taken in the church at his installation. But that offering simply disappeared, and no record had been made of what had been given.

The provost meekly asked the standing committee where the money had gone. He didn't realize he was stepping into a minefield.

The majority tribe in the church was Yoruba, while the majority in the diocese were Igbo. The Igbos controlled the money that came into the diocese and withheld their support from this outsider. Meanwhile, the indigenous members of the church, who, like the provost, were neither Yoruba nor Igbo, rallied to the provost's side.

They took one another to court. The previous bishop had to fight so many court cases his ministry became a wild goose chase. He was forced to retire. Some members of the congregation claimed to have been falsely accused over the lost funds. Others were counter-suing for defamation. Evangelism was neglected and many people, young and old, left the church.

Eventually, the matter was referred to the diocesan board, which set up a committee, and that split the church.

St Luke's Cathedral, which should have been raising funds to support the bishop, was divided down the middle and in crisis. They didn't have enough money to run the diocese or support the bishop, and they refused to support the provost financially at all.

The matter was referred up to the archbishop, who set up two powerful committees to try to resolve this issue, but both failed. From there it went to the incoming primate of the Anglican Church of Nigeria.

Archbishop Joseph Adetiloye had a heart for the poor and for mission. He declared the north a mission field and created nine new dioceses. In addition, he split Jos into three. This reduced some of the tensions from tribal competition.

Now I was coming into the picture, and I was neither Igbo nor Yoruba, but Angas. Some were convinced I would further the interests of my own people, but time and events have proved them wrong. My only interest is in promoting the gospel.

Nigeria is riven by division, and not all those divisions are tribal. Some are denominational and some based on envy. These petty resentments of class and anti-colonialism were imported into Nigeria many years before. And they gained a foothold.

The weakness of the Anglican Church in the north was that it had turned its back on its roots, the evangelistic missions of the early 1900s. The Anglican Church neither integrated evangelism nor trained local missionaries.

Most of the Anglican churches in the north were looked on as foreign vestiges of colonial oppression. The indigenous people kept their distance. They preferred to worship in the mission movements brought in by the Sudan Interior Mission, Sudan United Mission (SUM), or, latterly, the Pentecostal churches. The Anglicans were considered to be the educated rich.

Historically, those Cambridge-educated Anglicans were resented by the Baptists, while the UK-centric Anglicans were resented by the Americans, who were still smarting from their War of Independence.

The white, well-educated Anglicans in the north were few but effective. They taught people how to read and write and brought in education and health. Meanwhile, their rivals, the SUM, attracted tradespeople, who struggled to find acceptance with the CMS and felt inferior.

The British colonials made matters worse by favouring the educated Anglicans. They employed them in their district offices where they became the important people with money. Yet many of these newly wealthy Nigerians simply reverted to type and took second wives.

My grandmother led the revolt of the first wives against the second wives. They refused to go to the same church as their husbands and instead joined the SUM. This was considered to be the church of the properly married, while the Anglican Church became known as the church of the second wives and drunkards. The Anglican Church suffered from this for many, many years.

That was then and this was now. What I found before me in Jos were Anglican churches who kept themselves to themselves. They acted as though they were doing the local people a favour by inviting them to church. There was no biblical urgency for evangelism. Outreach had failed and the church was haemorrhaging members. It was even actively throwing people out.

At St Paul's, one of the biggest Igbo churches, some of the younger generation challenged the church over its conduct and were excommunicated. By 1991, they were holding a large Bible study group that was on course to become a Pentecostal church.

This was what I was heading for as bishop. You can see why I didn't want to take up the post! How was I going to set this right? I was born in Jos. Many people who had known me as an infant were still alive. I had buried my father in 1990, but my mother and my aunties and uncles were still there. So was my old headmaster, along with my primary school teachers – even my old Scoutmaster was still in Jos.

Everybody knew what I had been like as a child and everybody would have a position on every single matter that affected the church. I couldn't see how I could navigate through this labyrinthine crisis without some uncle, auntie, or senior sister informing me I was sadly mistaken and doing their level best to set me back on the straight and narrow.

Why would I want to come back to this? It had to be a clear call from God. And it was. I came as a blank sheet, trusting God. There was no way, humanly speaking, that I could ever resolve these deep and complex issues that were tainting every relationship.

On top of that, the diocese couldn't even pay its bishop. There was no official residence for the bishop and not even a car. The first bishop lived in a rented house for five years. The next inherited nothing, and this crisis crashed down on his head until he was asked to retire. When he went, he was owed several months' salary.

The diocese had no property or resources to its name. It was supposed to serve some seventy-five churches with just seventeen clergy. The territory was vast, around 600 miles long by 400 miles wide, and spread over two states. Most of the diocese was rural, yet the church remained stubbornly focused on the cities. Evangelism was nothing more than an empty word.

The church had not only lost respect, it was held in contempt. People in Jos were ashamed to be called Anglicans. This had been going on for at least four years, and this was what I took over on 9 February 1992. I confess I had low expectations of this appointment.

I was consecrated that day and enthroned that same evening. I called a staff meeting for the following day, before everybody could disappear back home. They were demoralized and flat broke. All we had in the coffers was 500 Naira, the equivalent of just £1. The clergy had not been paid for three months.

I informed them my calling was to evangelism and administration and they needed to brace up for change. The message on their faces was clear: that wasn't going to happen. They were so sure this crisis could never be resolved and we would never be able to move on to evangelism.

They cited the disagreement between the Igbos and the Yoruba at St Luke's Cathedral and St Paul's. A third church, St Piran's, was just doing its own thing, in its own little world. St Piran's was originally set up by miners from Cornwall. Its priest had just been made a bishop and they were searching for a nice English vicar to come and run the church along colonial lines.

§

Sunday was my first opportunity to see for myself what the cathedral was like. There were about 300 people, their numbers swelled by those curious to check out this new bishop. Even so, the cathedral was barely half full. After the service, people formed into little huddles and pockets of discussion trying to work out which side I would take.

One of the women was like a mother to me: she had known me from birth. Elizabeth Pam was a small, brightly dressed godly woman in her fifties, who was noisy and forthright and never hid her feelings. Her husband was a lieutenant-colonel who was killed in the 1966 coup. Elizabeth was close to my family and declared herself worried for me. She advised me not to take sides.

I had already written to one of the archdeacons and dismissed him. He was an Igbo, while my predecessor had been a Yoruba. This archdeacon had two cars, while the bishop had none, and the archdeacon refused to allow the bishop to use one of his. The archdeacon was older than me. He was the real power behind the diocese. I didn't see how I could survive under his leadership, so I asked him to go.

I needed help, so I asked the Lord what I should do. I had with me a CMS missionary, who was just about to leave. Susan Essam, a small, feisty Englishwoman in her fifties, knew a lot about the situation. I begged her to stay and she and the CMS agreed.

I spent a few days searching the mind of God. I paced up and down in my office in my rented house. Over two or three days I didn't get an answer. I wanted to hear an audible voice, or get a sign, or be given a Scripture, but I didn't get anything. I cried, "What should I do first? How should I do this?" I was confused. The more I sat down in my office alone, looking at the pile of files Susan had provided for me, the more confused I became.

The women's ministry was dead. The youth group was dead. Nothing was moving. Even the college was out of control. It was all down to these two large groups of Igbos and Yoruba who were fighting. I didn't know where to begin. And God said nothing.

When I was leaving my office I said, "Oh, dear God, honestly, if You don't support me, I don't know what to do. I need Your help."

I went back to my house and Gloria took one look at me and said, "Ben, are you sure we are doing the right thing?"

I said, "I don't know."

She shook her head. "This is going to backfire!"

"I don't care."

She said, "Look, do you know what the Lord is saying?"

"Honestly, I don't know."

Gloria was worried. Our latest little son, Arbet, was just two months old. Gloria was nervous. Every day we prayed and prayed. We said, "Lord, if we're doing the wrong thing, please show us. Don't lead us into disgrace." But He said nothing.

What I had to learn was how to keep heading in the right direction. My broad direction was to put the accounting of the diocese right and the mission of the church straight.

I took a step of faith. On the Monday, I called a meeting of the standing committee of the cathedral. They thought they were going to be consulted over all these various problems.

I resolutely refused to address the issues they were presenting. All this infighting was their problem. What interested me was mission and evangelism. Instead, I thanked them profusely and immediately dissolved the entire committee. I have never had a committee since I was ordained and I didn't need one now.

One of the barristers warned me to be careful: we had a constitution. He brandished a copy. I had studied this massive constitution the week before and hadn't understood a thing. But I had asked God to help me, and He did.

I looked at them straight and said, "Friends, I am the bishop of Jos, and by divine commission, I now suspend the constitution of the Diocese of Jos."

The meeting lasted less than twenty minutes. They were shocked into silence. They were utterly convinced I could not succeed. And I was utterly convinced I would.

What they did not know, but I did, was that their constitution had never been passed by the Church of Nigeria. It had never been formally endorsed.

I asked every officer to bring their documents to my office by 8 a.m. the following day. By some miracle, all did, except for the committee secretary, whose books contained all the minutes. He refused to bring them.

I fired them all, even my office secretary, who couldn't type. I gave myself to prayer for the next two weeks and appointed a caretaker committee.

Even before my consecration, the story had spread that I was coming to sack all the Yoruba. The archdeacon had been an Igbo, so at a stroke I had spread my unpopularity equally over both factions.

I called the diocesan board and announced I was going to replace them all. I would be the new dean of the cathedral as well as its senior pastor. I would be the overseer and signatory. Morning prayers, evening prayers, and Bible studies, I would do them all.

They went out muttering, "Oh my! This boy thinks he can run the diocese this way? We shall see." They were so sure I was going to fail. As for St Piran's, they could abandon their search for an English vicar: I would be their new priest. They were in disbelief, but they had to accept it. I was now the pastor of the cathedral, St Paul's, and St Piran's. I had to juggle all three.

The phone rang. It was the primate of the Church of Nigeria. He challenged me over suspending the constitution. Archbishop Joseph Adetiloye asked me, "Is it true?"

"It is true, Sir."

"You dissolved your diocesan board?"

"Yes, Sir."

"How did you do it?"

"Sir, I just did it." I braced myself for the flak.

After a moment, he said, "Ben, could you come and do it in Lagos?"

From that time on, he nicknamed me Wild Wind. In Hausa it is called Guguwa. The name stuck.

By now the clergy were beginning to kick off. They accused me of undermining the Anglican structure.

I told them, "As long as I'm bishop, no one is going to tell me what is Anglican. I will decide what Anglican is."

A canon retorted: "You are destroying the Church and you are destroying the structures of the Church. You are disgracing Anglicanism." He announced this at a staff meeting in the cathedral. I said nothing, but just sat back quietly watching. Then he walked out on me with his wife and effectively fired himself.

That news reached the ears of Bishop Titus, who rang me. He said he was not prepared to take up the issue but asked me to write a letter of release for the priest. He would find a way to absorb him into his diocese.

I said, "Sir, do you want to hear the truth?"

He said, "Ben, I know you. I don't want anything. Don't worry. Let's just put this behind us."

The problems marched on. Another archdeacon walked out after informing me I couldn't tell him how to administer his archdeaconate.

By now, most of the bishops were convinced I had ruined the church. It no longer looked Anglican, respectable, or structured. But I was not interested in structure and, God help me, I have never been interested in respectability. For ten years I had no canon or archdeacon, nor any of the usual structures.

The clergy were watching and waiting for me to fail. The ordinary people were watching too. So was God.

MISSION, MONEY, AND A WHIFF OF CORRUPTION

My heart was set on mission, but the people didn't believe me. They didn't see how it could happen. In the twelve years of the church in Jos, only three churches had been planted and two of those were breakaways. But I had seen it happen in Zaria and Zonkwa. And it was going to happen in Jos.

In my first few weeks in the cathedral, I told the congregation that while I had grown up in this church, I'd had to go to Lagos to find out about Jesus. "If you people knew Jesus," I said, "you would have given Him to me. But you didn't. So now you listen, when I describe who Jesus is."

And I would explain to them that the resurrection was real. It had happened. The people who jailed Jesus and had killed Him, their names were known.

All the time I had been going to this church as a little boy, all I had been offered was religion. Just the *Common Book of Prayer*. Nobody cared about young people like me, who were indigenes and Anglicans by birth. They were too busy fighting their battles between the Yoruba and the Igbo. I would not even have been considered for the ministry, had I remained at St Luke's.

But today, that was going to change. What I was looking for were people who believed that the mission of Jesus Christ was not only to one tribe or another, but to everybody, to the world. What I wanted was to lead a revolution in the heart of the north, to take evangelism to Igbos and Yoruba, to settlers and indigenes and foreigners – to everybody, anywhere in the world.

But first, there were a few stubborn obstacles to clear out of the way.

Sex, power, and money. Those are temptations that can bring down a minister and destroy a church. And the love of money had resulted in Christian taking Christian to court in Jos.

There is no room for corruption in the church. I set out to address the finances. I wanted to see all the records of bookkeeping. Everything had to be transparent. No money should be transferred without proper invoices and accounts. I was looking for honest people to lead the cathedral. And where there were to be elections, it would be me that set the guidelines.

By Synod in May, I had raised enough money to pay my predecessor the salary we owed him. I paid his debts and the old man blessed me. I had paid all the salaries and arrears of the clergy and I had money enough for mission. How? People trusted me and they gave.

I centralized the payment of salaries for all the church staff and set a quota system for every church. "You contribute this, and I will contribute the rest." I wanted every clergy to be on the same salary scale. For some of them, this would amount to a pay cut, and they were unhappy. But I wasn't about to change. One archdeacon tried to withhold the salaries from his staff, with the excuse that I hadn't paid them. I challenged him, and he left.

Things were beginning to get exciting. At the end of my first year, I insisted that every church must produce a financial statement and publish it openly on the boards of the churches. I wanted everyone in the congregation to see how much they had given, and where their money had gone.

The cathedral refused. They argued that the Bible says the right hand should not know what the left hand is doing.

I said, "In that case, go and report me to Jesus, but until I am satisfied that I'm dealing with honest people, the left hand will know what the right hand is doing." They didn't like it. And at the end of the year we published everything on the noticeboard.

There was war. Women, men – everybody – huddled round the church entrance and raised a hullabaloo. They said, "Bishop, this account is not correct! I paid my tithe! We paid more than this!"

They were screaming. "Bishop, this is wrong!"

I set up a committee to investigate. They discovered money was being stolen. Despite that, we saw a 300 per cent increase in finance coming into the cathedral. Giving rose from 300,000 Naira to more than a million.

I had two trusted advisors, who had known me forever. One of the elders, Ayo Kehinde, had known me from birth. He was a godly man, a well-respected, committed Christian, and the treasurer in this diocese. Earlier he'd warned me to be careful, now he was excited. He was a millionaire, who had made his wealth in mining. Although he was rich, he didn't show it. He was a thrifty man and a deep thinker. Ideas mattered to him. While I tend to act on impulse, he would think deeply about the pros and cons before giving advice.

Mr Kehinde was short and stout with a head that was always freshly shaved. He was smart, neat, and well organized. He was completely honest. I trusted him.

And I trusted Elizabeth Pam. She had raised six children, and considered me one of her own. Her offspring became doctors, a judge, a bank manager, and lawyers. She had done a good job on them, and she was not about to let me down.

She would say to me, "Ben, Ben, Ben! What are you doing? I don't understand – but I am praying."

Mr Kehinde urged me to train my staff and train them well. He gave me 32,000 Naira as a gift to get me started. I began the training in my own parlour with eleven people, many of whom I had known for years. What started in my front room grew into the Christian Institute. My vision was to train able and qualified men who were fired up with a vision for the gospel. My first ordination service was to ordain four of them to be priests and deacons.

What I was looking for were committed Christians who had a clear testimony of knowing Jesus. It was irrelevant to me whether they were Yoruba or Igbo. The mission of Jesus is to everybody, not one tribe or another.

By 1994, I had ordained sixteen people. Then I set up a mission team headed by a godly man, the president of Campus

Crusade for Christ in West Africa, Professor Timothy Gysue. He and his wife Elizabeth were professors of education and committed to the gospel.

He had known me since I was a young man, and had brought Campus Crusade into my church in Zaria, to great effect. Now he had joined me in Jos, and we were one in mind and spirit about reaching the whole world for Christ. He was among the first eleven to be ordained from my little school in the parlour. Together we mapped out our strategy for outreach. And it was blessed by God!

The cathedral embraced my evangelistic appeal and church attendance doubled. But we needed to work out a way to reach the rest of the city. So I did a survey of the population of Jos. Out of 500,000 people, on a typical Sunday morning, there were only 130,000 in church. Given that there were 50,000 Muslims, we were left with a question: where were the remaining 320,000?

My mission team were incensed. They said, "We thought Plateau State was Christian!"

I said, "No, Christians are in a minority. We need to look for the remaining 300,000." And that was how we began our central city evangelism. Within the next two years, we had planted some twelve churches in the city of Jos. Within four years, we had grown to eighteen. And all of them were thriving.

We equipped the congregation with booklets and pamphlets on Bible studies, teaching, and witnessing for Christ. People were getting excited about their faith in Jesus.

These new churches offered fresh opportunities for leadership, and more young people were coming forward to respond to the call to ministry. But before I ordain a person, I throw him into the bush to see if he can start a church. If he can't start a church, then I don't need him. I need only those who can start and nurture churches, and look after vulnerable, suffering congregations.[6]

In six years we had grown from about thirty churches in Nasarawa to almost ninety. The growth was exponential. It was

6   Adapted from an interview with Ben Kwashi on Clayton TV from Word Alive
'11: www.clayton.tv/new/0i0/690

unbelievable. The Primate of Nigeria, Joseph Adetiloye, decided to make Nasarawa a diocese of its own with a bishop. Local indigenous ministers were jumping up left, right, and centre.

From training leaders in my parlour, we bought a piece of land and set up a permanent Christian Institute. That institute became a powerful place of training. We were growing. Then Peter Akinola took over as primate. He broke the province into four dioceses, each with an archbishop.

My focus was evangelism, and the evangelism that will win my heart until tomorrow is in the style of Ajayi Crowther. So everywhere I went, I started a primary school, a boarding school, and a church, and wherever possible, a little clinic.

Plateau State had been evangelized in 1907 and neglected for years. There were no Anglican ordinations until 1976. In the meantime, churches and schools had collapsed. I took over these forgotten schools and lands that had belonged to CMS. Excited younger generations came forward to help look after the abandoned mission stations and property. And then we bought more and built more. Everywhere I went, I bought land and moved on.

I had acquired land and started building the Bishop's Court, along with six or seven secondary schools. I had started boarding schools without a single contribution from the diocese – and some bishops were demanding to know how.

Where was I getting my money from? The church was only giving me enough to pay stipends. After ten years, the rumours were running wild. The clergy began to suspect me of getting money that I was not declaring, of being neither transparent nor sincere.

I was getting invitations to speak and lead missions around the world. Rumour had it that I was using diocesan money to join the jet set.

Eventually, some of the members of St Paul's, the Igbo church, insinuated they would no longer contribute to the diocese, the Bishop's Court, or any other project. They said I had done wrong. I was shocked.

It came up in discussion at Synod in Bukuru. I was proposing to centralize the education policy. But the delegate from St Paul's was in fighting mood and he refused. He accused me of wanting to take over the school. He said they didn't know where the money was coming from or where it was going. He accused me of flooding the Synod with clergy who were loyal to me.

It wasn't quite like that. I believe every church should be run by local leaders. But until recently, the non-indigenous people of Jos Diocese – the Igbo and Yoruba – had been in the majority while there were no indigenous clergy. It's these local leaders, who live in the area, who should own the work of mission. So as I established new churches, I appointed local clergy to run them.

It meant putting out of joint the noses of the out-of-town Igbos and Yoruba. They expressed their disdain by withdrawing their financial contributions. And along with that came rumours of corruption.

The Synod became rowdy. There were 300 people present – a mixture of clergy and laity. People started fidgeting and murmuring in their dark wood pews. Some were saying, "It's true!" Others, "It's not true."

The uproar continued.

I calmed them down. I asked one young priest to lead the prayers. He led those prayers in a most spiritual manner, and the anger subsided.

In all of this, God showed me what to do next. Construction at the Bishop's Court had reached the lintels. I announced I was abandoning the building plan.

I told them, "I'm not working for a Bishop's Court, in case you think that I will be asking you for money for that. I am working for a home in heaven that is not built with hands. I don't care where I live, so let that not bother you."

For ten years, we had been living in a rented house. I continued: "The reason I wanted to build the Bishop's Court was to let you know that we needed an institution, so that the bishops coming after me will have a house. I assure you, before I retire, that those bishops will have a house, but I will not live in it."

So, I suspended the Bishop's Court, and I promised full accountability over the fundraising for all the schools.

What they didn't realize was that much of the money that had gone into those schools was mine. When I went to preach, people gave me money as an individual, and when the need arose, I used that money for schools.

The story of my mission work was spreading. I was asked to speak in England and then the US. When people heard, they wanted to support the work. They trusted me and gave me money. It was God who was raising the support.

The sums were not large, but prudence made them go a long way. And the staff that I had at that time were willing to work. They moulded the bricks and built the schools. Then once the schools were built and the pupils came, their school fees followed.

These were the principles established by the earliest missionaries – to use indigenous people who would make the best possible use of what they had. I used guys who could manage effectively and would invest back into their schools. This way all the schools succeeded. It was the same in all the villages: all the land was given. We put what we had to best use.

But what use is a school without children? I have a policy that all my mission schools must give room for those who cannot afford an education. You are on their land, and you must not benefit from their land without them benefiting from you. As a result, people wanted to join the Anglican Church because they said the bishop cared about their children.

Gloria had bought a brand-new grinding machine, a Lister, from England. We took it to a church so the children wouldn't have to carry their grain four miles to town. The principal at the school there was ingenious. He adapted the grinder so it could be used as a generator to provide light for the whole school.

The land for that school, St Paul's, Kwatas, was given to me by the community, at no cost. And the land for St Benedict's school in Pankshin I bought with my own money, along with funds given by friends to support the ministry.

I have learned never to complain about a lack of resources. Resources will always follow your mission activities. If there is no mission activity, your resources will not come to you. Start the work from where you are, with what little you have. You will be amazed at how God raises the resources, and soon you will be able to do more. He will never fail you, no matter how far you have to go. Look at the feeding of the 5,000.

What have you got? Offer it completely. And then whatever you've offered, it has to be broken. If you allow God to break it, then before your eyes, you will be amazed at what God will do with it. What He breaks He will bless and will multiply. Don't wait for provision.

For God to supply you with seed, you must decide to be a sower. We shouldn't wait for others to help, not even governments. If you're waiting for money, you will do nothing. Let God bless and break whatever He gives you and it will be as the waters that cover the sea.

So we gave what we had and God made it go further. That's the way we did things. But people who lived away from where all this was happening didn't know that. They assumed these new local schools we were setting up were like those in the cities – money-spinners for those who ran them.

What interested folks like these were the school fees. So, hearing that I was going to centralize education management, the people running those wealthy city schools were afraid I was about to snatch them from their hands. At the same time, they were casting envious eyes on the schools I had set up. So they put out the word that I couldn't be trusted.

I can understand outsiders wondering how all this expansion could be possible. I can also understand how some would wrinkle their noses and fancy they could catch a whiff of corruption. But I was living in a two-bedroom rented house with four children by now, sharing a single room. We had no running water, and the well went dry each year. I no longer even had a car of my own. I had given the Mazda away to my younger brother, Jacob.

I kept full records of everything that had been given, and insisted that every gift went through the episcopal accounts, which were audited. Those who contributed from the UK and the US would rightly insist on seeing the records. If the accounts were not available, they would stop giving. But when they could see that level of accountability, they wanted to support the work even more.

When I gave my life to Christ, my past life was gone. I used to lie and cheat and drink. But all that was behind me. Any form of corruption in the faith is repugnant to me. I believe in principles of personal accountability – absolutely.

And then there's Gloria. Gloria is my policeman! She always asks, "Where is this money from and how did you raise it?" From the day I became bishop to date, not a dime has disappeared in the history of Jos Diocese. I demand that each church must be audited by chartered accountants and given their stamp and seal, otherwise I refuse to accept those accounts. External auditing is a principle of Jos Diocese. It's all in the open.

Where we found clergy who were corrupt and taking money, we would call a Commission of Inquiry who would produce a report. The clergyman in question would be given an opportunity to respond. If needs be, it would go to trial in an ecclesiastical court. One priest ended up in criminal court and took my judgment to appeal. He lost. Corruption used to be common, but it has been reduced, drastically. I have fired more than a dozen priests for corruption.

But all of this is just a distraction from the real work of the church – mission.

As I said, thanks to the new primate, Peter Akinola, we now had four dioceses: Bukuru, Pankshin, Langtang, and Jos. Given the rivalry between Yoruba and Igbo, I had to teach afresh that there were twenty-four other tribes and kingdoms in Plateau State that needed to hear the gospel.

Wherever we planted churches, we raised local leaders from among the people. You have to do this for the people to stand. Paul gave Titus the responsibility to raise local leaders, not to import them. Anything else is just colonialism. Colonial Christianity was weak when it came to expressing the gospel of love. You cannot love when there is segregation. Jesus' love raised women, the forgotten, the poor, the orphans, and the widows – right across society.

Whatever the divisions in Nigeria, Christ came to tear down every wall that divides. And He has committed to us that ministry of reconciliation.

When Gloria and I came to Jos Diocese, there were seventy-five churches in Plateau and Nasarawa, which became a State in its own right in 1996. I concentrated my mission work there and we added almost sixty more. Within a few years, people were flooding into the cathedral in Jos and the building was full. The congregation had forgotten whether they were Yoruba or Igbo and people were giving their finances. And God had raised up eleven people who were willing to offer their services as key volunteers – unpaid. We were then able to concentrate on mission in Plateau State, where we were able to add a further 320 new churches. God was on the move.

SECRET SOCIETIES

Nigeria is plagued with cults and secret societies. Rooting these out of the Church was another challenge.

Bishop Titus Ogbonyomi had had to fight his own battles with these shadowy groups, and he had learned a thing or two. At my ordination, Bishop Titus made me take an extra oath. With the Bible in my hand, he made me solemnly swear that I had never been a member of any secret cult and never would be. If, after taking this vow, I joined any secret cult, I put myself under the wrath of God, in the name of the Father, Son, and Holy Spirit.

Among the secret societies in Nigeria were the Rosicrucians, Freemasons, Ogboni, and a host of others. Their members included top civil servants, judges, and police officers. Some had been recruited from their university days.

St Luke's Cathedral had become their playground, and some of these cults were seeking to establish their authority within the church.

When I started as bishop, my very first sermon was from Matthew 6:33 (NKJV): "Seek first the kingdom of God and His righteousness." Whatever my own agenda, I had to lay it down. My first task in Jos Diocese was to seek the kingdom of God. It was also my second and my third. I would never deviate from that. I would seek to establish the rule of God in the hearts of men and in the affairs of men. In heart and in practice, God must rule.

This ten-minute sermon made a stir. It was reproduced in print and in the news. And for the next twelve years, at every anniversary of my ordination, I would preach that sermon again. I left nobody in any doubt: anything that competed with the kingdom of God would meet with spiritual and physical opposition from me.

My bishop had fought these secret societies in northern Nigeria and God had given him the victory. Many members recanted from masonry and other societies and turned to Christ. They became on fire for God.

When I became bishop, I did the same thing in Jos. I took an oath that if I knew anybody who was in any of these cults, ancient or modern, I would remove their name from the church. And when they died, they should look for somebody else to bury them. No church would bury them.

That may sound harsh, but I had seen some of their ceremonies. They gathered round corpses and wore uniforms, and it was rumoured they cut off bits of dead bodies and took them for their rituals.

As a little boy, I had seen them, screaming in the middle of the night. Everybody feared them.

Then many years later, I went to a funeral in another town. A group of men raised a shout outside and then came in and ordered everyone to leave. They said, "Out, out, out!"

I was there in my clerical collar and I was not prepared to obey them. Everybody else was running away, apart from me and a few relatives of the deceased, including the wife.

These men were dressed in dark-blue garb or traditional costume. They surrounded the casket, opened it, and reached inside. They were busy doing something, but they were so tightly packed around the casket you couldn't see what. They stayed like this for some minutes, then bowed and screamed.

There was nothing Christian about this ritual. It disturbed me in my spirit. This was something cultic, for sure.

It was the Freemasons who were the leading cult in St Luke's Cathedral. They were usually wealthy and influential, with followers.

Those who have come out of the Freemasons say the deeper you get, the closer you get to worshipping Satan. There is a spiritual power at work in this. Your loyalty will no longer rest upon Jesus Christ and His resurrection.

The Freemasons made themselves appear respectable with Bible verses and recruited people by confusing them. But if you join, you must take a vow of silence. You are not allowed to divulge what you know and have been taught. The brotherhood was so strong that if you offended one, you would offend them all.

The Church of England battled with Freemasons many years ago, before the House of Bishops finally ruled that Masons were incompatible with Christian doctrine.

The Christian gospel is Jesus Christ *alone* – Jesus alone can save. God needs no help from cults and societies. He shows Himself a jealous God. It must be Him and Him alone. We must serve no other. Jesus reinforced this by pointing out that He alone is the way, the truth, and the life. He alone is Lord. Jesus must be supreme at all times, or at no time. These cults can add nothing to Him.

Freemasonry demands your loyalty above everything else. It was the same with the Ogboni and the Rosicrucians. They demand your loyalty, faith, and brotherhood, over and above the fellowship of Jesus Christ and His people. But Jesus said you cannot please two masters. It is simply not possible.

For me, once I reached this conclusion, I was absolutely sure that nothing on earth could help me live this life and be fulfilled – nothing. No money, no intellectual or academic attainments could give me a fulfilled life outside of Jesus Christ. Once I had found Jesus, He directed my life path for His glory, to be used in His kingdom.

I knew I had to tackle this head-on. I preached an Easter sermon at St Piran's that insisted the cults had no part in the kingdom of God, and those who belonged to cults had no part either, unless they renounced them and turned to Christ.

After this, I got opposition, which is a good sign. People threatened me. They withdrew their monies and said they would not support me any more. They tried all sorts of things. The aim was to intimidate me.

They even went as far as hanging dead cats from my window handles – twice. My son had a vision of a hand reaching for him at night, beckoning him. He woke up and ran into our room. We spent many nights in prayer.

People kept saying, "Be careful of these people, Ben." People were unwilling to talk about it. They were afraid. And sometimes I also had a sense of dread. When you experience spiritual forces attacking you, they cannot be explained. Their intention is to frighten.

One Sunday morning, I was holding a youth service at the cathedral. As I was going up to preach, a man strode in from outside and headed straight for me. He was an untidy-looking figure in his late twenties, with a fierce expression on his face. He seemed to be trying to prevent me from going to the pulpit. He got within a couple of feet of me, looked me straight in the eye, and pointed. Then he laughed, "Ha! You are afraid."

Everybody was watching. His voice was clearly picked up by the lapel mic clipped to my chest.

I said quietly, "Thank You, Lord, it is good they come physically."

Then I said to him, "In the name of the Lord Jesus Christ, I command you…"

I had not even finished my words, when the man spun round, lost his footing, and fell. He rolled over, then got up and ran. The wardens chased him, but he didn't stop. We never saw him again.

The church burst into choruses of "Jesus is Lord" and began to clap. The young people were much encouraged.

When I am in church as pastor, I am also there as leader. If anything shakes me, it will also disturb the flock. So when I come to church, I submit myself to God's authority to lead the people. I kneel at the altar and prostrate myself. I ask God to take sovereign control and pray that all who come to the church will come under the authority of Jesus Christ. And that includes me.

A few years later, an older man we knew to be a Grand Master, whose name I had struck off the cathedral list, came to the church. I'll call him Yousuf. He was a wealthy businessman in his sixties, with many houses, always immaculately dressed.

Yousuf came each year at Easter and Christmas, and every time, he always tried to put me down. He would tell me how the

Masons had built the church and how his own money had gone into the building. He told me I could not remove him: I wouldn't dare. "We are Christians!" he insisted.

I used to say to people, "If you give us money, it will be useful in the church, but just be sure that your money will not buy you membership in this church as long as I am bishop."

For nearly ten years Yousuf continued to take issue with me. And then, when he turned seventy, he decided to hold a thanksgiving in the church. We held the thanksgiving to celebrate his age, not his financial support.

People came from everywhere. I prayed, and before I could reach my second sentence, he began to cry uncontrollably. They had to take him and sit him down. After the service, he waited for me in the vestry, and I braced myself for the usual put-down.

Finally, I came out to greet him. For the first time, he bowed his head and said, "My Lord Bishop." I couldn't believe my ears. He just said, "Thank you, Bishop," shook my hand firmly, and left.

The next Sunday he was in church again, unusually so. I was preaching, and after the service they told me this man was waiting once more for me. Again, I braced myself for a telling-off. It never came. Once again, he said, "My Lord Bishop."

I said, "Lord have mercy," under my breath.

He shook my hand and looked me in the eye and said, "Pray for me: the Lord's will must be done."

I said, "Wow!" After that, he never missed a Sunday. At the end of the year, he came to me before the service to show me some letters. He was resigning from at least three major cults.

He returned all his regalia, including his rod of Grand Master. He said to me, "Seventy wasted years."

He said, "Only Jesus can save," and he gave his life to Christ. "I wasted seventy years: don't waste yours." He's in his eighties now.

One Easter at St Andrew's Church I preached that all of these cults and secret societies were worse than trash. They were toilet paper, they were filthy rags (I went further than that…). They could add nothing to the gospel.

A professor of medicine was in the congregation. He booked an appointment with me the following Monday and brought with him several books on masonry and mysticism. He asked me to study them, so that I would know better. I looked at him and said, "Sir, I don't want to know more than I've preached!" I was already saved. But he didn't understand that.

A few years down the road, this professor became terminally ill. By now I was a bishop and he had risen to Grand Master in the Masons. He phoned me and I went with Gloria to see him. We went to his bedroom with his wife and hugged him. He pointed to his stomach and said, "Ben, I'm dying."

I said, "No!"

We cried and we prayed and he said, "Listen, I'm dying! What shall I do?"

I said to him, "Where are your books?"

He said, "Ben, they won't help me now." I knew that – but at last so did he.

He went and brought them out and prayed to receive Christ. His local pastor came and took all his regalia, from the Masons and all the other cults he belonged to. That's the thing about cults: when you rise to a height in one, you are drawn into the others. They burned it all. And after burning everything, he turned to Jesus fully. His only regret was that he hadn't listened earlier. He died such a wonderful death: he died in peace, ready to go.

It was the same time and again. Whenever you preached, these cult members would listen to pick holes in your teaching and destroy your joy. They would put you down as though you knew nothing. They were gnostics, who believed they alone possessed true knowledge. They were marked by an absence of joy and were utterly opposed to evangelism. It was all down to power struggles and who would be in command. And all the time they were seeking to put the priest under their thumb. But they couldn't do that with me. I was pursuing what God had asked me to do.

One old widow prayed for me regularly. She was illiterate, but a strong and dynamic Christian in her sixties, who followed her convictions and raised nine children in the faith. One evening she came and prayed for me in her tribal language. I couldn't understand most of it, but she kept it up for about forty-five minutes. She assured me, "These people can do nothing against you. You are a child of God, Ben. They can't do anything to you. Hold on to Jesus." She always prayed for me.

Eventually, when all these cultic people had left the church or repented, the older people who knew the truth grew excited to see that the Lord was winning. They wanted to see people set free for Christ.

The difference became obvious. Formerly, the cathedral had been packed with old, frowny-faced people sitting in the front, forbidding clapping, music, or dancing, and drawing the line at praying out loud or in tongues. Today, tongue speaking is commonplace in the cathedral. If you love Jesus, you express yourself! The place became free, and the younger generation began to come in, until 80 per cent of those in the cathedral were aged under forty.

I can confidently say that in the cathedral today, nobody knows of anyone who is still in an occult society. That is true in the churches across most of Jos Diocese.

That vow I had taken became a vow for every council member. If you are going to serve in any committee of the diocese, you have to know the Lord, you have to be a leader who is not given to alcohol or violence, you must not be in any cult, you must attend Bible studies and support the church with your giving and your time, and be a leader who is willing to serve the cause of the gospel. This is now the canonical standard in Jos Diocese. If you can't do that, then sorry: you cannot serve. We adopted biblical methods and they work.

The leading Pentecostal pastor in Jos summed up the change that he had seen. He said that when he started his ministry, the Anglican church in Jos had been his fishing ground. It was full of cultic people, it was joyless, and there was no evangelism. Those who turned to Christ would come to the Pentecostal churches. He said, "But when Ben came, our fishing pond emptied. Ben is now fishing from our churches!"

People who had run away from the Anglican Church were returning, because the Spirit of the Lord was at work, the Word of the Lord was being taught, evangelism was being pursued, and people were free to exercise all the spiritual gifts the Lord has made possible.

If you have been involved in the occult or a cult, then you must seek prayer to make sure God can cleanse you. Cults are spiritual. You need to be sure there is nothing left in you, no ground to which they will keep coming. Every connection needs to be broken. Ask your pastor to pray for you, let him watch out for you and talk to you from time to time about your experiences. You should hide nothing. If you feel any strange experience or have dreams, or feel things around you that you don't understand, then without hesitation, let your pastor know.

Pray through Psalm 139. God knows you inside and out, and wherever you have been, He knows. But it is His intention to restore you. Restoration is a gift of God and He will assure you that you have been set free. Micah 7:8 says, "Though I have fallen, I will rise."

So don't let your feelings deceive you. You can always trust in God. You may have let God down, but it is God's will to lift you up and restore you.

JOS ABLAZE

Everybody remembers 11 September 2001. We remember where we were and what we were doing when the planes ploughed into the Twin Towers in Manhattan. Everybody, that is, except the people of Jos. We were caught up in a crisis of our own that the rest of the world does not remember, because their eyes were fixed on CNN, and CNN's cameras were fixed on the World Trade Center.

Jos was set ablaze four days before the Twin Towers. And the fuse had been laid many years earlier…

§

Jos was a city with a comfortable Christian majority. Which was an anomaly, because Plateau State was toward the north of Nigeria, and the British colonials had declared the north to be Muslim. The British had given instructions not to evangelize Muslim areas. Christians were permitted to live there, providing they knew their place and kept to it.

Anyone who became a Christian in the north would risk losing their place in society. They would forfeit every opportunity for leadership in the economy or political life. But Plateau State was different. Plateau had never fallen to the jihadis.

The governor and his deputy were Christians, and most local officials were non-Muslims. Jos enjoyed a degree of autonomy that was unprecedented in those parts. Inevitably, that centrality and autonomy made Jos a target for the ambitions of northern Muslim politicians. Whichever direction you were travelling, you would have to pass through Jos.

Decades earlier, Hausa communities had settled in Jos. They intermarried and were peaceful. The same was true for the Yoruba and the Igbo. But from the mid-1990s suspicion began to grow towards the Hausa.

The Hausa community declared themselves the bona fide indigenes of Jos city, the Jasawa, the original people of Jos. They claimed to have had the first chief and started calling for an emir, a king, to rule over both them and Jos.

The tribes who had previously sold land to the Hausa pointed out that those who had bought the land must have done so as settlers, not as indigenes. They went back to the British historical archives to research the claim. There, they discovered the first king of Jos had been a Berom, not a Hausa, and furthermore had been a Christian evangelist.

It seemed as though the Hausa were taking their lines from a familiar script, an old script that called for the north to be recognized as having a distinct Muslim identity. This notion, introduced by the British, was carried over into the first Jasawa Hausa government after independence in 1960. The Jasawa equated tribal identity with religious identity and believed that to be Hausa was to be Muslim. They wanted a north with one religion and one people. What they were seeking was segregation.

In 1994, Nigeria was still ruled by a military regime. To everybody's surprise, a Muslim local government officer was appointed to Jos North. And in 2001, a Muslim officer was again appointed by the federal government to handle poverty alleviation, also in Jos North.

People objected. How could a non-indigene represent the Berom, who were in a majority, and the Anaguta and Afizere communities? They were concerned he would represent the Hausa community alone.

The appointment, they said, would drive forward the Jasawa agenda and the movement for segregation.

So many objections were raised that the president was forced to suspend the appointment.

The indigenous people, including Muslims, were beginning to feel the squeeze. A division began to open up between those indigenes and the Hausa settlers.

That division cracked wide open on Friday, 7 September 2001. A girl was walking home in Jos as usual, and had to go past Muslims who were praying. She had done so many times before, passing between the worshippers to reach her house. But on this particular day, the cry went up that she had desecrated their prayers.

It was the excuse some people had been looking for. A mob set about burning churches and destroying businesses and homes. They were also killing Christians.

In those first few days there were at least 150 casualties. Most were non-Muslims, who had been caught unawares. The girl passing by at Friday prayers had become the pretext for an organized attack on the Christian community.

I was 180 miles away at the time, preaching in Gombe, with Rinji, who was fifteen. Gloria was in the UK with the Mothers' Union, while Susan Essam, my administrative chaplain, was at home, looking after our other children. I needed to get back to them, and quickly.

I got as far as Bauchi. The next leg to Jos should have been a two-hour journey. But for the next five days, I got stuck there, because the crisis dragged on and on.

The Hausa Muslims were also killing Yoruba Muslims. All the Yoruba had to leave. They ran for their lives. Most of the non-Muslim houses around my rented home were burned down. Somehow, my own home escaped. People didn't know what to do. They were waiting for the government to act. But the government failed woefully to contain the crisis.

My children and Susan were OK, thank God, but some of my Christian neighbours had been killed and my house was at risk. I had to phone the governor to get my children out.

In Jos, even though the Muslims had started the slaughter, the story they fed the BBC was that it was Christians who were killing Muslims. Pictures were broadcast purporting to show the bodies of scores of Muslims who had been slaughtered by Christians. To make matters worse, the bloodshed had reportedly taken place in a mosque.

The story spread quickly to CNN and Al Jazeera. Journalists were pouring into Jos from all over the world. I had my doubts about what had really happened.

It was days before the roads were reopened. As soon as I could, I drove back to Jos with Rinji.

My heart was heavy. I would never have thought that in Jos – where Christians and Muslims, Hausa, Igbo, Yoruba, Berom, and all tribes and races had lived together – people could allow their anger to overflow into wanton destruction.

On the outskirts of the city, the first thing you see coming in from the direction of Bauchi is the university campus. From the windows of my Mercedes, as we waited in a growing line at a military checkpoint, I could see the chapel we had built. It had been growing, but was now completely burned. The roof had gone, and a mob had pounded on the walls and totally destroyed it.

Deeper into Jos, I saw houses that had been flattened. There was evidence of widespread looting, where rioters had removed windows and emptied houses and shops of their contents. They had strewn the leftovers across the streets.

Christian home after Christian home had been set on fire. I saw block-built bungalows with doors that were smashed and walls that were broken. Twisted ribbons of red corrugated roofing were hanging down inside. And between the rows of burned-out houses, you would see one here and one there that was untouched. These were the houses of Muslims.

It was from this area that two Youth Corpers, National Service boys who had been members of my church since their twenties, were killed. They had been cut down with knives in the house where they were staying.

I was sorry for my country and afraid for the future. This was not a place to raise children or build a community. My family had been evacuated to a government guesthouse, and I wondered where it all might lead.

Whatever the soldiers had been doing, it was not peacekeeping, at least to begin with. They would stand by and watch as people were being killed. People ran to the soldiers for protection and the soldiers shrugged and said they had not been given any orders. The army later disputed this, but at the time the people were helpless and afraid.

Things began to change when the soldiers were finally given orders to arrest the rioters. Arrest them, they did – in their hundreds. And when the order went out to shoot on sight, the crisis finally began to simmer down.

§

The army commander called me into the barracks with a Muslim leader, the city's senior Sharia judge. Everywhere were hundreds of ragged, barefoot boys, some as young as twelve, who had been arrested for looting and arson. They had been held there for days under armed guard and many were begging to be set free. The general ordered them to shut up and keep quiet. Then he made them sit down.

Most were not from Jos. I suspected these boys had been hauled in by truck from out of town. The general was at a loss. "Bishop, what should I do with these ones?"

I turned to one boy who could have been fifteen at most. He was in tears. I asked him, "What made you do this?"

He said, "Please, I was given five Naira. I don't know anything." Others said much the same. They had been paid small sums to carry out the attacks. But they didn't know, or couldn't say, who had given them the money.

Most of them were Muslims. I had seen this before, in Zaria in 1987, when the churches and my home had been burned. There were young children like this, who had been arrested by the police and then released.

We said to the general, "These are not the people we need. They have been used. We want the sponsors of this violence."

We needed those who would have known which houses were Christian and which were not, which were to be targeted and which were to be spared. When Islamic State fighters destroyed houses in Iraq, they daubed their walls with the Arabic letter "N", for Nazarene. But in Jos, no symbols had been painted on the houses. These out-of-town kids couldn't have known which houses to attack. But there were others in the community

Benjamin Argak Kwashi.
"I was spoiled and I knew it…
I made the very most of it.."

A grandfather's legacy. Gideon's Bible, prayer book and reading glasses.

Ben (right) with his younger sister Anna and his father Jon Amos Kwashi.

"What are you waiting for? Get going! Let the adventure begin!"

The widest smile at TCNN, class of 1980: Ben Kwashi, front row, second from left.

Private Benjamin Kwashi (eighteen).

Ben and his older brother Isaac at Ben's ordination in 1982.

Married at last! (December 1983).

All smiles - Gloria finally agrees to marry Ben (1983).

Arbet Kwashi.

Homeschool uniforms run up by Gloria. Rinji (top left), classmates, and Arbet (bottom right).

Homeschooling with Gloria in the Bishop's Court.

Baptism at Amper, Ben's home town. After Ben preached the gospel in 2002, thirty-six people gave their lives to Christ and were baptized immediately.

Archbishop Benjamin Kwashi with orphans at a camp for the displaced in Jos.

Ben and friends at his ordination in 1982.

Ben Kwashi, succeeding Archbishop Peter Jensen as General Secretary of GAFCON in 2018.

"The joy of the Lord is my strength." Ben preaching in Virginia, US.

Benediction at the All Saints gathering in the open air at St John's College, Jos, 2018.

Archbishop Benjamin Kwashi praying at an IDP camp near Jos, 2017.

Ben Kwashi (left) with Mark Lipdo of the Stefanos Foundation. Both provide aid to persecution victims in Nigeria via Release International.

Archbishop Benjamin Kwashi at camp for the displaced near Jos.

CALL TO GLORY !!!

With deep regreat the entire members of St. John Bosco Society, St. Augustine's Parish Alishes to announce the Death of our Beloved Sister & Member which sad events took place during the 18th February 2006 Crisis which also include the Mother, Elder Sister, and her Junior Brother as Pictures show below:-

Nkiru Obodo
Born in 1991
-15 Years

Felicia Obodo
Born in 1963
43 Years

Uchenna
Born in 1994
12 Years

Chizoba
Born in 1989
17 Years

WAKE KEEPING AT ST. AUGUSTINE'S PARISH DATE:....5....06 TIME:.....
BODIES LEAVE FOR HOME VILLAGE AFFA, OGOR TOWN IN UDI L.G.A ENUGU STATE ON:.....
MAY THERE SOULS REST IN PERFECT PEACE ..... "AMEN"

Courtesy of: St. John Bosco Society of St. Augustine's Parish

Burned to death by militants in Nigeria.

Abednego Solomon was ten when he was slashed by the Fulani militants who attacked his village.

Orphan Juliet (fifteen) recalls the day Fulani raiders struck her village.

"As for my country, please pray for Nigeria. That out of these ashes will rise revival."

Church destroyed by Islamist militants in Borno State.

Rinji's family with Gloria and Ben. Helen (left) with Rinji (right) and their daughters Wuni and Lerit.

Orphans no more. Ben and Gloria (middle right) with quite a houseful.

A ready smile. Ben Kwashi photographed by the author Andrew Boyd.

who would; there were those who had given them directions, and these were the ones we needed.

We never got the ringleaders. The police and the army had no capacity to look after 300 street kids. So they let them back on the streets to find their own way home. And as they vanished into their backstreets and boltholes, so did all their evidence.

But there was a body that did have the capacity to find out exactly who was behind this action on 7 September – and that was the federal government. I believe they knew exactly who had started this.

The crisis had been organized, clearly. There were pump-action shotguns and AK-47s. There had been guns, there had been bullets, and there had been rioters to fire them – and they were all brought together at one time, in one place: Jos.

A later Commission of Inquiry heard these guns were being stockpiled in the central mosque which was guarded by heavily armed police.[7] Had they attacked with machetes, there would not have been so many deaths. But 150 died, mainly from gunshots. And the later judicial inquiry reported: "Arms were illegally stock-piled in the state and freely used during the crisis."

And then there was the question of the 139 bodies in the mosque.

I began to ask around for the names and addresses of the dead. I wanted to know who these people were. Until today, no one has provided an answer. I still dispute that these were the corpses of Muslims. Many Christians had gone missing and are still missing to this day. Could some of those bodies have been those of the missing Christians?

When the corpses were carried away, there were people who said they saw crosses around their necks. This is anecdotal and unverifiable. However, to date, no evidence has been found to demonstrate that those were the bodies of Muslims, as claimed.

---

7   *Report of the Judicial Commission of Inquiry into the Civil Disturbances in Jos and its Environs*, September 2002, Chapter 4, Section 4.10.

Even so, everybody believed the story that Christians had slaughtered Muslims in a mosque, including Christians all over the world. The use of the media was very effective. The campaign had worked.

That display of the dead in a Muslim religious building provided a ready excuse for the killings to continue, for revenge attacks that could be dignified as reprisals. As a result, the crisis on Plateau continued to unfold as if to a master plan.

Because the government was unwilling to defend its people, many resorted to defending themselves. Shopkeepers and householders began to take up arms to protect their property. What would you do, if the police and the army refused to protect your loved ones?

As for the police, they were even worse than the military. They appeared unwilling to intervene. I believe they were deliberately being withheld from protecting and defending the Christians. This resulted in a clash between me and the police commissioner.

§

Some two weeks into the crisis, the Bishop of Lagos, who was travelling abroad, began to gather assistance. He rang me to say he had arranged for fourteen U-Haul boxes of relief aid to be delivered to Jos by public transport.

I asked him for the consignment details because the shipment was to travel unaccompanied in the hold of a long-distance bus. I passed on those details to Emmanuel, my finance officer, who was a quiet, composed man in his thirties. Meanwhile I was called away to an appointment in the US.

The morning after I flew out, the police arrested Emmanuel and took him to their headquarters. The story had gone all over town that a Christian leader was picking up a consignment of fourteen containers, and that these containers were overflowing with enough assorted weaponry to arm a small militia.

Gloria got wind of the story because she was chair of the Women's Peace Committee of Plateau State. She heard from the governor's wife that a top religious leader was importing arms into Plateau. No names were given, but all were deeply concerned and were praying against it – including Gloria.

Meanwhile, the police commissioner had taken steps to intercept the shipment. The police headed off the bus and its bewildered passengers some fifty miles before Jos. They commandeered the vehicle and drove it to police headquarters, where the contents would be inspected.

How could the police possibly have known about this shipment? And why would they have assumed those fourteen U-Haul boxes were brimming with arms?

The only possible answer to that first question is that my phone was tapped. There's nothing new in that. I have grown used to it. But the second question only the Muslim police commissioner could answer.

The commissioner had been so sure his intelligence was good that he had called in the press for the grand reveal, when this massive arms shipment that filled the hold of this juggernaut would be exposed. But as they ripped open container after container before the waiting cameras, they found nothing more than food and clothes, all generously donated to bring relief to the troubled citizens of the city of Jos.

It was a spectacular public embarrassment, and the police commissioner had no option but to send my finance officer home, along with our fourteen cases of relief aid, which had now all been checked by hand and passed as fit for purpose.

When Emmanuel met Gloria, she was fresh from the prayer meeting, doing battle in the heavenlies against this so-called arms shipment. Emmanuel had to explain to Gloria that the supposed villain of the piece had been me, that her own husband was suspected of importing arms.

She was furious. She said, "Do you realize what this means? If they believe my husband is behind this violence, they will kill him!" Her blood was up, and I was not around to cool it. The police commissioner would have been well advised to join those who had already fled the area.

Gloria hit the phones. She called the lawyers, press – everybody. She held a press conference the following morning, inviting journalists from national and state TV. With the cameras rolling, she denounced "a master plan by the police to kill my husband". And afterwards, she led the march on police headquarters.

A Commission of Inquiry was called and headed by Niki Tobi, an associate justice of the Supreme Court. It concluded in 2002, but a full eight years passed before its findings were published.

The Inquiry was scathing in its criticism of the police commissioner. It heard evidence that he "not only failed to avert the crisis, but took certain active steps to facilitate it, for which he was accused of bias and even complicity..." He took sides "to aid the Muslims against the Christians in a crisis that had long been planned by the Muslims... He gave police protection to the mosques in Jos, especially the Central Mosque, while he deliberately left the churches to the mercy of the rioters..." and his "policemen looked the other way when the churches were burning".

All this led the Inquiry to the "inescapable" conclusion "that the former Commissioner of Police is guilty of, at best, gross negligence and at worst, sheer incompetence".

Its conclusion, it said, was that the former Commissioner of Police "contributed to the crisis and must be held responsible". It added, "He clearly showed his bias for the religion of Islam and his hatred for the religion of Christianity."[8]

The police commissioner, who has since died, denied the allegations. In 2012, two years after the report was finally published, he was appointed Inspector General of Police – the head of the Nigerian police force.

The crisis erupted in Jos on 7 September 2001. Four days later, Al-Qaeda flew a plane into the Pentagon and two others into the Twin Towers in New York. The Jos crisis was utterly overshadowed by 9/11 and the world paid no attention to it.

But it wasn't over yet.

---

8   *Report of the Judicial Commission of Inquiry into the Civil Disturbances in Jos and its Environs*, September 2002, Chapter 4, sections 4.13, 4.20, 4.27, 4.39, 4.41, and 4.42: https://groups.google.com/forum/#!topic/usaafricadialogue/yKgOCiB84Tg

§

From now on, when anything happened to offend Islam, Christians were killed. A howl of outrage went up again in 2002. The previous year's winner of Miss World had been a Nigerian, so Abuja, the capital, was chosen to host the forthcoming beauty contest.

Then things turned political.

Some of the contestants decided to boycott the pageant in solidarity with a Nigerian woman. An Islamic court had sentenced her to be stoned to death for adultery.

One Nigerian journalist appeared to defend the beauty pageant and, perhaps unwisely, wondered aloud what Mohammed would think, asserting that in her view he might have happily chosen a wife for himself from among the contestants. Realizing the offence that had been caused, the paper later published an apology. But it was too late.

Clerics took offence and issued a fatwa against the journalist. Riots erupted in Kaduna, killing 250 and driving upwards of 20,000 from their homes. The journalist in question had to flee the country.[9]

One thing led to another. The crisis was no longer being contained in Jos, but the city was becoming increasingly fragile and divided. As Christians were killed in one area, they would move to another. And the Muslims were beginning to feel uncomfortable in areas where they were in a minority. They too began to leave.

In Kuru and some of the Berom villages in the rural areas, some of the Muslims were killed. There were reports of Muslim deaths from Vwang, and other areas too. These were revenge killings.

As the tit-for-tat murders set in, the troubles began to take on a tribal hue, between the Berom and the Hausa settlers. This developed into a conflict between the Berom and the Fulani who

---

9   "Religious Violence in Nigeria Drives Out Miss World Event", Alan Cowell, *New York Times*, 23 November 2002: https://www.nytimes.com/2002/11/23/world/religious-violence-in-nigeria-drives-out-miss-world-event.html

were sympathetic to the Hausa cause. The tribal element of the conflict was widening.

Most tribes on Plateau kept cattle. The Fulani have always kept herds there. The Fulani accused the Berom of stealing their cattle and took revenge. Then the Berom retaliated.

But the reports that get into the media never seem to show the Fulani or Hausa killing local people – only ever the indigenes killing the Fulani.

Once the international press had seized the notion that the Fulani were on the receiving end of both cattle-rustling and violence, sympathy shifted towards the Fulani.

The conflict was being narrowed down to "Berom versus Hausa/Fulani", with the largely Christian Berom portrayed as the aggressors.

I said we couldn't simply accept this: we had to find out the truth. I wrote to the state government and made my case to the attorney general.

I gathered my own reports, and the evidence they uncovered offered a different picture from that of the world's media. This was not about a couple of warring tribes. In 2001, everybody had suffered; the Yoruba, the Igbo, all the indigenous people were being killed. And as the crisis dragged on, Christians were still being killed.

But how could we build community if we were to embrace segregation as a way of life? I knew many Muslims whose parents had been born in Jos. I had gone to primary school with Muslims, and there were Muslims among our relations. We had grown up together. How could we say they no longer belonged to Jos? We needed to put this thinking behind us, that to be Hausa was to be Muslim. We needed to talk together.

I called for discussions with top Muslim, Berom, and Igbo leaders. I brought them together with the help of a Dutch NGO. The Dutch gathered the arguments and allowed everyone to speak frankly and to be heard.

Our first meeting was in the home of a Christian leader. The Muslims were uncomfortable with that, so they asked us to meet in the office of a Muslim leader. We agreed, and eventually we continued to meet on neutral ground.

The process took years. Several times it broke down, but we never gave up. We developed a rapport and grew closer, particularly myself, the Catholic bishop, the Muslim imams, and the mosque leaders.

But overarching this was the political element to the troubles, which is difficult to separate from Islam. This is the major fear of Plateau, that the troubles serve a long-running Muslim agenda to overrun Plateau and turn it into a Muslim state. Most of the people believe this to be true. Sadly, it does appear to be the case.

The state government was not sympathetic towards my work of mediation. And the federal government had declared a state of emergency in Plateau and removed the governor, a Christian, by force. They were trying to make him a scapegoat and impeached him. Senior political figures were speaking negatively about Plateau. The atmosphere had turned to poison and the people of the state felt hated by Nigeria.

Hated, perhaps, but helpless – never.

Muslims in Jos have always felt they were denied equal opportunity. But if I believed there was discrimination, I would raise the case. It would be a matter of justice. There can only be peace when there is justice for all. But there cannot be justice until truth is established.

I have built with Muslims, played basketball with them, and we have worked together. I value and defend my friendship with Muslims. I have learned that if I do not work for their safety and security too, they will never listen to my gospel. And I have learned that once they trust you, and know you will protect their interests as well as your own, they will get behind you.

Trust is a long walk, but the destination is worth the walk. And I have had to learn to walk in wisdom.

My life is in the hands of God, and I do not take that for granted. I have a message that is authentic and is changing lives. Over forty years of my preaching I have seen how the gospel has blessed people, and I want to do more gospel preaching before I die. I have a lively message and a living message. But if I am careless and let them kill me, how will I be able to preach it?

Troubles have a way of spreading. And before long, our troubles in Jos had erupted in other parts of Nigeria, and further afield too. It was the publication of a set of cartoons in a Danish newspaper in 2005 that lit the blue touchpaper.

The Mohammed cartoons, one depicting his turban as a bomb with the fuse burning, sparked riots all over the world, claiming some 200 lives. But it took extremists five months after publication to seize the opportunity to cause mayhem in Nigeria.

Militants rioted in Kaduna. They burned churches, killed Christians, and attacked their homes and businesses in Maiduguri, a town that was later to become the base for Boko Haram. There was rioting in Jos too. I was abroad at the time.

And I was abroad again when the bloodshed visited my own home.

ENEMY AT THE GATES

The Carmelite sisters in Reading, England, had been using the same machine to produce their communion wafers for more than sixty years. The wafer machine was even older than the nuns. Now the nunnery was closing and the machine had nowhere to go – until Gloria made it her own. Gloria had seen a wafer machine in Sokoto Diocese and it had caught her imagination, turning out communion wafers rather like waffles. Heated elements would fry the liquid flour mixture between two large plates, to create a large circular wafer.

Such machines were rare in the north of Nigeria. Gloria wanted one to supply our own churches and generate an income that would support the ministry. So she asked for one in faith and some English friends became the answer to her prayers.

The Carmelite sisters, who were vowed to silence, never saw the buyers for their wafers. Reverend fathers would come to the nunnery, drop their money in a slot, and walk away with their purchase. Buyers and sellers would never cross paths.

Gloria's wafers proved popular among churches of all denominations. They were healthier and safer than the local bread. Most of the local churches came to the house to buy them, and we went on to supply the cathedral bookstore and a big Christian bookshop.

Gloria or the children would cut the wafer into pieces, put them in bags, and sell them for about 300 Naira. Whenever we had the generator on, we would make as many as we could.

It had the makings of an excellent enterprise. But I only realized just how enterprising when Gloria announced one day that she had bought some land.

I said, "What! Where did you get the money?"

"From the bank." I was none the wiser.

"Out of the savings from the communion wafers."

Three hundred Naira per bag was now worth less than a pound, but Gloria's business skills proved so successful that she soon turned into a Naira millionaire!

She bought land for a school, with a library and a laboratory. Her communion wafers contributed to a football field and a basketball pitch, along with essentials such as shoes, clothes, and toothpaste.

I was away from home in London for an international meeting and staying at a mission hotel. It was February 2006 and I was already supposed to be back in Nigeria, but there was more to do and I had to extend my stay at short notice for several days.

I had just finished catching up with Gloria over the phone. It had been a late call – after midnight: our time zones were the same. Gloria had been making communion wafers with the children, when the generator had failed, plunging them into darkness. When the power came back they had to continue, or the flour would have spoiled. After they had finished, Gloria and I talked until about 1 a.m., and then I turned in for the night.

Half an hour later, as I was slipping into sleep, the phone snatched me awake once again. It was Hannatu, my daughter, who was studying medicine in the Ukraine, and she was raising the alarm...

Hannatu sounded panicky and anxious. She said Rinji had called to say our house was surrounded by armed people. They were banging the door and trying to break in through the windows with huge boulders. She said, "Daddy, Daddy, they are armed! There are many of them. Please, Daddy, don't let anything happen to Mummy. Help her!"

Had I really been chatting away to Gloria only half an hour earlier? We had been blissfully unaware that trouble lay just around the corner. By now I was completely awake.

§

Gloria's phone was dead, so I called Rinji, who was in his room. He was twenty-one and calm, as always, but I could hear the stress in his voice. He confirmed Hannatu's message.

I said, "Fine, let me call some people. I'll be in touch with you." But at that point, the credit on my phone ran out and the call was cut off. I felt powerless and afraid.

I got down on my knees by my bedside in the mission hotel. I prayed for Gloria, for her safety, and for her life. I prayed for the children, begging, pleading, "Please spare the children, please spare Gloria." If only I could have been in Jos at that moment. I was desperate and angry. I was asking God to do some miracle, to rescue Gloria and the children. I cried for them all, "Lord, show Your power, show Your greatness, blind the killers, may they never get in!"

I hurried out of my hotel in central London in the middle of the night, searching for a corner shop that was still open. I bought tons of credit and loaded my phone. Then I started to call every influential person I knew. I rang the governor of Plateau and many others. But it was 3 a.m. and none of my calls got through.

I got back to Rinji. The attackers had still not got in. I said, "Not to worry, hang in there. I will call again."

Then I rang even more people and started calling my own staff. I got one, described what was happening, and said, "Please get the police." Then I called Rinji again. His phone was ringing, but now there was no reply. I tried again and again. No answer.

At this point, I broke down. I was sure they had killed Rinji and killed my wife. It was cold in London, but I didn't feel it. I just felt broken. I believed the end had come. I went back to my room and began to pray.

By now, it was almost 4 a.m. One of the officials I had been working with in London had seen me moving around. He came to check on me. "Are you OK?"

I broke down and fell to my knees. Eventually, I regained enough composure to tell him what had happened. He woke up the others and they came and surrounded me in prayer.

I kept calling Rinji's number, over and over again.

Then at about five in the morning he answered the call. I said, stupidly, "Rinji, are you alive?"

"Yes." He said he had just come to, because they had beaten him hard and he had passed out.

"What about Mum?"

"I don't know," he said. "I'll check her room."

There was a pause while he looked. When his voice returned, he said, "I don't know where Mummy is, but there is blood everywhere."

I swallowed hard. "What about Nanminen?" He was just six years old.

Rinji replied, "He is here, but his mouth is bleeding."

It was now 5:30 a.m. I rang the secretary of the state government, who was close to the governor. Finally, I got through. He said, "I will rush out of the house immediately." And he was true to his word.

I managed to get through to one of my clergy in the cathedral, Odige, the principal of St John's College. By now Gloria had been found unconscious on the floor of my office. He said, "We are heading to the hospital."

"How is she?"

"She should be all right." The words were reassuring but the voice was not. He sounded worried. I thought he was holding something back, so I put him on oath. He said Gloria was in the teaching hospital.

I could scarcely believe she was still alive. I just wanted to get home. Nobody was telling me anything and I needed to see for myself. I cancelled an appointment to meet a Nigerian uncle living in the UK, Panchen Large, and he arranged to meet me at Heathrow.

I tried to exchange my return ticket for Monday for a flight that was heading to Abuja today. But none of the airlines would make the swap. The only option was to buy a brand-new ticket for that day. It cost about £1,000 and Uncle Panchen promptly paid for it.

I was still burning through credit on my phone. I rang one

of my closest friends, Sam Banwat, who worked as a pharmacist. He and another prayer partner had already been to see Gloria.

Sam said, "Ben, Gloria is going to recover. She has just gone into the theatre. They are doing a lot of work. They have managed to stop the bleeding from her head, her legs, and her private parts."

I was relieved, but worried about the implications.

I spoke to another friend, Dr Nambol Zwandor. He was calm and reassuring. He was a vet and used to blood. "She should be fine."

"Tell me the truth: you're a doctor."

"Ben – she should be fine."

They couldn't, or wouldn't, go into further detail.

My rebooked flight wasn't for hours. I stayed in the airport and found a charging point for my phone.

I rang every hour and spoke to Rinji. He had a cracked rib and a headache. Nanminen was getting treatment for a broken jaw. I called Hannatu in the Ukraine and updated her on the situation. She was crying.

I was phoning every few minutes to hear when Gloria would come out of theatre. Around midday I phoned Sam again. He said, "She's out, but she's yet to come round."

Later, Sam was able to tell me the surgery had been successful. I said, "Well, we thank God."

He said, "Yes, yes." But I was sure there was more that he still wasn't telling me. I asked, "Sam, what really happened to her?"

His wife, who was a nurse, had put him in the picture. But Sam was holding back. I sensed that, but I could see the wisdom. There was little I could do from this end of the phone in London. He said her injuries must have been inflicted by a stick.

By the time I got on the plane, all I knew for sure was that Gloria was alive.

§

I touched down in Abuja at 4 a.m. and my driver sped me

towards Jos. The journey took three agonizing hours. Gloria had been taken to the old hospital. It was built in the colonial style, in a noisy, bustling part of the city called Terminus Market. By the time I arrived it was seven on a Sunday morning. My friends were there to greet me. I hugged them quickly and demanded, "Where is she?"

Gloria was in a side room in the female surgical ward. To reach her, I had to march down the long hall with patients either side and through a green-painted door on the left.

There was Gloria. She was battered and bandaged. She looked like the victim of a plane crash. But she was alive.

I was grateful to God. Her forehead was swollen and bloody. She struggled to open her eyes. She didn't seem able to see. But she heard my voice and stretched out her arm, which caused her pain. I came close and hugged her. She said, "I'd rather have you, than be a widow."

Had I been there when the assassins came, they would have killed me. Instead, they had taken it out on her. "They were looking for you," she said. Gloria was bearing my death.

At that moment, I was so grateful to God for giving me a wife like this. Her value was beyond measure. She was more than a gift. God had a purpose for our lives that only eternity would reveal. I told her that whatever it would take in the grace of God, we would make sure that she recovered.

Parts of her head had been shaved and stitches ran over the top. There were bandages over her legs and hands. She could barely open her eyes.

In the room were large bowls, one smelling of disinfectant. Gloria had been made to sit in this bowl, while they cleaned her up. Oversized cotton balls were strewn around. Her bed had been lifted to raise her head, and she was supported by pillows.

When she heard me, she tried to gather her strength, but I urged her just to lie down. She was clearly in pain.

She was not as bad as I feared. She would live. There was hope and I was grateful. I said, "Whatever it will take, wherever we must go to get you better, we will do it."

She had a wrapper over her chest. She wanted to show me what had happened to her. But at that moment, I had seen enough. She was a mass of wounds. She wanted to talk, but I said, "No, we'll talk later." Tears were running down my face. I hushed her and hugged her, carefully.

It felt like decades had passed since we chatted inconsequentially over the phone about making communion wafers.

I went outside and was comforted by my friends. Later that evening, as I sat with Gloria, when everyone else had gone, she was able to tell me what had happened.

"WE ARE DEAD"

After I had rung and Gloria had finished with the wafer machine, she had locked all the doors and checked the children were sleeping. Tired by now, she switched off the lights and quickly began to drift off to sleep.

Fifteen minutes later, at about 1:15 a.m., she heard a large bang at the front door. She surfaced with a start, frightened. She pulled back the curtain and demanded, "Who's there?"

A voice came back: "We are the ones. We are coming for you. Where is the CAN chairman?"

She said, "He's not back."

They said, "No, we are coming!"

It was then she saw our security guard lying on the ground. He was yelling. They told him to shut up. Our guard dogs had fled. Both of them. They had run away to a safe distance where they could bark to their hearts' content.

Under the security light, Gloria could make out a crowd of about thirty people who were surrounding the main building. She couldn't tell whether they were armed, but from their voices she believed they were in their twenties or thirties. She realized the situation was dangerous.

She ran to Rinji's room and announced, "We are being invaded!" She told Rinji and Nanminen to stay put while she worked out what to do. She knew the first thing they had to do was pray. Rinji said, "I'm going to find them." Gloria managed to restrain him and he went back to his room, where he grabbed his phone and started dialling.

The front door was sturdy, silver-painted steel, and set back into the wall. It was designed to be impenetrable. They tried to crowbar the locks open, but failed. Then they tried to smash their way through with boulders. Then they set about the windows, which were protected with solid iron bars. They shattered all the glass in every window, but still couldn't find a way in. Then they redoubled their assault on the door.

It gave Rinji the opportunity to keep making his frantic calls.

For some reason, the mobile phone network was patchy that night. But Rinji finally got through to someone who worked with the divisional police officer and explained we were being attacked by armed robbers. The policeman assured Rinji that officers were on their way.

By 2:30 a.m., Rinji and Gloria were still waiting.

Meanwhile, the mob continued hammering at the door.

Inset into the door was a small glass panel. It was supposed to be for security, so you could see who was there from inside. But that night, this glass panel worked against us. The intruders had already broken that window, and one of them taking a closer look realized the key was still in the lock on the inside. In her sleepy state, Gloria had left it there.

He reached his hand through the shattered glass and pulled out the key. When Gloria heard the door swing open, she said, "I know now that we are dead."

She braced herself for the inevitable with her children in their room.

From downstairs, she could hear the house being ransacked. They broke anything and everything; the television, tables, and plates. And as they were coming upstairs they were screaming, "Where is the bishop? Where is the CAN chairman?"

Rinji stubbornly stepped out of the door of his room to confront them. He was the first to take a beating. They hit him on the head and chest, and then saw Gloria and dragged her out.

"Where is the bishop? Take us to his room!"

"The bishop is travelling."

"No, you are lying. We know he is back. He is hiding somewhere. You must bring him out."

Then one of them grabbed a huge glass bottle we had filled with peanuts and brought it crashing down on Gloria's head. The next thing she knew, blood was streaming over her face and into her eyes.

Some of them went to check the rooms. Another set about Gloria with a club. She caught a glimpse of five hefty men with guns, knives, and clubs.

They threw open the drawers and looked under the bed. Then they dragged Gloria into the room and threw her on the floor. She screamed out the name of Jesus. They shouted at her to shut up. "We want the bishop." They hit her so hard on the shin she thought her leg was broken. She could no longer stand.

"Please, please, he's not here. I'm telling you the truth."

"You're lying."

With every word, they hit her again hard on her head. She couldn't stand, she couldn't see, and she was dizzy.

One of them said, "Remove her dress."

Another said, "Let her remove it herself. Get up!" And he hit her again.

Gloria struggled up and managed to take off her dress. Two men held her shoulders while two others held her legs. They grabbed a metal mop handle and rammed it inside her. Gloria was screaming, "Jesus, Jesus, help me!" Each time she screamed "Jesus!" they hit her on the head and yelled at her to shut up. They pushed the aluminium handle so hard that it broke inside her. So they yanked it out and forced a broken bottle into her instead, ignoring her screaming.

She was bleeding profusely. Yet still they beat her, on her back and on her head. One of them said, "Let's kill her."

Another said, "No, don't kill her. Let's check everywhere." They beat her again and she was drifting out of consciousness. By now she could barely see or even talk.

One of them demanded, "Where is his office? Take us to it." They thought my office would be in the compound, somewhere nearby. Still naked, they pulled her downstairs. Gloria uttered a prayer that God would give her strength, because she believed her leg was broken. She had reached the point where she no longer felt the pain of the beating.

When she came out naked, she said the cool breeze was like the Spirit of God giving her fresh strength. She said to them, "How can I take you to the office naked? Let me at least cover myself."

One of them threw a wrapper at her. They ordered her to carry a carton of orange juice so they could enjoy refreshments on the way. She hauled this box of twenty-four cartons onto her bleeding head, and felt her strength renewed as she breathed in the night air.

After a couple of steps, she fell. Through eyes that were sticky with blood, she saw a crowd of up to thirty in the compound. She realized this attack had been well planned. Then she fell again. At this, one of them, a young man, took pity on her. He said, in Hausa, "Mother, please get up and try to get us to the office." She struggled up, and they helped themselves to cartons of orange juice from her head on the way.

Then she fell again, in the gutter. Someone said, "Let's just shoot her." She could hear it all in Hausa. The young man who had encouraged her said, "Leave her, leave her. Let her get up." Somehow, Gloria managed to stagger more than a mile to the office.

At the office gate, she called out for Susan Essam, our assistant chaplain who handles all our logistics and correspondence. By now, Gloria was passing out. Susan heard Gloria's voice and peered out through the window. She believed Gloria was on her own but had been attacked. What she didn't realize was that there were men behind her, with guns. Susan came down in her nightgown, took one look at Gloria, and said, "What's this?"

Then the men with guns came out and asked where the bishop was. Susan was more concerned about Gloria than their firearms. She didn't know about the others surrounding the building. She told them, "Put your guns away and get out of here."

But they slapped her, knocking off her glasses, and threatened to shoot her. Gloria pleaded, "Susan, give them whatever they want, please!"

Susan is a small grey-haired English woman in her sixties with a will of iron. She is unflappable and courageous. Susan is the sort of woman who could make the trains run on time – and heaven help any that didn't.

They demanded, "Get the bishop!"

"The bishop isn't here," she insisted.

"Where is the bishop?" some ordered, while others demanded, "Give us dollars, give us pounds."

They told Susan to take them to the bishop's office. Gloria agreed.

Susan said pointedly that if they wanted her help, then they would have to find her glasses which they had knocked to the ground, so they scrabbled around and returned them.

She gave them whatever money she could find in the office. Then they spotted a suitcase and broke it open. Inside were brand-new cameras and a laptop provided by British parliamentarian Caroline Cox to record the crisis that was unfolding in Jos. Too bad they wouldn't be able to record this.

Susan handed them over.

It was about 4 a.m. when a face appeared at a small window. The gang member insisted time was up and they should leave without shouting.

They told Gloria and Susan to lie on the floor and melted into the darkness.

When the dogs stopped barking Susan knew they had gone. So in the pitch dark, she picked her way over to the bishop's desk and dialled the cathedral. In a matter of moments, pastors and police arrived in cars and took Gloria to hospital.

But not before time. It had taken the police three long hours to respond to our calls.

§

When I got back to the house, I met Rinji and Nanminen. Both were nursing their injuries and were very sore. Mercifully, the other children were in boarding school and Hannatu was abroad.

I walked around the house with Rinji to try to retrace the steps they had taken. I was trying to imagine what had happened. Without a doubt, had I been there I would be dead. There were bloodstains everywhere, over the wall and on the bed sheets.

Our home had become a crime scene. Our bedroom was a theatre of evil. They had tortured Gloria beyond speaking and beyond imagination. And they had left her half dead, half blind, with a broken head, chest, and leg.

Rinji gave me his side of the story. After I'd called, he had a running argument with his mother. He wanted to take action, but she said just pray.

At first, Rinji had thought they were armed robbers, but when they came in, they kept on asking, "Where is your father? Where is the bishop? Where is the CAN chairman?"

Gloria told them, "He's not the CAN chairman." That was true enough, because I had just resigned from that office to concentrate on my mission. But they must have thought Gloria was lying.

Rinji had tossed his phone under the bed, so after they finished beating him and he came to, he was able to fish it out and call me.

§

That night, it was impossible to sleep. I began to pray, "Father, it should have been me, not Gloria." I was in anguish on her behalf. Her pain had become my pain.

Since 1987, we had known nothing but attacks and persecution. Now it had come through my door.

I got up and went to the guest room. I prayed until almost 1 a.m. "Lord, why not me? I'm the big mouth; I'm the troublemaker! Lord, why was it not me?"

I laid all these complaints before Him and sensed that He was saying, very gently, "Did you have phone calls?"

"Yes."

"From where?"

They were from all over the world – Singapore, everywhere.

"Did you get emails?"

"Yes, from every country."

The conversation went on. He said, "Did you realize that widows in England are praying for you? That they pray all day and when they fall asleep, those in Australia start? Did you realize they have been knocking on heaven's door 24/7 on your account?"

I burst into laughter and fell backwards on the bed. I said, "OK God, more persecution, so my name will always be at the gates of heaven!" And I laughed some more.

Whoever these attackers had been, they were the losers. Gloria was alive, and I was alive. And they had failed. I felt grateful too, because I believed Gloria would get well.

What the devil intended for evil, God had worked for good. When I thought of all of those prayers around the world, a new determination came upon me. I said, "Lord, no more fear. I'm going to be an unrepentant preacher, an apologist for the gospel of Jesus Christ."

I was screaming to myself, "I will not be afraid any more! I will stand against evil, I will preach against Satan and all his works!" A fresh dynamo began to turn inside. I was ready to seize any opportunity to live the gospel more powerfully. I told myself, "There are people who have died, who are voiceless. I will compel governments, I will do whatever I can to bring the attention of the world to this evil."

Morning broke, and I went to see Gloria. She told me she was able to get up on her own. She said, "Ben, I was able to go to the bathroom!" She tried to show me and managed to stand up without wobbling. Her eyes were still a problem, but she was greeting people in the ward and praying for them. And it was only the following day.

I was encouraged. I didn't doubt the goodness of God. I was excited – we were alive! The would-be killers had lost – twice. The miracle was happening, and I was grateful.

Two things had protected my heart. I was grateful that Gloria was going to recover, and I was grateful that the attackers had failed. It was gratitude that softened my heart.

FRESH DETERMINATION

ome husbands bring their wives flowers, but I brought Gloria a mosquito net. She had asked for one. There had been none on the ward. And when I was fixing that net in place, she asked me, "What about the other patients? Could you buy nets for each of these women, please? I wouldn't be happy being under a net when they are without one." It was typical of Gloria to be more concerned about others than herself.

The following day I brought fifty nets for the ward.

Gloria spent eight days in hospital, but although she was healing well, her eyesight was a worry. She began to tell me, "Ben, I can't see clearly."

I said, "You'll be OK." But when I finally got her home, I noticed she was walking unevenly and had slowed right down. I told her to take her time, that she would recover, just give it time.

But you know Gloria. As soon as she came back, she went to buy more mosquito nets – this time to distribute in the villages. She took the car and when she returned she admitted, "I'm having difficulty driving. Everything seems dim."

Her driving may have been uncoordinated, but her spirit was undaunted. She insisted on driving out to the villages to give out her nets. She had also been visiting an orphanage, and now redoubled her visits. It seemed a new urgency had come into her life.

But as the weeks went by, it became obvious that her sight was deteriorating. In fact, she was going blind.

We had no idea why. We went to an eye doctor, who gave her sunglasses. But after six weeks, Gloria was tripping over steps, and bending down and peering. She said, "Ben, I can't see." Then I became alarmed. Gloria, who is usually unstoppable, had stopped most of her work and needed help with the cooking – with everything.

Three months had passed since the attack. I had called for prayers, and we got a letter from Chuck Collins at San Antonio in Texas. His church had surgeons and ophthalmologists. They invited us to bring Gloria.

By the fourth month, I had to take her by the hand to help her get around. Everything was now on hold. Gloria was urging me to go to the office, but how could I? I was trying to get my reports together for Synod, to give an account for our work and begin planning for the coming year.

I would go, then rush back to see how she was doing. She was having to feel her way around the house. Gloria had begun homeschooling the children, but she could no longer read the schoolbooks. By now, our six-year-old, Nanminen, was having to lead her by the hand.

All I wanted was to finish Synod and get Gloria to the US.

§

Just before we left for the States, three men came to see me unannounced. One was big and strong, another a fraction of his size and obviously his sidekick. I had no idea who they were.

The big man opened his mouth and said, "Sorry, Bishop, I am the divisional police officer and I have now come…"

I couldn't believe my ears. "You are the *what*…!"

"The divisional police officer…"

Now they come?! Where were they when we needed them… when Gloria was being attacked?

I saw red. "If you don't leave my house, I'm going to kill you!" I went into the kitchen to grab anything I could find. But by the time I returned they had run out. They had not even troubled to appear in uniform.

I thank God they fled. I had already sinned in my heart. When I saw them running away, I came to my senses.

Later, another police officer came to say, "We deeply apologize, Sir."

He tried to explain away the three-hour delay between Rinji calling the police and their arrival. "We went to the wrong bishop's house," he told me, "and when we got there, nothing was happening."

My mouth fell open. This police officer claimed they had gone in search of the Pentecostal bishop, not the Anglican bishop. Even then, they had managed to turn up at his church, rather than his house, which was miles away. And once there, it had taken these razor-sharp sleuths some three hours to work out that there might just have been a mistake…

That was the first time I'd seen these so-called police officers. And it would be the last. The divisional police officer was sacked before the year's end.

There were only two possibilities. This had to be either crass incompetence or collusion, and I suspected the latter. Whoever organized the attack on my house must have had someone in the local police in their pocket. Rinji had called the police before the criminals had broken in, but they only showed up the minute the deed was done and the culprits had left.

The attackers had been acting on intelligence. That intelligence had been flawed, but it had been intelligence, nonetheless. Somehow the attackers knew that I was due to come back from the UK on Friday night. What they didn't know was that while I was there, I had extended my stay in London.

For some reason, these thugs were confident that they would be able to attack my house for hours, banging on steel doors and shutters with a boulder, making a racket that could raise the dead, without any passing fear that the police would turn up to stop them.

It's hard to avoid the suspicion that someone in the police had a hand in it. Whoever was behind this must have been rich and influential. Someone had paid for this to be done.

Their intelligence had been correct, but they had overlooked God's timing. In the end they took out their anger on the wrong person.

Nobody was ever arrested for the crime.

President Obasanjo ordered an investigation from Abuja. They concluded that the attack on our house had not been a robbery. They spoke to armed robbers who insisted it was not their style. Whatever the motive had been, they couldn't say. The case was closed.

Even today, I don't know who was behind the attack. I had received no prior threats or indications. But I had taken a stand against corruption and against the killing of Christians, which was fast becoming a sport in northern Nigeria.

My argument was that if the government allowed the killing to continue without defending the people, the day would come when people would be forced to defend themselves. And when that day came, the authorities would struggle to tell the difference between those who were defending and those who were attacking. There would be little to choose between them.

It's human nature. Unless you arrest the criminals, it won't take long before good people turn bad as well.

Sadly, my concerns were soon realized. When the young men began to retaliate, they reverted to cannibalism, to eating the flesh of their enemies. The young men ran wild while the police ran away.

I put a high value on life. It doesn't matter to me whether the life being killed is Fulani, Muslim, or Christian. The taking of life is wrong! I had challenged the systems in the country and in the state. I had challenged the Muslims to stop the killing and to keep their children under control. There were those who thought I was just a troublemaker, and others who considered me hungry for publicity. Many people had a reason to silence me.

I had a meeting with the chief of the Nigerian police force. I knew him well. We had grown up together in Jos and I trusted him. He told me he would find the person behind the crime.

I said, "Don't waste your time: I'm alive and Gloria will recover. Forget it."

This surprised him. He said, "Why?"

I explained. "While they were planning this, God knew. He knows each of them by name. I may have shaken hands with them, eaten with them, or visited them in their homes. If I find out who did this, how will I be able to eat with them and how will I be able to preach if I see them? Not knowing means I can preach my sermons and love them as I should without any shadow in my mind."

He said, "Bishop, are you sure?"

"Yes. I don't want to know." I said, "I want to preach the gospel, please, and I want to preach it freely. One day, God is going to bring all of this out into the open. God will judge this. I leave it in His capable hands."

I hadn't always felt this way. To begin with, I badly wanted to know who did this. Then on my first night back home, I had that encounter with the Lord, which put the whole thing into a different perspective. I simply lost interest in who did it.

I have forgiven Gloria's attackers. And as for Gloria… as soon as we got home she said to me, "How can I meet that young boy who was helping me, that one who was with the killers?"

I said, "*What?*"

She said, "My heart goes out to the boy. We should pray for him."

The next day she asked me again. "How can I get to this boy? He is somebody's child. He has a mother. The negligence of one mother has led to this. Let's pray for that boy. Maybe somehow or other, he'll get saved." So we did.

Gloria has always had a heart for the children. But now, I began to see a change in her. She had always cared about children, but now she was redoubling her efforts.

§

We managed to get away to the US for Gloria's treatment in June.

The journey from Nigeria to San Antonio was a trauma for me. I cried all the way through it. My tears had come on when we went to the boarding gate. I was dragging her bags, while my little boy was dragging Gloria by her hand.

Nanminen was fed up with her. "You're too slow, Mum, the plane is going to leave us! Come quickly! Follow me! Hold my hand!"

When we got to Heathrow for our connecting flight, Nanminen needed to go to the toilet. Gloria said to me, "Ben, why are you crying?" How could she see that?

I said, "I'm not crying."

She said, "I can feel you are crying." I sighed and started to sob. Gloria squeezed my hand. "Don't worry," she said.

My ministry had come to an end. It was now about Gloria. She had done everything for us. She had looked after us and raised the children. And now, here she was, helpless. We even had to take her to the bathroom. That was how it was going to be.

Gloria said, "Ben, it will be all right. Even if I turn blind, it will be fine."

For the next three months, they gave Gloria treatment and the church covered all the costs. A team of doctors took responsibility for everything. At the end of the first week, they brought out the results of the MRI and CT scans. The neurosurgeon told us Gloria had two cracks in her skull, but they were healing. There was no need for any internal surgery. A cracked rib and a cracked leg were healing. A toenail that had been torn off was regrowing. The pains in her back they put down to bruising. Even the damage to her private parts had healed, even though they had been torn to pieces. Her womb had not been damaged.

The neurosurgeon complimented the surgeons in Jos. He said their work had been beautiful.

This left the problem of her sight, which was failing. The ophthalmologist said he could treat her. It would be a long procedure and they would deal with one eye at a time. He would attempt laser surgery, and if it were successful, they would move on to the other eye.

He operated on the first eye while I was there. When Gloria opened it, she looked around and she was excited. She could see the women who were looking after her. She said, "Thank you, you look like angels!" She was so delighted, she ran out. She said, "I can see the sky, I can see the sky!"

I was so happy. I was glad for this one eye.

Both operations were completely successful.

Gloria recuperated in the States for another month, before coming home. She arrived in September, in time for the dry season in Nigeria. It had taken nearly nine months, a miracle of God, and the prayers and support of brethren around the world for Gloria to recover.

§

The attack had quite an impact on us all. It was after this that Rinji decided to go into the ministry.

That troubled me a lot. I asked him, "Young man, can't you see this is costing me my life? Why do you want this kind of life?"

He didn't respond. It is only recently that I have stopped badgering him, "Are you sure?"

Before joining the ministry, I had never seen persecution. For me, persecution had no vivid and tangible reality until then. So, for my son to see persecution first-hand and still want to go into the ministry was a worry. But I was afraid of putting him off, because I didn't want to find myself working against God.

I took consolation in telling myself that this boy just wouldn't last. Of that I was sure. Rinji would give it up after two or three years. I made certain he had no special support to cushion him. He got nothing extra. No luxuries. He laboured like every other evangelist. If this wasn't God, he would soon give up.

Rinji now tells others who are coming into ministry, "Don't think it's about my dad. If it was about my dad, I would have been dead."

They don't believe him, but it's true. I posted him to places that were dangerous, including Rustu, a village close to where people were being killed. There were families in Jos who came to me to ask why I was being unfair to Rinji. One even demanded,

"Why do you wish your son dead?"

I said, "Those who are being killed are also other people's children. If they kill my child, I will cry, like other parents. But Rinji has joined the ministry. That's his lot. Let him die, if needs be, with his people."

But what's the alternative? Favouritism? There is something in a father's heart, though. You try to deny it when you're training your son, but it's there. I was always looking out for him, I was always praying for him. I would keep asking people, "Where's that rascal? What's he doing now?"

Rinji had no house. His house in Rustu caved in with the rains. He slept in his car, got tuberculosis, and almost died. People were very angry with me, but Rinji went through it and he recovered. He loved the villagers and they loved him.

Rinji never complained. If he was resentful, he never showed it. Now he understands. He looks back and is grateful. I'm sure I did the right thing. Church ministry is dangerous. If I had treated him any differently, I would have had to do the same for all the other clergy, and I would not have trained them honestly.

It was the making of Rinji. He became a man. He is not afraid of anything. He's my official chaplain. He understands me. He has to work harder for me than anyone. He had to tell a clergyman once, "When the bishop has finished roasting the clergy here, he calls me in and I get it again. He roasts me twice! You guys are lucky."

It's worked out well for Rinji: he's a good leader. Way after I'm gone, Rinji will be able to stand on his own, and not just because I am his father. That's my aim. He's doing a great job. He has a great ministry.

WAIFS AND STRAYS

The attack on Gloria gave us all a fresh determination. If this gospel is worth dying for, then it is certainly worth living for!

God seems to work like this: He takes your inclinations and He gives you a nudge in that direction. But sometimes He gives you more of a shove! Who could have guessed that homeschooling would lead us to setting up schools, and that caring for waifs and strays would turn into running an orphanage? Not us. But the writing had always been on the wall...

From my earliest days I had seen the helpless Almajiri kids, the little boys put out of their madrassa to beg for food, while I had plenty of food on my table.[10] Even as a little boy, I wondered why the world was like this. These kids needed to eat, and I could help them forage for food. Today I know the gospel doesn't save me to bless me alone, but it saves me so that I can be a blessing to others. Gloria feels the same; my problem is this woman has a heart the size of a planet!

Perhaps it was this that drew us together. Before we got married, I had a string of young men staying with me who needed just a little help to get their lives back on track. Guys like Henry, who had been released on probation from prison. I was also working to reconcile young people with their families, whatever their faith. One of the boys living with me was a Muslim. I remember explaining to Gloria that I just liked to help people. She said the same. Neither of us ever imagined where that would lead.

While I was still a bachelor, my younger brother used to come to me on holiday. I would help him and others with their school fees and pay for some of their training.

10   "Nigeria's Almajiri Children Learning a Life of Poverty and Violence", Christian Purefoy, CNN website, 8 January 2010, http://edition.cnn.com/2010/WORLD/africa/01/07/nigeria.children.radicalization/index.html

If it wasn't me, then it was Gloria. From the moment we were married, we had a houseful. Her younger brothers and sisters came to us for support. Then some of our relations who had finished secondary school came to stay and we took over responsibility for their training and the cost of their upkeep. There were always people staying with us long term.

This is normal in Nigeria. This is what families do. Families believe they are raising up older children to take responsibility for the younger ones. So now it was my turn to look after my nephews, nieces, and cousins.

Attitudes were changing, though. Those who trained abroad adopted the model of the nuclear family. In my view, that was all well and good for the West, but not for Africa. Western countries had developed their own social care systems to cushion their citizens. Not so in Nigeria. If we cared only for our nuclear families, then others who were less fortunate would never see the grace of God through our lives.

How could I look after my own children and educate them alone, when others in the same community didn't have the means to send their children to school? How could I turn from those unable to care for their own? Nigeria can be a harsh place. But whether or not the government or any others care, my faith tells me that I must.

When Gloria came into my house, what she saw struck a chord in her heart. Together we continued the work. We had only two rooms, so some of these younger ones slept in the parlour while others had to bed down in the garage. But it worked out.

One is now a manager in an oil company, another a pastor, and a third an archdeacon. They used to call themselves the BQ Boys, the Boys' Quarter Boys. All went into business and prospered. They are big men now, my BQ Boys.

It was my responsibility to get them married off. They would find their own wives, but we would need to approve them, and I paid their dowries. One of them brought a girl to meet me one evening, and I said to him afterwards, "That is not your wife." He trusted my judgment and is now happily married to another girl.

They looked on me as their pastor, elder brother, or uncle. They trusted me, because I looked after them. From the little I had, I would share.

All this laid the foundation for what was to follow when I became bishop. In Nigeria, the higher you rise, the more responsibility everyone expects you to take. So, our relatives didn't care that my stipend was just 1,000 Naira per month (around £225 at the time): I was a bishop!

And with every child that arrived at our door, we would be expected to pay their school fees. I had to learn to manage our finances wisely and become Chancellor of the Exchequer for my entire extended family.

Our rented house had four rooms for the boys. This luxury of space meant our relations descended on us with a vengeance. At one time, we were looking after twenty-two relatives while we were both still in our thirties.

Then, as if we didn't have enough on our hands, Gloria decided to start homeschooling, and it was without my consent.

It was in 1994. I was in the bush, preaching, while Gloria was at home with the children. By now, Hannatu was at nursery school and they were teaching her to hold a pencil. Hannatu is left-handed, and they beat her because she refused to hold the pencil in her right. And when we got to Wusasa, the same thing happened at primary school. These educators forced her to write with her wrong hand. There was nothing right about it.

Next, Rinji turned into a typical Kwashi. He was a lively five-year-old and full of mischief. He was jumping everywhere. His teacher despaired of him. Her constant cry was, "Is it because your father is the bishop?" Those comments haunted him. Rinji wasn't being a bishop's kid – he was simply being an irrepressible Kwashi.

By now, Gloria had met missionaries in Jos who were homeschooling their children, and she began to develop grand notions of her own. One missionary, who was with the Sudan Interior Mission (SIM), was helping other parents to do the same. And before I knew it, Gloria had bought up all the teaching materials.

I came home one day to find none of my children at school. They were all at home. The reason, I was informed, was that our home was now their school. Gloria was so excited. All my protestations were like water off a duck's back.

And that was a good thing.

Her homeschool became so successful that our unruly kids were soon reading and behaving well. By the time Hannatu was ten, she had sat her common entrance to secondary school. She passed everything, and our other children all followed suit. I had been sitting on the sidelines watching while Gloria worked wonders, and now I was convinced.

Homeschooling is an enormous commitment. Gloria's time was fully taken up with the children. She kept to discipline and followed the programme. The children began class at 7:30 a.m. and observed the usual school hours. Each sat at their own table and worked through their individual assignments. Gloria enforced the break times and graded all their work. But they still called her "Mummy" in class.

And then the inevitable happened. I should have seen it coming. Gloria started taking in other children. Distant relations bundled their offspring in our direction, and my finance officer handed over his two. Gloria gathered them all in, like a mother hen, at absolutely no cost.

Our own immediate family was growing too. After Rinji, we couldn't have any more children for several years. So we adopted Pangak. Pangak was the son of my half-sister who is mentally ill. My mother looked after Pangak until she died, and then we brought him up as our own child.

We took in Pangak three years after Rinji was born. Then, three years later, we had Arbet. Then, for some reason, we couldn't have children again for another six years. After that, robbers killed my older brother's wife. Their child, Nendelmwa, was barely four years old, so we took her in. She was the blessing, because then Gloria became pregnant again.

We were in England and Gloria was working hard at Lambeth Conference, even though she was about five months pregnant. But one morning she woke up to find she was bleeding.

The doctors were convinced she had lost the baby and they insisted on a scan. The results were confusing. "Somebody's alive in here!" the doctor said. It turned out Gloria had been expecting twins and we'd had no idea.

In fact, we lost one baby, but the other survived: Nanminen. Had we not been in England, we probably would have lost them both.

Gloria homeschooled them all. And it worked. At the time of writing, Hannatu is a qualified doctor. She is married and planning to specialize in paediatrics. Rinji has a Master's in theology and is a priest, as you know. He is married with three children. Pangak is a graduate automobile engineer. Arbet is in medical school, while Nendelmwa has graduated in law and is a barrister. And Nanminen is at university studying to be a vet.

I have to concede that Gloria did a pretty good job – despite all my misgivings. Our children have travelled the world on their own. Not only that, but she taught them the very best old-school manners. She trained the girls to curtsy and the boys to bow, and wherever they go, people are taken aback by their comportment.

I said, "Gloria!"

"Yes?"

"Do you think we are the von Trapp family?"

Gloria is good. But she benefits from a bit of teasing, from time to time. Still, you cannot cut Gloria down to size. Or our family, it seems. Because all the time, Mother Hen is plumping her feathers and scanning the horizon for waifs and strays.

My wife is generous to a fault – usually at my expense. In Amper, my home village, she saw a woman who had just given birth. Someone sent a boy to fetch water to clean up the mother and bath the baby. The boy went to the only source of water for the entire village, where cows and pigs were competing with people to drink. He came back with a container on his head and a bucket. Both were full of filthy brown water.

Gloria couldn't believe it. She said, "Look, lady: you and your baby, I'm taking you back to Jos." And she drove all the way. I was away at the time.

At this point, the baby had no name. Hannatu had just returned on holiday and she named the baby Moses. By the time I came back, Gloria had taken a team of geologists to examine the whole village to find a place they could sink a borehole to provide clean, fresh water.

The only place they could find such water was on my own inheritance, land belonging to my father. To dig a borehole would have cost 700,000 Naira, all I had in savings, and that money was set aside to pay Hannatu's school fees when she went back to Ukraine.

Gloria asked me for the money and I refused. But Gloria wouldn't listen. She argued that while her daughter was going to school in Europe, these others on our doorstep didn't even have the chance to live!

"You're talking about money for school!" she rebuked me. "God will provide, but for *this* one, this money is already sunk. I have committed myself. We have paid for this survey and they are about to do the digging. You *must* pay!"

What could I do?

When Hannatu went back, it was without her school fees and with the bare minimum of pocket money.

We left this woman and her baby in our house and went to preach in the US. After we finished, we took a holiday with my younger sister in the States. Her pastor asked me to preach, and the following morning, they came with an offering of US$ 6,000. I couldn't believe it. It more than covered Hannatu's school fees and her pocket money.

Time after time, God has provided.

Once Gloria has made up her mind to meet somebody's need, God will meet our own need elsewhere. We never keep anything to ourselves, if we can help someone. Gloria just goes ahead and helps people and God provides. Our children have learned that lesson too. They never panic. Every one of our children knows that God will care for us. We have learned to be faithful, because God is faithful.

§

The moment Gloria returned from the US where she had been receiving medical treatment for five months, she made up for lost time.

Before the attack, Gloria had been helping out at an orphanage, which was in financial crisis. Most orphanages in Africa are run by NGOs and depend entirely on overseas support. If that support dries up, then the orphanages just die. This orphanage was being run by a white woman from America. Giving had slowed down and the finances were stretched to breaking point. The staff were not being paid and it was becoming hard to feed the children. Then Gloria discovered evidence of sexual abuse.

A lawyer who lived next door to the orphanage began legal action. He had photographed children who were clearly underfed and walking around naked. But because Gloria was involved, he brought this up with me. He asked me, "Ben, what should I do?"

I told him he should take up the case with the board of the orphanage. They conducted their own investigation and decided to close the place down. They wondered aloud whether Gloria should take some of the children. She jumped at the chance.

I was away at the time. When I returned, there were twelve extra children in the house whom I didn't recognize. I did some more travelling, and when I came back there were even more. And it didn't stop there.

I couldn't understand her. I said, "Gloria, where are we going to keep all these children?" But this was just the beginning.

Gloria had taken it upon herself to start feeding scores of children in the village and now she was asking me to come and admire her handiwork. Admire it? I was angry.

I said, "Honestly you've got to stop this. Gloria! You have started something you can never finish. You can't raise people's hopes and dash them!"

She just told me to shut up. "Ben, you're not angry, you're just screaming. I know your heart. If you see this thing, you will help me. We're going to do this together. Come!"

"I'm going to the office."

"You're not going to the office. You're not going anywhere. Let's go. Come and see!"

So I went, and the place was alive with children in a state of excitement about nothing more than cocoa and water. They had neither sugar nor milk, but these children were beside themselves with joy.

I insisted, "No, Gloria, we can't do that. We have to get them sugar, milk, and bread too – please!"

So I gave her the money. In the evening, she said, "Ben, I knew you would do this. All your screaming was nonsense."

"We have to feed them every day."

Our work with orphans was underway. Just as well, because the Boko Haram terrorists had begun to emerge – and creating orphans was their speciality.

§

Gloria had done her research. Around us, where we lived, were 500 orphans who went to no school at all, who were roaming around and scavenging, with no one to help them. They had fled to the village to escape the gathering crisis.

Gloria's first priority was to give them playground equipment. Why? She reasoned this would draw the children in, so she could feed them and give them classes in the open air. Then our neighbour let us use his unfinished building. It became our schoolhouse. By now there were more than 100 children. Gloria split them into different ages.

At the same time, she looked around and saw a different need – widows. She gathered thirteen widows from the community and brought in a teacher to train them to sew. When their training was complete, we were able to get a sewing machine for each of them.

It became clear that some of the children were in a desperate condition. A girl arrived at the school wearing nothing but a dressing gown – she had no clothes, no pants, nothing. Gloria followed some of them to the place they called home. There were eight of them in a shack, huddled together in only one room, with scraps of zinc for the roof. They were packed in like sardines.

Even where families were trying to look after these children who had been displaced by conflict, they were unable to feed them or take care of them. An offer of a simple shack to sleep in was the best they could manage. These refugee children had to fend for themselves. So Gloria built a proper feeding centre. We had moved on from cocoa without milk and sugar to proper meals.

As Gloria's health recovered, Gloria was recovering more and more children. She talked to each ragged child she saw and went to visit them at home, if they had one. She interviewed the hard-pressed host families, who were only too willing to release these displaced children to us. Before I knew it, my own house was overflowing with sixty-two children. There were mattresses everywhere. It was chaos.

I would come down at 5:30 a.m. and wake the children for prayers. There were children sprawled across the entire parlour. Their blankets were soaked in urine. You could almost feel the stench. I would sit with them and lead them in the Anglican morning prayer, read the Bible with them, and we would sing songs from my hymn book.

Until then, our family prayers had always been conducted peacefully in this same living room. Now our prayer time was chaotic. The children were disorganized, mumbling in their sleep, and the smell was terrible. I wondered, "How long can we continue?"

Dealing with sickness was another thing. We had a girl and a boy who had epilepsy, and children would fall ill in the middle of the night. One would get ill and you would somehow cope with that, and then another and another. But Gloria remained confident that this was not beyond our ability to manage.

After struggling through morning prayers, I would go to work and come back, and then have to deal with all our problems until midnight. The sink was broken, the toilet overflowing, the outside tap had stopped working. There were too many people using too few facilities. Everything was breaking and falling apart, and no one owned up to anything. Even if they had, what would you do?

These children didn't know how to tidy their room or make their beds. They threw their things about carelessly everywhere. They knew nothing. Some of them had been crammed in, fifteen to a room, just surviving, when we picked them up. I was back to raising three-year-olds.

So, Gloria's solution was to build an extension. We moved out all the boys aged nine to thirteen, and then we built another extension on the other side for the girls. The rainy season was setting in, so we had to rush it through. It meant we could keep them to a maximum of six to a room in bunk beds.

Through all this, Gloria was still recovering from her attack. I didn't see how on earth we would ever cope. Most people thought we would never be able to continue the work with the orphans beyond two years. The sheer expense and the time commitment would make it impossible.

People were expecting us to have to go round begging, cap in hand. Never. What the enemy intended for harm, God worked for good in our lives. The attacks and opposition just made us stronger.

WITCHES, WIZARDS, AND HIV

T hankfully, our own children took everything in their stride. Hannatu would call me long-distance from her medical school in Ukraine and tentatively ask, "Daddy, has Mummy brought any more?"

If I said, "No," she would say, "Thank God! Daddy, how are you coping?"

And I would say, "You know your mum: she won't stop. She wants to save the whole world. The only thing that could slow her down is a lack of money, and even that wouldn't deter her."

Then we would talk about all the children whose names she could remember.

When Hannatu came back on holiday, she was eager to check out her new brothers and sisters. She would say, "Which ones are new?"

Hannatu was the senior sister and got on with them all. The moment she came in and dropped her bags, she would throw open all the windows because of the stink. I used to tease her, "You are a doctor, what's the problem?" By this time, even I was getting used to the smell.

Our children realized that these newcomers posed no threat to them in their home. God understood that the time was right for these new ones to come in. Nanminen, our youngest, grew up with them. And he was the one who felt closest to them.

Distance was no object for Gloria. Someone phoned her and told her about a boy 150 miles away. He had been found wandering in the market. No one could understand a word he was saying. All he could do was babble. We never found out what had happened to his parents. He had been on his own for about a year. Gloria tracked him down and took him to the village chief and signed off documents for him.

Joseph had never worn shoes and couldn't tell his left from his right. He was a challenge for everyone. His only way of communication was violence. Everything for Joseph was a fight. He was physical with everybody. Yet, that began to change.

When Joseph was learning the national anthem, he made us all laugh. No one could understand what he was saying: he was mumbling and juggling all the words. And to cap it all, he was tone-deaf.

Today, Joseph is a tall seventeen-year-old with plenty to say. We were able to take him back to his village, where we had found one surviving relative.

When Gloria went to another village in the north-east for a funeral, she saw a little baby under a tree, on its own. She wondered who was looking after her. She asked the villagers, "Why do you leave babies like that?"

They said, "Everybody is tired. Her parents are dead. Nobody knows what to do any more." People were barely surviving. One family might take the children for a day or two, then another would take over. When there was no longer enough food to go around, the children would be left to scavenge on their own.

Gloria picked up the baby from under the tree. A little later, her older sister, Nana, who was no more than four or five, returned and started searching for her. She was crying and crying. So, Gloria took them both to the village head, signed off their documents, and brought Mimi and Nana back to live with us.

Mimi, the little one, grew to love songs and nursery rhymes. When it came to the song "States and Capitals of Nigeria", she didn't know all the names, so she would come up with something that sounded sweet in her mouth and sing it out with all the confidence she could muster.

Mother Hen then gathered a seventeen-year-old girl who was pregnant and had been rejected by her parents.

She was a very pretty girl, but a first-class thief. Gloria delivered her baby, and the girl delivered Gloria's watches into her own not-so-safe keeping. Within two minutes of entering your home, she would steal something. But you could never catch her.

She hid everything carefully in her room. And as for money – well, any currency would do.

When we had guests from England, she pilfered around £200 from them. She stole everything – including their biscuits.

I couldn't believe it. I was mystified. "Surely not," I said to Gloria. "Now, how could this be missing? What would she do with British pounds?"

Gloria said, "Ben, just wait."

She confronted our little kleptomaniac and said, "Give me the money."

The girl began to cry, "Mama, I didn't take any money!"

"OK, bring me all your clothes, everything you have, and everything your baby has."

Gloria started searching her baby things.

Earlier, I had given Gloria 200,000 Naira for building an extension, but that money had gone missing.

We recovered almost half of it in one of the pockets of her baby clothes. We also found wristwatches and dollars, and Hannatu's missing fees for her Ukrainian studies.

This girl had inspected every room and lifted everything of value. After we confronted her with the evidence, she ran away and left us with her baby, who went on to live with us. He was a handsome little boy, who grew up well.

No one is too hard for Gloria to handle, or beyond the reach of the Almighty – that is my wife's complete conviction.

At one point, we were praying for Hannatu, who was twenty-one. I prayed, "Dear God, now Hannatu is twenty-one, You might find somebody who wants to marry her. But as head of the family, I am begging You, please, never let any of my children wander from the way to find a spouse who is a son of the devil. I'm not ready to have the devil as my in-law."

Everyone was laughing, but I was serious. I knew that if Satan turned up in front of Gloria, she would just look at him and say, "Satan? Is that you? Come in and stay in our house!" And she would put him to work.

§

We employed a woman to help us cook for the children, another to help us look after them, and a third to do the washing and cleaning. It was costing us a fortune, but whatever we did, we were not seeing the children's health get better.

Rather, the women we employed insisted these children were demon-possessed. All of them were complaining of not sleeping at night for fear of these children who had demon powers and were witches and wizards who wanted to destroy us all.

This came to my attention when I was about to go travelling and was on my way to say goodbye to the children. This woman insisted, "Don't tell the children you are travelling, because if they know, they will orchestrate their evil powers to pursue you and cause a car accident for you on the road."

I couldn't believe my ears. After saying my goodbyes. I said to Gloria, "Did you hear? Are these the kind of people you've employed to look after the children?"

She was as troubled as I was.

I had read several articles about children in Nigeria being accused of witches, and being killed for it. I was determined this was not going to happen here.

Some of the children in our care had been rejected by their parents, who believed they were witches. They had a pagan belief that spirits hovered around and possessed children to use them to harm others, especially their own parents. If a mother dies in childbirth or a father dies from AIDS-related illness, they blame the children. They say the infection was created by one of their kids.

All this talk of demon possession makes me angry. Don't get me wrong: demons are real enough, but where demons do exercise their powers, we have the power of Jesus to cast them out. I have powers from God to confront Satan himself! I'm not afraid of witches and witchcraft. I have cast out secret societies from the cathedral. Why should I be bothered about little demons? Let them come!

But I have *never* had to exorcise one of our children. Some families who don't understand child development interpret a child having bad dreams and screaming at night as being demon-possessed. But this is just children being children! Children are also susceptible to the influences of the community and the troubles of the day.

Gloria has taken family members to social services and the court and had them arrested for attempting to kill their children. She has become known as the champion of these cases, and most of the child lawyers in Jos know her.

Social workers and local government know her well, and refer cases to her. They invite Gloria to come to the aid of children who have been accused and abused. By the time I returned from my travels, Gloria had moved these children into the Bishop's Court.

That didn't trouble me. What did concern me was that we had eight children who were infected with HIV. This was the most difficult part for me. Gloria wanted to move them in to live with us and our own young children. I found that tough. I had my own irrational fears that our children might catch HIV, or that these children could infect others. But I was wrong. That hasn't happened. Over all these years, nobody has been infected.

We did, however, lose two of these children to HIV, Daniel and Raymond.

When we picked up Daniel, nobody thought he would last three months: his heart had grown so weak. But Hannatu had just come back from her medical training and looked after him in person. Daniel lived with us for six years, until his heart just gave out. He was nine when he died.

Raymond was a different matter. I believe he wanted to die. We took him to his grandmother in the hope that he would regain some of his zest for living. But he died there during his visit. We later found out that instead of taking his medication, he had hidden some of it under his mattress. He was tired of living.

There were success stories too.

Comfort and Paul had HIV. Comfort finished her secondary school and Paul returned home to take care of the farm. They know how to take care of themselves too.

It is hard to imagine what would have happened to these children if we hadn't taken them in. The street is no place for a child. We often see pregnant girls with several children in tow, and we see boys who have become thugs and thieves. Some have died of illness, and others have been killed. Even more have become part of the army of ragamuffins around the town.

One young girl who was already sexually active didn't stay with us for long. We saw her again when she was seventeen, with two children of her own.

Men take advantage of girls such as these. But we have introduced a strict local rule that carries the weight of law. If the boys who don't want to go to school are found to have violated any of the schoolchildren, they will go to jail.

Gloria has drawn in the village head and the entire community in this. Anybody who touches these girls, or sexually induces them to leave school, will end up behind bars.

We are safeguarding these children. We want to ensure that they finish their schooling and have a future, so that they can come back and be a blessing to the community. It has been a fight, but these children are worth it. When Gloria calls a meeting, everyone comes running. They say, "Mama Bishop is calling a meeting! Let's go!"

By now, our own little school had outgrown its borrowed premises. So Gloria bought a piece of land in the village and relocated it. The school expanded from 100 to 200. Guess who was paying! The money came from the savings I had built up over the years.

But Gloria wasn't interested in my complaints. She said, "Our own children are doing well. We must now look out for others."

And there were many others now to look out for. Boko Haram terrorists had begun their mayhem, burning churches, driving families from their homes, and turning children into orphans – orphans in need of new parents.

The story of Gloria, this woman who would take on all and any children, spread over the areas where the attacks had taken place. People as far away as Langtang, 150 miles distant, heard about her and brought children to her. All of this became normal life for us.

Eventually, Gloria became completely exhausted. I could see it coming, but she refused to recognize it and just wouldn't give in.

I managed to persuade her to take a holiday, when our children were back home and could look after all the others. Gloria would never spend money on herself, so I took her away on air miles. I was able to fly her business class to New Zealand. It gave her great pleasure to know she had been to the uttermost ends of the earth. She loved picking up stones from the bays. "Lord, You have brought me here!" she would say. "Here's the ocean!"

Gathering stones was one thing, and gathering orphans was another. Gloria did them both. And then she turned her attention to... monkeys.

We had always had cows, goats and sheep. I grew up with them as a little boy. Nanminen had loved horses since he was four. He started saving his money to buy a horse.

What hurt Nanminen the most about the attack on our home was that he lost his wallet. It was a beautiful wallet, and it must have caught our attackers' eyes, because they took it. It was difficult for six-year-old Nanminen to forgive them, not because they were killers in waiting, but because they took all the money he had been saving for a horse.

After that, we bought him a horse. And we added to that another which I had kept in the village. We also had two donkeys. But then Gloria took it upon herself to provide these children with a proper zoo of their own.

§

She was on a trip to the north-east when she saw ostriches and decided we simply had to have them. So she hired a bus and drove these ostriches back with her.

Next, two monkeys turned up in a taxi. I have no idea how Gloria persuaded the taxi driver. Then a pick-up arrived, laden with pigs.

You can blame me for the pigeons. I have always kept pigeons. They are easy to keep. When you take the first two pairs and put sugar in their water, they will never leave you. We now have hundreds of pigeons.

But you can blame Gloria for the rabbits. She thought it would be a good idea to buy rabbits, and Cracker agreed. This was the new Cracker, a black-and-tan German Shepherd. Cracker number one passed away at the ripe old age of fourteen – older than the children. Rinji conducted his funeral.

One balmy night, the new Cracker made for himself a fine feast of Gloria's rabbits.

So she decided to buy something with armour plating that would keep Cracker at bay. She bought a tortoise. I drew the line at having it in the house, so it stays in the school.

Gloria has her animals, and I have my plants. I bring back plants of all kinds from all over the world, as much as they will let me. I have fruit trees of every kind: pomegranates, bananas, guavas, and mangoes of every description. This is my hobby. And Gloria has finally learned to keep her pesky animals away from them.

As for the orphans who live with us, we have adopted them into our family and given them each our name. Every one of them is a little Kwashi.

We look after more than 400 children in the school we built ourselves. These children don't have to bring fees: they only have to bring themselves. The school is called Zambiri Nentapmwa. *Zambiri* was the name of Gloria's mother. In the Bachama language it means, "Life is not an accident." *Nentapmwa* is Angas for, "God watches over them."

Ours is a busy house and everyone has their own responsibilities. But with so many children comes opportunity for a little cultural and sporting indulgence. We have set up a school choir, football team, basketball team, and athletics club. Well, we have to do something to keep them all occupied!

Across the road we are building a health clinic, to serve the school and the entire community. Our clinic will be close to the place where I still hold out the hope of one day retiring.

But it is only a hope, and that hope is gradually fading. With every month that passes, Gloria undertakes some new rescue operation. The work and our household continue to grow.

VALLEY OF THE SHADOW

t was 2007. A year had passed since the assassins had struck and failed in their task. We were planning a Thanksgiving for Gloria's miraculous recovery and the continuing gift of life.

All our family were to be there, and almost everyone was already at home. Hannatu had returned from her medical studies in Ukraine. My younger brother, Jacob, was with us from Kaduna, as was Gloria's younger brother, who was preparing to go to the UK to do a Master's degree. We were bringing together all of our birth children, along with many of the children Gloria had rescued. Every room in our house was full. We decided to have an early night to save our energies for the Thanksgiving the next day, so we prayed and went to sleep.

Between midnight and 1 a.m., a huge bang woke me suddenly. It was a loud metallic pounding on the solid back door. It could mean only one thing: the assassins had returned, and this time they had come with a sledgehammer.

Instantly, I jumped out of bed and went to the window. I was wearing a long, flowing clerical robe that had been given to me by an Egyptian priest. It had grown old, so I used it for nightwear.

The security lights were on, but there was no one in sight. I could hear footsteps and movements in the dark.

Gloria was making many calls, but in her confusion, she was dialling lots of wrong numbers. None of them got through.

So I grabbed my phone. I no longer trusted the police, so I called a friend, a former classmate, who was now a group captain in the Air Force. He was in Kaduna, miles away.

I told him, "If these guys get me and kill me, then you need to know where to find my diary, and this is what you should do for Gloria…"

He said, "Ben, no, that's impossible!"

I told him I was sure my time was up. Gloria heard me and insisted that wouldn't happen.

He said, "Ben, drop your phone. We will get this done."

Gloria was pacing up and down, praying and working the phone. She was telling me, "Don't give up. Nothing's going to happen. We are going to survive this."

I was calm. I called one of my priests, who was five miles away. I told him, "If my time is up, don't worry. I have made my peace."

I was expecting to die, and I was ready.

At that stage I had no idea how many people had come against us. But I refused to do anything to protect myself. I had made my calls, and now I sat down. I was calm and relaxed, and decided to pray.

The assassins had come from the rear of the house, using a ladder. They captured the two security guards and locked them in a room. They were well prepared. When they realized the metal door was too thick to break down with the sledgehammer, they turned to a breaker they had brought with them. They used its sharp metal spike to dig out the door. They were unconcerned the racket they were making could alert the authorities.

Gloria kept trying to phone. She kept saying, "The phone is not working. It's not working."

I said, "Don't worry, Gloria, there's no point. Before any help will come these guys will just shoot me straight. I'm ready."

Gloria hid herself in the bathroom so she could make phone calls up to the last moment.

It took them thirty-five minutes to wreck the door. After they burst in, they came straight up the stairs to my room. They knew the way. Three came in, one with a gun, one with a club, one with a knife. I was kneeling in prayer.

These men were not masked. They were untroubled that anyone might see their faces. That could mean only one thing.

The oldest of the three, a short, stout man in his late thirties, was the first to speak. I had never seen him before. He was wide-eyed and fierce and brimming with assurance. And he was holding a pistol. He said, "Man of God, get up and let's go! It's not time for praying now."

I said, "Fine."

As well as the three in the room, there were two others by the door outside. They were big men. One also had a gun. There were two more by the stairs. They led me down. Nobody grabbed me, nobody touched me: I offered no resistance.

Gloria was still hidden in the bathroom. Seven-year-old Nanminen heard them come and wanted to fight. Last time he had tried to tackle our would-be assassins, they had broken his jaw. Rinji was awake too. To try to restrain Nanminen, he locked him in the wardrobe.

Instead, Rinji came out to accost them, just as he had done before, and just as they had done before, they beat him down. They stood on his back, forced him to the ground, and put a gun to his head.

When Nanminen heard this, he burst his way out of the wardrobe, yelling, "You can't do that!" He was ready to fight them. They hit him in his mouth again and he was bleeding. At least they didn't break his jaw.

The two by the stairs were watching to see if any others would hear the commotion and venture out. One of our adopted daughters, Becky, stepped out of her door. They beat her hard about the head, and she retreated.

My younger brother's sleep had been disturbed. He peered out of his window and saw a crowd. Realizing the danger, he kept quiet. In the other children's room, they were sound asleep, dead to the world. Thank God.

Gloria dropped her phone in a bucket in the bathroom to hide it. It did more than hide it. It incapacitated it. The bucket was full of water.

When I emerged from the house, a large crowd converged in a circle around me. Up to forty surrounded me, while others were at the gate, keeping watch over my guards. They were mostly in their twenties. One was very tall. He looked like a Fulani and wore a knee-length flowing baban riga robe, which he tied like a

Fulani. He also tucked his trousers into his boots in the style of the Fulani.

Their speech was slurred and their eyes were red. They were on drugs and ready for anything.

I was focused and quiet. The man with a pistol was behind me, and the two big young men with their pistol and their club stood beside me.

I was certain I was going to die. I wasn't panicky or troubled. I stood with my arms crossed, ready for whatever they would do. But in my heart, I was praying, "Lord, if I'm going to die, let me die alone. Let there be no other bloodshed in my house."

Then one of them said, "Look, man of God, give us money and we won't kill you."

I looked at him. He was young and serious. He said, "Give us money and I will tell whoever asked us to kill you that we didn't find you."

I said, "How much?"

He said, "Three million Naira."

I grinned and said, "You should have told me this yesterday!"

The money was a red herring. Even if I had money to give to them, they would still have killed me. They knew I was not afraid.

Then somebody from the back shouted, "No, don't kill him here. Let's kill him upstairs in the presence of his wife."

I couldn't see this man, but the voice was unmistakably that of a leader. He added, "Let's go to his room."

The man he was addressing, the one who was supposed to murder me, was shaking. Adrenaline, and perhaps more than that, was coursing through his body. He was poised for action.

They escorted me back up the stairs to the slaughter. Some stood outside the door while others went in, including the older guy with the pistol and the shakes. Seven came into my room. Three of them found Gloria in the bathroom and pulled her out.

I said to them, "Please, before you kill me, let me pray."

The older gunman said, "OK, you can pray."

I kneeled down and got my Bible, a small brown leather ESV. I realized I didn't have my glasses, so I couldn't read. They allowed me to get my half-moon reading glasses from my bedside and I returned.

I kneeled down on our big red rug, put on my glasses, and opened my Bible. I started reciting Psalm 23, "The Lord is my shepherd; I shall not want… Even though I walk through the valley of the shadow of death, I will fear no evil…"

I was reading it under my breath. Something told me they might hit me, so I prostrated myself on the ground, with the Bible in front of me. I put my head on my hands and I closed my eyes to pray.

I heard footsteps back and forth. I didn't even bother to look. I couldn't say how much time passed. The next touch was from Gloria. I know her fingers. I was going to say something, but she said, "Shh – just pray."

She prostrated herself on the ground beside me. We held hands. I believed they were going to kill us both. I was ready to go. There was no fear, no panic, I was calm and very peaceful. I was already dead.

Gloria was more agitated. One of them hit her on the buttocks. I was praying, *Lord, let them kill me alone, not Gloria. Only me, Lord, for the sake of the children.*

Gloria was praying, *Lord, there shall be no bloodshed. Deny them the opportunity of bloodshed.*

Those were our thoughts, but we prayed silently in our hearts, with our eyes shut. Still, nobody touched me. The place went quiet. Then I heard footsteps and I knew my hour had come. This was it.

And then the footsteps stopped.

Curiosity made me look, and I saw the legs of my son, Rinji. I said in a hushed tone, "What are you doing here?"

He said, "Daddy, they are gone."

I couldn't believe it. But Rinji had been under armed guard. I had to believe him. But I hadn't heard them go. Why was I still alive?

I said, "Rinji, are you sure?"

He said, "Yes."

Gloria's recollection is that a man came in and told the assassins, "OK, drop this thing. Get out now." But I heard nothing. The house was silent.

We ran down. There was nobody there. I went to the gatehouse and freed our security guards who had been beaten up and locked in. They were surprised to see us.

Just then, the Air Force Police turned up. They missed the crooks by minutes. And they were beside themselves with disappointment. They were spoiling for a fight. Fifteen of them arrived in several vehicles, ready to take on an army.

Apparently, the message had been delayed. It had got lost somewhere in the chain of command. Where had I heard that before?

The officer in charge looked around, bristling. "Where are these bastards?"

"They're gone."

"Oh God!" The air turned blue.

He looked me up and down in my flowing white nightgown: "Sir, are you OK?"

"I'm fine."

"Oh God, why didn't the signal come earlier?" He was raging. "We could have got these beggars!" They were ready for war, but it had been denied them.

And then they left.

Much, much later the police turned up. Then they left too.

First assassins with sledgehammers, then a belated army of blaspheming vigilantes, backed up, eventually, by the boys in blue.

Amazingly, most of my household slept through the lot. So we woke them, turned them out of their beds, and together we began to sing:

"Praising the Lord, always,

"Praising the Lord, always,

"Praising the Lord with all my heart…

"Hallelujah, the Lord is good, is good to me.

"What the Lord has done for me, I cannot tell it all."

We sang these songs over and over, the younger ones raising their own choruses of joy and thanksgiving.

But in the middle of singing, we suddenly realized Hannatu wasn't with us. Where was she?

We ran into her room.

Hannatu had slumbered through it all and was still soundly asleep. So we woke her too.

"What is it? What's the matter?" She staggered up and saw the broken doors: "What!"

Her eyes widened. She saw the mess: "What!"

And then she saw the breaker the killers had left behind: "What!"

God in His kindness had spared her. He had not allowed her to hear anything at all. If she had woken up, she would have screamed the place down.

We kept up the singing and dancing until 7 a.m. or 8 a.m. Thanksgiving had come early. It was a frenzied time. There was joy that morning.

Gloria was so grateful that God had answered her prayer. She had prayed, "Let there be no bloodshed," and there was none. Every single thing she'd asked of the Lord, the Lord had answered. She had asked God to spare me. She refused to let me die.

I told her, "You didn't want me to die, because you wanted to empty my bank account!"

She said, "Yes, I have work to do! I need your money. I need you alive until this job is done!"

I think only eternity will reveal why these armed assassins turned tail and left. What they saw, what drove them away, why they didn't carry out their plan, only God knows. And I don't need to know, because He knows.

Gloria was convinced that some of the voices she heard were familiar. She recognized them from the previous attack. They knew the route to my bedroom and came straight to my room. They took nothing, not even my watch or phones. In fact, I had $500 in an envelope in my Bible and they even left that. They had come for one thing only – to take my life. But once again they went away empty-handed.

§

If the previous attack had made us more determined, then this failed assassination was a transformation. It changed my preaching. In fact, it changed my life.

I preached what I had learned: I knew that when I die, it will not be by the hands of useless men. I will die when my time is right and not before, but I must use the time I have well. It left me with an urgency to do every ministry, every good work, every sermon, every teaching swiftly and to the best of my ability, vigorously and strategically without wasting time or resources.

It brought a new boldness to me. And it did the same for Gloria. She concluded that her security was in the Lord and she set about developing her own ministry with renewed vigour.

I have to confess a certain sense of loss. I saw less of my wife than I used to. But I couldn't complain, because I could see a new person emerging. She wasn't driven, but peaceful. She no longer had any sense of fear, even behind the wheel of a car. She would drive for hours at any time of the day and night to find an orphan. She took hold of the Mothers' Union and grew it rapidly. The Jos branch has since become a model for the organization and Gloria went on to become the trainer for the Mothers' Union for the whole of Nigeria.

Gloria was motivated by some inner strength that I cannot explain. She became a different person. And rather than wanting her for myself, I was grateful to God. I was glad to release her and encourage her in this. I love her now more than ever.

§

Shortly after the crisis, Romans 8:28 really came alive to us: "And we know that in all things God works for the good of those who love him, who have been called according to his purpose."

We went to visit Baba Kehinde who had funded the Christian Institute. Gloria shared her vision to build a girls' hostel. Even though Jos was a university city, it didn't have enough hostels for girls. They had to rent in the community, where some had been abused. Gloria wanted a hostel with a chaplaincy and a chapel where Christian girls could come and be safe. Mr Kehinde said to Gloria, "My daughter, would you take a plot of land?"

He had land in Jos he had bought in the 1940s, complete with a bungalow. He fished out the papers and gave them to her.

A few months later, his daughter died in a car accident on her way to school in Bauchi. Gloria named the hostel after her: Jumoke House.

Our local and international ministries continued to grow. We received help from all over the world. We began training pastors to degree and Master's levels.

The building of the hostel for girls took off. The orphans now have a school. I paid for the scholarships of fifty-eight Muslim children in my primary schools and another fourteen in my secondary schools. We held joint projects with Muslim women and youth. Our aim was and still is to establish a peace-building community.

From that time onwards, the urgency to accomplish these things has been heavy and our focus has never slipped.

The lesson we would share with others is this: don't wait for a crisis to strike before you give yourself fully to what God has put you on this earth to do.

PART THREE

UNLIKELY ARCHBISHOP

never set out to be Archbishop. In fact, in 2008 when it happened, I almost missed it. I was sitting quietly in the House of Bishops, at the back. I had switched off to what was happening and was working on my laptop. The nominations came for the elections of the archbishops. The next thing I heard was, "Congratulations, Bishop of Jos!" I had been elected. I was shocked! Archbishop of Jos! What happened?

As a young man, all I wanted was to be known as an evangelist. That's where my drive was. I wanted to be known for preaching a convincing message that would move people to action. That was always my dream. I wanted to walk in the ways of those great evangelists like Ajayi Crowther.

I wanted to change the world. Why not? This world needs changing! Perhaps that's why people keep yelling at me to stop rocking the boat and sit down.

As a young pastor, I had my fair share of misunderstandings. Even in church there is a hierarchy where the strong and determined wield considerable power. I have had to learn to trust God to get me out of my many mistakes. And He has.

I've had some arguments which I suspected would get me into deep trouble. I've learned to challenge things that are not right and to trust God to get me through.

I don't regard myself as a man of courage or immense confidence in God, but both have grown with the fiery experiences I have gone through. The more the Lord has saved me, the more my confidence and courage in Him have grown.

But when they appointed this turbulent priest as archbishop,

I was as astonished as anyone. Before the vote, which I hadn't even bothered to observe, one bishop had come over to me and looked me in the eye and said, "Do you think you're the only one in Nigeria? You're always travelling. You're always abroad. We will not vote for you."

People were telling me what they thought of me. Another one complained, "Ben, you're only popular abroad. You are not popular at home. No bishop likes you. Nobody will vote for you."

Did I want to be an archbishop? Why were they bringing all this to me? There were accusations upon accusations. I just kept quiet. I didn't defend myself. My colleagues had made up their minds. Nobody wanted to find out the truth.

I had learned over the years never to harbour any bitterness. This one is a struggle. You'll be pained, you'll be injured, you'll be slandered – but you must always take it to the Lord.

Years earlier, I had been at a service in Kenya where the benediction taught me an early lesson as a young pastor. They would say, "All your sorrows…" (and they would point to the cross), "take it to the cross." They would continue: "All your sadness…" (and they would point to the cross), "take it to the cross." It was a practical demonstration that settled the struggle and will remain with me forever.

Bitterness will rob you of every dividend. Never get bitter. Always rely on the Lord.

There have been many accusations. But whatever anybody does, I will take it to the Lord and I will leave it with Him. It may take a long time, but God will always vindicate His truth, and if His children will stand in the truth, He will vindicate them. Never give in to slander and never cave in to people's wishes, when you are working for the kingdom. Just focus and get on.

So when I heard, "Congratulations, Bishop of Jos!" I prayed, "Lord, do they really mean it? Is this true?" Had I stopped travelling? Had I lost my popularity abroad? What had changed their minds?

My archdiocese will tell you that I'm just an archbishop by title. I have confidence in what the young bishops in Jos are doing. Talking shops are not my style. I believe that actions speak louder than words. So why should I call for meetings or stamp my authority with burdensome visits? My style of leadership is a light touch. I'm happy for clergy to call me if they have a problem and need my help. I'm happy to serve them in that way. And if they don't need me, then that's fine.

Every diocese in Jos is under persecution. They have enough on their hands. My priests don't need me to add to their troubles.

But worse was still to come. The crisis had visited our home and passed over – for the time being. But in the state and in the city that crisis continued to gather steam. Then inflaming it, beyond anything we had known, was a new menace that entered my nation.

BOKO HARAM

T hey called themselves Jamā'at Ahl as-Sunnah lid-Da'wah wa'l-Jihād, the Group of the People of Sunnah for Preaching and Jihad. That's a bit of a mouthful, so people gave them a nickname: Boko Haram.

Boko Haram, a blend of Arabic and Hausa, means roughly, "Western education is forbidden" or "sacrilegious".

The movement was led by Mohammed Yusuf, an Islamist and socialist, who wanted to impose an Islamic state. Yusuf was preaching against the corrupt Muslim elite and all the ills of society. He drew in many of the poor in Maiduguri, Borno State, and bought vast tracts of land in the north, where he settled with his followers.

The story has it that in 2009 some of Yusuf's followers clashed with the police. One was killed. On the way to the funeral, there was another clash. More were killed. Boko Haram retaliated by attacking the police in their barracks, killing men, women, and children. It became a federal issue, and they widened their attacks to government offices, security services, churches, and schools.

Yusuf was arrested and killed in custody. This encouraged his radicals, who were even more left-wing and felt Yusuf had been soft on government. They were convinced the only way to deal with Nigeria was to Islamize the entire country. They believed that until they could institute the reign of Allah, there would be no peace.

Yusuf's successor was Abubakar Shekau. Under his leadership, Boko Haram became well armed and well supported. Many believed he got their weapons from Turkey and Libya, using funding from Saudi Arabia and Qatar. The police and the army were unable to withstand them. Within a short time, Boko Haram had occupied some seventeen local government areas in the north-east of Nigeria.

Shekau set out his agenda in a one-hour video message to the world. He described the jihadist Usman dan Fodio, founder of the Sokoto caliphate, as his father. Then he declared, "It is a jihad war against Christians and Christianity... This is what I know in Quran. This is a war against Christians and democracy and their constitution. Allah says we should finish them when we get them."[11]

Under Shekau, Boko Haram extended their front line from Maiduguri to Jos. They developed their bombing techniques in Jos. They bombed the market, churches, and centres where people gathered to watch television. All their bombs were in Christian areas.

One of their bombs went off close to my house. In a bomb-making factory only two miles away, fighters were practising how to detonate a bomb when it went off in their hands. Three young men were severely injured. One lost his face. Somehow they survived and were taken by the police to Abuja.

Logistically, Boko Haram realized Jos was too great a stretch from their base in Maiduguri. So they regrouped to Maiduguri, Bauchi, and Gombe, in order to inch their way back towards Plateau.

They pursued a strategy of attacking and occupying – and it was working. They were taking territory in Nigeria. They slaughtered Christians wherever they could find them, filmed themselves doing so, and posted the bloodshed on social media. Islamic State could have taken propaganda classes from Boko Haram.

According to reports, the authorities uncovered a list of potential targets in Jos. The six churches included St Luke's Anglican Cathedral, St Piran's, and the COCIN headquarters. My home was also on the list.[12] Abubakar Shekau had announced he was coming to Jos. So we braced ourselves for the worst.

---

11 "Boko Haram Leader Pledges War Against Christians", *The Christian Post*, 16 May 2014: https://www.christianpost.com/news/boko-haram-leader-pledges-war-against-christians-scoffs-at-gays-saying-even-animals-know-better-119884/
12 "Nigeria Suicide Bomber Targets Church in Jos", CSW, 27 February 2012: https://www.csw.org.uk/2012/02/27/news/1148/article.htm

The worst of times always seem to come at the best of times – Christmas.

St Luke's Cathedral was in the lively heart of the city at the Terminus, next to the market and all the big stores. We and they were making ready for Christmas 2011. St Luke's was signposted for all the world to see by its Christian cross lifted high on a spire.

The congregation were well aware of the risk. I made sure to spell it out for them. I was always calling for prayers for the persecuted church. By now, around 100 had been killed in attacks on places of worship in Plateau State. I didn't want us to ever forget them. And I wanted us to be ready.

We were ready.

The week before Christmas, as we were preparing for the festivities, I said, "Well, folks, they have struck at other churches and some people have become martyrs. And you can easily guess on your own who shall be next."

Someone called out, "We are the ones!"

I laughed and said, "I'm not saying this to frighten you, but to tell you to be prepared and pray the more. Let's hold on to the Lord. Some might die, but if you must die, be sure to die in the Lord."

It did our spirits good, because the confessions and the repentance were real. People became real Christians through these difficulties.

And when it came to Christmas Day, even though I had put the fear of God into the congregation the week before, still they poured into the church.

Our Christmas Day service was at ten o'clock and we carried out our security checks as usual. We blocked the road and closed the lane nearest to the church. The only route through was the outer lane farthest from the building. The army and the police directed the traffic, and our barricade and tyres on the road would deter anyone from driving in our direction.

St Luke's is one of those old-style buildings. It's about 100 years old, with windows of painted glass. Part of the chancel ceiling is vaulted, but the effect is more warehouse than Westminster Abbey.

The pulpit is elevated and made of white marble, with a matching lectern and altar. In the pulpit I had the Bible on my left and my phone on the right. I was expecting a security call at any time. The air was alive with rumours.

The church was packed with some 700 people. I was surprised by the number.

I asked the congregation to be sensitive and prayerful, just in case of bombs or gunshots. "Our faith is in God," I said.

I was preaching on Hebrews when my phone lit up. It was on silent. I continued to preach Christ, the image of God. I glanced again at my phone. It showed a missed call. I tried to see the message, but couldn't read it. Then the phone flickered again. I wrapped up my sermon early to check the call. It was a text to say there was trouble in town. They had bombed the Mountain of Fire and Miracles Church.

Why that church? My suspicion was they had hit the wrong target. The small Mountain of Fire Church was close to the much larger Living Faith Cathedral, which seats more than 3,000 and which was the more likely objective.

Bombers had struck with three devices and a dozen gunmen. In the event, only one of their three bombs went off outside the church and one policeman was killed in a gun battle.

We closed the service and told people the routes they should avoid. I said, "Pray for our brothers and sisters, and take care on the way home."

Bombers had launched coordinated attacks in Jos, Gadaka, Damaturu, and Madalla, near the capital, Abuja. That attack in Madalla on a Catholic church killed around forty and injured many more. There were not enough ambulances to ferry all the wounded.[13] Boko Haram claimed responsibility.

I asked my staff to help folks go home gently and quietly after the service. There was no talk of reprisals by Christians and

---

13   "Hell on Christmas Day: Nigeria's Deadly Bombings", Monica Mark, *Time*, 25 December 2011: http://content.time.com/time/world/article/0,8599,2103091,00.html

no fear of attacks by Muslims. We were all clear this was the work of Boko Haram and nobody wanted to confuse this with our own local issues.

I had set up a media team to gather timely, accurate reports. I sent them out with my welfare team to bring in correct information so we could get that out to the people of Jos, and they did.

In February, Abubakar Shekau tried again. His bomber arrived at COCIN Church in a VW Golf, the vehicle of choice for suicide bombers at the time.

COCIN Church is in the centre of Jos, next to the Central Bank of Nigeria. The bomber was accompanied by a man in military uniform, who got out of the car and was later arrested – but not before he was almost lynched.

The bomber forced his way through the gate, hit a motorcycle, and refused to stop. As his car bounced over the motorcycle the boot burst open, throwing out an industrial gas cylinder, which struck the ground, split apart, and ignited. It detonated the bombs, killing the bomber and several others.

The shrapnel from the blast injured thirty-seven worshippers. Had the bomber got any closer to the church, the casualties would have been far higher. The fact the attack was botched was God's hand – absolutely.[14]

Christians, Muslims, and the tribal groups pulled together to hold our ground on the Plateau. There was violence, but not on the scale anticipated by Boko Haram. So they tried again.

This time they struck at a viewing centre, where people had gathered to watch football. Again, their bomb failed to ignite widespread reprisals. So once again, they targeted the church. I believe they were looking for our Anglican church, but missed it. Instead they bombed a Pentecostal church nearby. Again, the people showed restraint. There were no reprisals and no Muslims were killed.

By now, the churches were beginning to resemble fortresses. After the bomb blast at COCIN, the church added

14   "Nigeria Suicide Bomber Targets Church in Jos", CSW, 27 February 2012: https://www.csw.org.uk/2012/02/27/press/1317/article.htm

a barricade manned by guards. This became a model for all the churches in Jos.

The best defence against the car bomb was to keep the cars away. Only the pastor's car would be allowed into the compound on a Sunday service, and even my own car would be checked in case someone had planted a bomb beneath it. People would have to park on the streets and walk to church, and before being allowed in, they would be checked by security. And there was a ban on taking handbags into church.

While the police stayed outside, scanning arrivals for potential suspects, the churches arranged their own security. This was provided by a combination of retired policemen and soldiers, and specially trained members of the Boys' Brigade and Scouts.

But even this didn't deter the bomber. A month after the COCIN attack, a car bomber struck at St Finbar's Catholic Church. Boy Scouts were standing guard. They saw the car heading towards them at high speed and refused to open the gate. So as the bomber struggled to get through, his bomb blew and killed the Boy Scouts. They were heroes. This time there were reports of reprisal attacks.[15]

Several times, it came close to home. Because of all the roadblocks, I needed to split one Synod over two venues. The first three days were held at St Christopher's, but we had to move the thanksgiving on Sunday to St Piran's.

When the bombers heard the venue had been shifted, they got lost looking for the Anglican church. It seems Boko Haram's map-reading skills left something to be desired. They went to a different Anglican church instead, and found nobody there. So, heading back, they looked for a target of opportunity. Any church would do. They found a Pentecostal church. The service had just ended and most of the members had left. It could all have been so much worse.

Then Boko Haram bomb-makers infiltrated communities around the nation. They began using child suicide bombers to

15   "Reprisals Kill 10 After Church Bombed in Nigeria's Jos", *Reuters*, 12 March 2018: https://www.reuters.com/article/us-nigeria-violence/reprisals-kill-10-after-church-bombed-in-nigerias-jos-idUSBRE82A05A20120312

slip under the radar. In 2015, one in five suicide attacks was carried out by children, three-quarters of whom were girls.[16]

But things didn't always work out for Boko Haram. Two sisters were sent to blow up themselves and others in Kano. One pressed her detonator, while the other hesitated. The girl, who was in a hijab, watched as her sister's head and limbs were torn from her body.

Her own hand was poised to press the button, but she was so horrified by what she had seen happen to her sister, that she became paralysed with fear. She started crying and screaming, "Please help me, please help me! I'm carrying a bomb. I don't want to do it!"

The bomb disposal people drove everybody away and were able to remove the explosives and rescue the girl. Later, they asked her questions. She gave one answer I will never forget.

She was told that as soon as the bomb exploded, she would automatically see herself in heaven, in the presence of God and all her relatives who had gone before. She was told it would be wonderful. But she explained to her interviewers that when she saw her sister ripped limb from limb, she knew there would be nothing left of her to take to heaven.

The indoctrination they give these suicide bombers is simply evil. And they drug them before they die. Many armies will do the same with their troops. But these are children.

§

When most people think of Boko Haram, they think of the kidnapped Chibok schoolgirls, the 276 female students who were snatched from their government secondary school in Borno State.

Boko Haram, having subjugated these other areas, had their eye on Chibok. And for good reason. Chibok was a Christian enclave that stood in the way of their drive to Islamize the north.

16 "Boko Haram Crisis: 'Huge Rise' in Child Suicide Bombers", BBC, 12 April 2016: https://www.bbc.co.uk/news/world-africa-36023444

Most of those who live in Chibok are Christians. They are well educated, which is a hallmark of the missions that evangelized the area. In the whole of Borno State, Chibok is the only local government area led by Christians with Christian representatives. Its people hold positions of influence within the police and the army.

The sheer audacity of the raid prompted many questions.

Boko Haram had the fighters and they had the arms, but their base in Maiduguri was a two-hour drive from Chibok.

The whole state was under strict security. Troops and police covered every inch. How could a militia convoy in pick-up trucks travel for miles, kidnap hundreds of children, then travel back for two hours laden with schoolgirls and simply spirit them away?

How could these girls be kidnapped with such impunity without raising the suggestion of some complicity from the military? And why did it take more than twenty-four hours for the kidnapping to come to the notice of the federal government?

More than 80 per cent of the Chibok girls were Christians. Boko Haram was targeting Christians certainly, but why set its sights on schoolgirls?

They knew that if you hurt the girls, you will hurt the parents, the grandparents, and the generations to come. If you ruin the women, you will ruin the future.

Abubakar Shekau had declared his intentions in a video in March: "In Islam, it is permitted to take the wife of an infidel. Soon, we're going to take those women and sell them in the market. Danger, danger, danger!"[17]

And after the successful kidnapping of the Chibok girls, he boasted: "God instructed me to sell them. They are his properties and I will carry out his instructions."[18]

The strategy of Islamization in northern Nigeria, as in other countries, is being worked out through forced marriage and forced conversion.

---

17 25 March 2018, https://www.cairn-int.info/article-E_AFCO_255_0043--the-words-of-boko-haram.htm

18 "Boko Haram 'to Sell' Nigeria Girls Abducted from Chibok", BBC, 5 May 2014: https://www.bbc.co.uk/news/world-africa-27283383

Kidnap and rape are all too often tactics of war. That is certainly true of this war. Abubakar Shekau later proudly announced that he had converted and married off the Chibok girls. These families now have Boko Haram fighters as in-laws. This is not just the destruction of girls, but of their families and whole communities. It's a terrible thing.

And it's not just Chibok. According to UNICEF, Boko Haram kidnapped more than 1,000 children in just five years.[19]

As a result, many Christians have now been driven out of the north-east. Some have come to Jos: many have fled even further. They have run away in their thousands. Some have been displaced time and again. By some estimates more than 14 million have been affected by the Boko Haram insurgency in the north-east.[20]

What Boko Haram is attempting is the deliberate religious cleansing of Christians from northern Nigeria. They must convert and become subjects. Or run for their lives. Death is the only alternative.

Successive military offensives have driven Boko Haram across the border into Cameroon, Niger, and Chad. These countries are now having to deal with these terrorists themselves.

They have learned not to travel with arms. Their weapons go ahead of them and are kept for them in communities. Their fighters infiltrate these communities and stay there, and on the day of action, they pick up their arms and launch their attacks.

There are splinter groups of Boko Haram everywhere. Some have been caught in Lagos. It is not correct to say they have been decimated. They are still making bombs and carrying out attacks. They are still causing fear and terror and have never been disarmed.

International observers believe their weapons, their vehicles, and their money come from the black market, along with supporters in Nigeria, overseas, and the Middle East – including Al-Qaeda.[21]

---

19   "UNICEF: Boko Haram Has Kidnapped More Than 1000 Children in Nigeria", CNN, 13 April 2018: https://edition.cnn.com/2018/04/13/africa/boko-haram-children-abduction-intl/index.html

20   "ACAPS Country Analysis on Nigeria": https://www.acaps.org/country/nigeria

21   "Paying for Terrorism: Where Does Boko Haram Get its Money From?", *The*

As well as adapting to function more like terrorist cells than a militia, their ideology has shifted too. In 2015, they pledged allegiance to Islamic State. And IS, by way of acceptance, announced that its ambitions for a caliphate had now expanded to include West Africa.[22]

In less than a decade, Boko Haram killed 20,000, abducted more than 4,000 women and girls, and drove 2 million people from their homes. And, after a dip in which the government claimed to have finished Boko Haram, their death toll has again begun to rise.[23]

Independent, 6 June 2014: https://www.independent.co.uk/news/world/africa/paying-for-terrorism-where-does-boko-haram-gets-its-money-from-9503948.html
22   "Nigeria: 2018 Humanitarian Needs Overview", ReliefWeb, 12 February 2018: https://reliefweb.int/report/nigeria/nigeria-2018-humanitarian-needs-overview
23   "Nigeria's Boko Haram Attacks in Numbers – as Lethal as Ever", BBC, 25 January 2018: https://www.bbc.co.uk/news/world-africa-42735414

CANNIBALISM AND REVENGE

n Nigeria, the thirst for revenge, turned – literally – into a thirst for blood.

When Nigerians reverted to cannibalism, it became clear to all that the country, and Plateau in particular, was in serious trouble.

In northern Nigeria, if you are a Muslim and you kill a Christian, you're most likely to go free. You can get away with murder – literally. There is a culture of impunity in Nigeria, and the government is either powerless or lacks the will to prevent the killing.

People can stand so much. But there comes a point where they will stand it no longer. If no one will come to their defence, they will take up arms to defend themselves. That is their right in Nigeria.

But from self-defence, it is but a small step to go on the offensive – to attack. And to take the next small step beyond, to revenge, is to plunge headlong into a downward spiral.

This is what happens when there is a culture of impunity, where evil is neither opposed nor punished.

§

It was a Sunday in 2007, and a crowd turned up to help a Muslim building a house in Jos. Christians going to church had to pass that house. The Muslims barred their way. They started beating them and throwing stones. They injured many women and children. And then suddenly, we heard gunshots. These young Muslim men started firing at the Christians, and the violence began to spread.

And here was the turning point. Some of the non-Muslims decided to fight back. They killed some of the Muslims and, having thrown off all restraint, took matters to extremes. They roasted the bodies of their dead enemies in the open air and ate them. And they called the place where they did this the Den of Satan.

This bloodlust erupted again a few years later, the day an extremist rode up to a church with a bomb. The crowd dragged him off his motorbike. He tried to run, but they caught him, killed him, roasted him, and ate his flesh. And they filmed themselves doing it. This atrocity was seen around the world. The video went viral. And these cannibals didn't even bother to hide their faces.

I watched as much of this as I could bear. I realized that people were returning to paganism. They were taking a stand, not only against their attackers, but against church and society. Their attitude was, "We are unbelievers and we will do whatever we want."

It was evil and it was cultic. But as far as the Muslims were concerned, this barbaric act had been carried out by Christians. It became a further excuse to attack us. And those attacks simply increased. Bombs were going off all over the place.

The government seemed unable either to protect the Christians or to arrest the criminals. And the government and the media kept referring to reprisals, as if to imply that in some way the killings were a justified response against an evil aggressor.

Revenge attacks became widespread and indiscriminate. And the government was doing nothing to stop them.

Young people felt betrayed by their country and abandoned by their church. Many stopped going to church. They were being slaughtered for no reason.

I met many young people who said, "If the government is not prepared to keep the rule of law, then we will have to take that law into our own hands. This has nothing to do with religion or politics. The Muslims want our land, and we will defend it."

They wouldn't listen to the church. They wouldn't listen to anyone. They left the church and armed themselves. Those who could afford it bought double-barrelled and pump-action shotguns. Those who couldn't took up clubs, sticks, knives, and bows and arrows. They fought everybody, including government troops. And they drove Muslims out of their homes in Bukuru and Jos. Plateau was sliding towards civil war.

This had to be halted, and thrown into reverse. Something had to be done to get Nigerians working together for the good of all. But what?

§

I felt the first thing that had to be established was the truth. In every circumstance. And that pointed a finger back at me.

I began digging deep into the stories of Wilberforce to learn how God had used one man. Wilberforce didn't set about reformation in a grand style, he began small. So, I decided I should face the injustices in Jos where I lived.

I focused on the local and I dug for the truth. I developed a media department to get at the root of the issues that divided us, even if the truths they uncovered proved painful for Christians. It became a respected authority in Jos and northern Nigeria.

So when I saw these young men eating human flesh, children whose families were Christian, but who were doing terrible, pagan things, I asked to meet with some of them.

That meeting took place on Rukuba Road. All around us were destroyed Toyotas, Peugeots, and VWs, damaged houses, and open sewers. It's hard to be sure what had happened here. Everybody had different versions of who was to blame, but what I gathered was this...

It was Eid. The Muslims were converging to pray on ground they had bought in the area. They were preventing the indigenes from getting into town, so to get their own back, the indigenes prevented the Muslims from gathering to pray. They told them to pray in their own part of town, rather than gather here. But the Muslims insisted.

When the Muslims arrived it was in a group and under military protection. The story went that the indigenes were fired on. They didn't know whether the shots came from the military or the Muslims. But when they heard the gunshots, they raised their own war cry and battle ensued. Hundreds were involved, on both sides. People were killed, and some of the non-Muslim boys reverted to cannibalism.

When the dust had died down, I posted a priest to the area as a missionary. I told him I wanted to meet with the youth.

The priest gathered about sixty young people. Most were in their teens or early twenties, jobless and living in poverty in ghettos. They came in ragged shorts or jeans, out of curiosity to hear what this bishop had to say. I greeted them with my black clerical shirt and dog collar, wearing my cross.

I was friendly towards them and they were easy towards me. I didn't raise the issue of the killings. The backdrop could speak for itself. Instead, I stood with them, in the middle of this scene of destruction, and I talked about their futures and the evils that any further crisis would do to their lives. I talked about the need to build up the local community to be prosperous and safe for everybody.

I defended neither one side nor the other, and offered no justification for what had taken place. I wanted them to know that I cared about their future and that some of us were working for a better Plateau State and a better Nigeria. We needed their support, so they should no longer take the law into their own hands; they should build instead of destroy. They listened attentively.

Some of these young men had eaten flesh, as had others at the second meeting that I called about a year later in a different part of Jos.

These young people had been into drugs and stealing. They were unemployed, rode motorcycle taxis, and whiled away most evenings playing football.

More than seventy gathered beside a school. It was midday and warm for Jos. The ground on which we stood was bare and uneven and the government school in the background was littered with broken windows and doors.

At the beginning this group was rowdy. They were calling for justice. "We won't let anybody overrun our land – whether they are Christians or Muslims. We are prepared to die for our land!"

I picked on that theme and told them simply, "Whatever you're going through, the attacks from those who want your land, from those who hate you for the religion you profess, in it all, you need to know that God knows, that God understands.

"However much you try to defend your land and your people, if you don't have faith in God, you could lose both your land and your life. At the end of it, whatever you were fighting for, without Jesus, you would have lost everything.

"So, it is safer now to turn to Christ and put your faith in Him. Our fight is the struggle of light against darkness. God is able to make your light shine in the darkness. So many lies have been told against you; so much injustice has been poured out on you, but God is able to do this.

"God," I said, "is the ultimate judge. He knows your circumstances, He understands your problems, and He can take all of your pain and all of your injuries."

One or two began to bow their heads. One was shedding tears, then another. They were ready to be prayed for. Some were broken. Some repented and some were changed. Other Christian leaders followed up on this. I was able to start a mission in their home area that is now growing.

§

I realized God wanted me to work for justice and peace for all peoples. I plunged myself into peace meetings across many different tribes and denominations. The Berom and Hausa received me, including the Muslims.

Many Muslims realized the stand I was taking was against neither them nor the government, it was simply for justice. And by God's grace, the Muslims began to listen to me even more. I drew closer to the chief imam of Jos and several other Muslim leaders.

We found ourselves on common ground. These were land matters that had become life-and-death issues between the tribespeople in Jos, and we were now working together for justice.

I was approached by Jonathan Onigbinde, a Yoruba businessman, who said, "Ben, look, we can't just sit down and watch the city burning. If you are willing to lead a group, I will facilitate it. The people trust you."

He convinced me, and we began to bring these different groups together. One of the Muslim leaders said the only reason he had come was to listen to me.

I met with Muslim youths too. They share the same concern for justice. In 2011 they held a huge conference at the University Staff Club in Jos and invited me to speak. I traced the history of the Nigeria I grew up in, particularly the Hausa Muslims of Kano. They came to Jos as businessmen. When they were persecuted by their ruling parties in Kano, they found a home in Jos.

I asked, "Where have we gone wrong?" We had allowed outsiders from beyond Plateau State to come to us and bring us their crisis. We who understood one another and had lived in peace, had found ourselves suddenly up in arms against each other.

All the time I was using Bible verses and they were clapping. At the end, one of the Muslim leaders, a lawyer, said, "Quite frankly, I'm confused. I don't know whether I am in a mosque or a church. Everything the bishop says, I agree with it!"

What the people were listening to, including the Muslims, was a cry for justice. They were responding to a cry for righteousness before God that would be worked out and walked out in society. And they continued to listen.

At the breaking of the Ramadan fast in 2014, I was invited to be a guest speaker at an all-Muslim gathering in Jos, held in a Muslim hotel.

They greeted me in the customary way, "As-salamu alaykum" – "Peace be with you." I related that to the desire for peace in the community of Islam.

I said that, as a Christian, I would not give peace if I didn't have it to give, because just saying peace means nothing. I had to desire peace for the other person, the peace that only God through Christ can give, the *shalom* that brings blessing, long life, preservation, and prosperity on the other person. I said this is what peace means when you say, "As-salamu alaykum."

Given the crisis and the killings in our community, I said that if a Muslim man and a Christian man were to meet, they could easily be wary. Each might fear he had encountered an enemy.

But I continued: "Your enemy is the failure of government to provide for both of you security, justice, and the amenities of life. These are rights they should have provided for you, but they have denied you. So even if you fought each other, you would not get those things. And if you killed each other, you would simply lose twice. It would be better for you to come together and fight to get your rights from government. They must give both of you security, justice, and the social amenities that are due to you."

These Muslim leaders received me well. They had heard me, thanks to God, and even asked me to pray. My cry for justice was reaching out beyond the Christians and to the whole community.

I had not taken this role of mediation upon myself. It was after visiting people on both sides that I began to get calls from both sides. It would seem that this is why God had put me in Jos. This was not a responsibility I was looking for, but it was a role that had fallen to me because people trusted me.

As terrible as the tragedy was, God had used it as a springboard to work for Him and to speak on His behalf. Again, it was a case of Romans 8:28, "in all things God works for the good of those who love him, who have been called according to his purpose".

This was something to hold on to, because in this darkest of times, Nigeria's troubles took on an even darker hue.

DEADLY CATTLE HERDERS

I have first-hand experience of cattle rustling – on the receiving end, that is. Keeping cows is in my blood. Holding on to them is proving harder these days.

The first time, I lost thirty-five cows and more than sixty sheep. Then, it was twenty-two cows and more than twenty sheep. The third time they rustled only the cows. But they took something far more valuable – my neighbour's life.

It was June 2018. We had woken up early to do our cooking in the Bishop's Court, when the young man who looks after our cows ran to tell us they were missing. We hurried to see. It was true. Whoever had taken them had broken down the back wall to get to them. They had taken nine.

I immediately phoned the divisional police officer. She said she had just got a report that somebody had been shot dead near my house. Maybe this incident was related. She said she would come right away. It was the first I had heard of this.

The broken wall opened up a back route past my neighbour's home. Bitrus Adamu was in his thirties and in our equivalent of a Neighbourhood Watch scheme. He had just come off duty at midnight, when he heard a commotion and went out to see what was happening.

He flashed his torch at the intruders, and they shot and killed him. We found a single cartridge case from a Kalashnikov assault rifle.

Bitrus had been a driver for another pastor. He had just moved in and had been working to build a house for his family on this plot of land. He had managed to roof it and partly floor it, but had yet to construct their kitchen and toilet. Bitrus was the breadwinner for his family. And he had been killed, before he could complete their home.

I didn't realize the struggles this family were having before I met his widow. Lydia had six children.

When I saw the children, I broke down completely. I cried for hours. But after I had gathered myself together, I called my archdeacon in charge of the area and we agreed that we would finish the building of their house, and make sure Lydia and her children were secure. We have taken those children into our schools.

You would think our neighbours might have heard these intruders knocking down the cement block wall, but with attacks by Fulani cattle herders on the increase, the people of Jos have grown too wise to come out at night, with the exception of our courageous Neighbourhood Watch.

This is not about cattle. It's about people. It's about Lydia and her children, left with no breadwinner. Bitrus was trying to protect our community, where armed herdsmen are becoming more commonplace. And he paid the price.

§

There are tens of millions of ethnic Fulani scattered across west and central Africa.[24] These herdsmen are part of our landscape. Yet, there are signs that some of them are now being turned into extremists. In recent years, these cattle herders have killed thousands in Nigeria, in Kaduna, Benue, Plateau, and Nasarawa.

They attack, typically, in the middle of the night while people are sleeping. They shoot in the air and create panic to drive the villagers out. When the people flee from their houses into the darkness, the Fulani lie in wait with their machetes and cut them down. Again and again. And the government seems powerless to stop them.

In 2013, the Fulani killed eighty people. By the following year, they had slaughtered fifteen times as many, until in 2015 the Global Terrorism Index (GTI) named Fulani extremists as the fourth-deadliest terror group in the world.[25]

---

24   https://www.britannica.com/topic/Fulani
25   "Global Terrorism Index: Nigerian Fulani Militants Named as Fourth Deadliest Terror Group in World", *The Independent*, 18 November 2015: https://www. independent.co.uk/news/world/africa/global-terrorism-index-nigerian-fulani-

And by 2018, the GTI reported: "Deaths attributed to Fulani extremists are estimated to be six times greater than the number committed by Boko Haram."[26]

Nigeria is being described as the largest killing ground for Christians in the world today.[27] First Boko Haram and now Fulani militants.

Fulani attacks have become today's big issue for Nigeria. And the reporting of the violence is often based on ignorance, with no sense of scale or history. Which is why I feel I need to set the record straight.

The problem didn't just come out of nowhere.

One common explanation is climate change, leading to the spread of desertification. We are close to the Sahara and our fertile land is disappearing. Trees are now being planted, which will help in years to come, but these herdsmen need water and green pasture, and they need it now. I sympathize.

Even so, there is space enough in Nigeria for all. In the past, Fulani herdsmen have come into communities and negotiated peacefully for grazing rights. Most tribes on Plateau kept cattle. The Fulani have always kept herds there.

Fulani cattle are mainly white or grey spotted longhorns. They would move them out from Plateau during the rainy season to avoid trampling people's farms. They would return in November or December when the harvest was in and graze their cattle on the leftovers of crops, before heading south. Then they would be back in April during the early rains, before the planting season, moving northwards again, away from the farms into the wilderness.

It worked for the benefit of all. The Fulani have long had a fruitful relationship with the farmers. The farmers harvested their rich acha grass, which is full of seeds for porridge, couscous,

militants-named-as-fourth-deadliest-terror-group-in-world-a6739851.html
26   http://visionofhumanity.org/app/uploads/2018/12/Global-Terrorism-Index-2018-1.pdf
27   International Christian Concern, cited in "Christian 'Genocide': Naming Nigeria's Mass Slaughter", Diana Chandler, *Baptist Press*, 7 August 2018: http://www.bpnews.net/51379/christian-genocide-naming-nigerias-mass-slaughter

and biscuits. But as they only harvested the tops, there was always plenty of goodness left for the cattle, who ate the rest. In return, the farmers collected the cattle droppings to fertilize the land. Everyone was happy.

I had grown up with Fulani who spoke my language. Some had become Christian, some had intermarried. Most people in my home area had Fulani blood. Some were still Muslim, but most had just integrated into the tribes.

But in recent years, as tribal and religious tensions began to rise, the Fulani accused the Berom of stealing their cattle. They killed the Berom and the Berom retaliated.

In one village, the Fulani had to run for their lives, but the pastor kept them in his church for safety. But then the Fulani turned around and killed the pastor along with his grandchildren. God knows why. But the cycle of revenge had begun, and it has continued.

This was all happening twenty to forty miles from Jos. While we were still facing a full-blown crisis in the city, another was already brewing in the rural areas. And it was spreading. The year was 2004.

About 120 miles away in Yelwa, Fulani herdsmen murdered worshippers in their church. A BBC report described the church killings as a reprisal for cattle rustling. And that line has become the prevailing wisdom. Tit-for-tat violence between herders and farmers is how this conflict is usually portrayed.

But that is simplistic and not the whole of the story. Document the evidence and you will see that this is far from being six of one and half a dozen of the other.

In the first quarter of 2018, Christian Solidarity Worldwide kept a record of the militia attacks on communities in central Nigeria. They logged upwards of 106 attacks that claimed 1,061 lives, an average of ten lives for every assault. These attacks appear to have been well planned – and cattle, frankly, had little part to play in them.

In return, over the same period, the indigenous people carried out seven revenge attacks on Fulani herders and communities. These inexcusable revenge attacks claimed sixty-one lives – the lives of sixty-one people who should still be alive today. No, it's not right. But neither is it equal: 106 attacks versus seven; 1,061 lives versus sixty-one.

Any life lost is a sin, a crime and a tragedy. But the figures give the lie to the notion that this is a conflict between two equal warring parties.[28]

Something has shifted, as my friend Baroness Cox observed in a debate in the House of Lords in Britain: "There has been a very disturbing change in the behaviour of the Fulani herdsmen... In the last two to three years they have adopted a new policy: attacking Christian villages, killing local people, destroying homes, driving villagers off their lands and settling in their place.

"There are concerns that the Fulani militants are now so well armed that they are possibly fighting a proxy war for Boko Haram, with the shared agenda of driving Christians out of their homelands in northern and central-belt Nigeria."

Whether they know it or not, Fulani militants are now serving the agenda of Boko Haram, whose overarching aim is to establish a fundamentalist Islamic state. That was the aim of the Sokoto caliphate, ushered in by the Fulani jihad of the nineteenth century. And some believe it remains the long-nursed ambition of some Nigerian politicians in the north today.[29]

So could we be seeing a conscious revival of that ancient impulse towards jihad?

The Christian Association of Nigeria has been following the trail of destroyed churches. They say herdsmen have ruined more than 500 churches in Benue State alone since 2011.

---

28   British human rights campaigner Lord Alton called a debate in the House of Lords, in which he asked: "Given the escalation, frequency, organisation and asymmetry of Fulani attacks, does the Minister believe that the references to 'farmer-herder clashes' still suffice?" https://hansard.parliament.uk/Lords/2018-06-28/debates/B694EEEC-7D52-4FBB-97E9-20C52519C332/Nigeria?highlight=nigeria#contribution-C14327EC-E2AA-475E-9B23-4DCEF5E8451B
29   The International Crisis Group noted in 2018: "Enmity is deepened by the claims of some Fulani elites... that 'a large chunk of what... some people prefer to call the Middle Belt today were actually territories belonging to the Sokoto caliphate."

"The impression has now been firmly established that the Islamists of northern Nigerian have 'legalized jihad' in Nigeria."[30]

Across the north, the mainly Muslim Fulani have been taking land from predominantly Christian farmers by force and occupying their villages.

And the violence cannot be contained in the north. In 2018, Amnesty International said the military were struggling to contain the attacks in thirty of Nigeria's thirty-six states, including the federal capital territory.[31] This movement, which looks, sounds, and smells like a jihad, is gaining ground.

Yet, these murders continue to be reported around the world as reprisals – summary execution for cattle theft. This is just lazy reporting.

The sheer scale of that revenge is hugely disproportionate to any crime. And the government appears to be doing virtually nothing to contain it.

Certainly, the Fulani deserve justice if their cattle are being stolen, but does the right to justice confer the right to kill?

Does the loss of my cows give me the right to take to the streets and start killing others? When did the value of human life sink to that of livestock? And are those they are killing actually the cattle thieves? What of the women and children who are being slashed to ribbons in their homes?

Whatever the motive for these attacks, it is certainly not justice. It is for the law to capture and punish cattle rustlers. But government ministers are simply excusing this wanton murder, destruction, and criminality.

Instead of facing the issue, the government is claiming the killers are foreigners from Niger, Chad, and Cameroon. If so, what brings them so far from their borders? And if Nigeria really

---

30   CAN Press Conference, 16 January 2018: https://worldprayer.org.uk/pa-worldwide/item/10186-can-press-conference-miyetti-allah-should-be-prosecuted-for-genocide

31   "Amnesty International Reveals How Many Nigerians Fulani Herdsmen Killed in 2018", by Ameh Comrade Godwin, *Daily Post*, 30 January 2018: http://dailypost.ng/2018/01/30/amnesty-international-reveals-many-nigerians-fulani-herdsmen-killed-2018/

is being invaded, then why is our government doing nothing to prevent its citizens being wiped out by armed foreigners?

Some of these attackers may indeed be foreign. On Plateau, some survivors overheard attackers who were not speaking Hausa.

But other survivors have confirmed their attackers were definitely Fulani – Fulani armed with machetes and Kalashnikovs and sometimes dressed in military fatigues: uniforms, but without any national badge.

What is making these attacks so deadly is the use of modern weapons.

As President Buhari told reporters: "Before now, cattle herders were known to carry sticks and machetes… but these ones are carrying AK-47s."[32]

Correct. In the House of Lords debate, Lord Alton raised a crucial question: "Armed with sophisticated weaponry, including AK47s and, in at least one case, a rocket launcher and rocket-propelled grenades, the Fulani militia have murdered more men, women and children… than even Boko Haram, destroying, overrunning and seizing property and land, and displacing tens of thousands of people. This is organised and systematic. We must ask where this group of nomadic herdsmen is getting such sophisticated weaponry from."[33]

Indeed. Who is arming the Fulani? According to the International Crisis Group: "The quality of the arms suggests the militias have well-heeled patrons."[34]

---

32 "How Trump Stirred Up Controversy in Nigeria", BBC News, 1 May 2018: https://www.bbc.co.uk/news/world-africa-43964932

33 *Hansard*, House of Lords debate, 28 June 2018, volume 792: https://hansard.parliament.uk/Lords/2018-06-28/debates/B694EEEC-7D52-4FBB-97E9-20C52519C332/Nigeria?highlight=nigeria#contribution-C14327EC-E2AA-475E-9B23-4DCEF5E8451B

34 They added: "Yahaya Abdullahi, the senator representing Kebbi north senatorial district, contends, 'This violence is paying some people, so they are sponsoring it.'" "Stopping Nigeria's Spiralling Farmer-Herder Violence", International Crisis Group, 26 July 2018: https://d2071andvip0wj.cloudfront.net/262-stopping-nigerias-spiralling-farmer-herder-violence.pdf

Perhaps that may explain why the government and the army are failing so dismally to disarm the Fulani and prevent these attacks.

If the rush to arms continues, what will become of our country? People are already taking up arms to defend themselves. Food production is plunging, prices are increasing, and poverty is on the rise.

Nigeria's military, and indeed President Buhari, have been criticized for doing little to stop the slaughter. Some have pointed out that President Buhari is himself a Fulani. The US Council on Foreign Relations documented almost 20,000 deaths within three years of President Buhari taking office in 2015.[35]

So many questions.

But there a few things we do know. These attackers are organized. They know what they doing, where they are going, the routes to get there, and the people they intend to kill.

They rely on people with local knowledge. They kill the Christians, but leave untouched the houses of Fulani Muslims.

Their route to attack is from the north-east. This also is known. And yet the army seems unable to stop them. In Kaduna State, the killers are taking over the villages they empty. You would have thought that would make them easy targets for the army. You would be mistaken.

Their style of warfare shows they have been trained in terrorism. If it were not so, they could be confronted and disarmed, but so far no one has been willing or able to withstand these killers.

§

As with Boko Haram, this lack of opposition has led to suspicions of tacit support by some in the military.

In Dogo Nahawa village, less than ten miles from Jos, Fulani slaughtered nearly 500 people, including women, children, and a

---

35 "Nigeria Has Recorded Nearly 20,000 Deaths Under Buhari, Says US Body", *This Day*, 1 July 2018: https://www.thisdaylive.com/index.php/2018/07/01/nigeria-has-recorded-nearly-20000-deaths-under-buhari-says-us-body/

four-day-old baby. That was in 2010.[36] The governor of Plateau called the army and the police, but nobody came.

In Kaduna State, the Fulani wrote to the villagers in advance to tell them they were coming. They even provided the date. They were true to their word. And nobody stopped them.

In 2018, Amnesty International documented an air-raid against villages in Adamawa that were being attacked by hundreds of herdsmen. Villagers described being bombed by a fighter jet and a military helicopter as they tried to flee the Fulani.

Amnesty couldn't work out who had killed the most – the military or the herdsmen. They spoke to witnesses who said: "The helicopter and jet started releasing bombs. Children started running for their lives. Mothers packed up their children and escaped with them. The jet burned our houses to ashes." Three thousand homes were destroyed.[37]

Air support for the Fulani? Or appalling military mismanagement?

Someone must answer these questions, if only to quash this persistent rumour of military collusion.

As Christians we must continue to question a culture of impunity – wherever we may find it.

While thousands have been killed, where are the prosecutions?

And why do those in power appear to be turning a blind eye to this endless bloodshed?

Given that Nigeria is torn in every direction by history, tribe, language, and religion, is it inconceivable that some elements within the military could be pursuing a sectarian

36   "Christian Villagers Wail as Hundreds of Nigerians Slaughtered in Machete 'Revenge' Attacks are Buried in Mass Graves", MailOnline, 10 March 2010: https://www.dailymail.co.uk/news/article-1256293/More-500-people-slaughtered-machete-revenge-attacks-Christian-villages-Nigeria.html
37   "Nigeria: Dozens Killed as Military Launches Air Attacks on Villages Beset by Spiralling Communal Violence", Amnesty International, 30 January 2018. See also: "Amnesty International Reveals How Many Nigerians Fulani Herdsmen Killed in 2018", Daily Post, 30 January 2018: http://dailypost.ng/2018/01/30/amnesty-international-reveals-many-nigerians-fulani-herdsmen-killed-2018/

agenda? Certainly, that is the view of a former Nigerian Army Chief of Staff.

During his debate in the UK, Lord Alton quoted former Defence Minister, Lieutenant General Theophilus Y Danjuma, who believed, "The armed forces were 'not neutral; they collude' in the 'ethnic cleansing' by Fulani militia."

Danjuma went on to warn: "The ethnic cleansing must stop… otherwise Somalia will be a child's play."

§

This takes us back to the most fundamental question of all: just whose interests are being served by this slaughter?

Like Woodward and Bernstein, we must follow the money. This killing campaign is amply resourced and funded. The question is: who stands to benefit from all this bloodshed?

A great deal of cattle are owned by the emirs and retired generals. Most wealthy politicians in the north have cattle. The Fulani herdsmen are their caretakers. In Nigeria, the herding business makes more money than oil. You can sell your cows in the east for cash, and the money you make is tax-free.

The principal interests served by the Fulani are of those who want to eject the Christians from Plateau State: the rich and powerful Muslims of the north and their Islamist allies worldwide, who want to impose radical Islamic law – Sharia.

Although Nigeria is secular by constitution, twelve northern states have already imposed Sharia, a parallel legal system.[38] And

---

38 Nigeria is becoming one nation with two laws. And that's impossible. For example, women's rights are protected under the law of the land, yet under Sharia, women have half the legal value of men. How can both be enforced at the same time? The security apparatus of Nigeria is controlled by Muslims sympathetic to these Islamist aggressors. They are sympathetic to the cause of making sure the Fulani acquire lands in the central regions. And they are sympathetic to the cause of stamping the authority of Islam in these areas by force – in short, Islamic domination. Muslim politicians who stand in the way of this invisible, open agenda get removed. The security apparatus of Nigeria is compromised. There has been a failure of Nigeria's government at federal, state, and local levels to identify this strand of aggressive Islam. There has been a similar failure by international governments throughout the world.

there are wealthy states in the Middle East who are willing to resource that Islamist agenda handsomely.

Their aim is to create a northern Nigeria that is one religion and one people – an Islamic north. If needs be, a northern bloc that can be torn away from Nigeria. And to do that, they must first thin down the Christians.

Violent Islamists are now armed the world over. And they are bent on redefining civilization.

So Nigeria's problem is a problem for the world.

Now, as in the original Fulani jihad, Plateau is becoming a backstop for many of the Christians who have fled the north. Of the 1.8 million displaced,[39] most are Christians, and the areas that have faced the most attacks are those where the Christian missions were most successful.

Many have moved here from Borno, Kaduna, and Adamawa. We are taking their displaced children into our schools and giving them scholarships.

Yet, our camps for the displaced are filling with orphans, including survivors who have been hacked with machetes: children, like ten-year-old Abednego and his five-year-old sister Goodness, whose faces today are riven with scars so deep you wonder how they could still be alive.

Abednego says the herdsmen killed his father and brother, and when he tried to run, they broke his legs. Then they set about him with a knife. The scars stand out as brown raised welts across his face.

Bright is in the same IDP camp in Jos. He was fifteen when the Fulani attacked, killing his father and mother. "They said the land belongs to them," says Bright. "They want to inherit the land. That's what causes the attack."

Somehow, Bright managed to escape. As did his attackers.

§

My sad conclusion is that in northern Nigeria Christian lives don't matter – at all. If you are an indigene and a Christian, who cares?

---

39   ACAPS country analysis, Nigeria, 2018: https://www.acaps.org/country/nigeria

The killing of Christians over the years, without reason or justification, has grown to such an extent that the practice has become acceptable. And when the police do arrest the perpetrators, they quickly release them.

This has been going on so long that some of those young men who began their killing back then will now be in their fifties. They will be the people of authority: judges, lawyers, politicians, and businessmen. If killing was their business back in 1987, then what could possibly trouble their consciences today?

The plan we see being executed is to wipe Christianity from the face of northern Nigeria. Those behind this plan have used Boko Haram to that end. And now they are using and arming the Fulani.

I believe the current system of governance in Nigeria gives Christians no hope beyond their trust in God. Any Christian who is living in any part of northern Nigeria is hanging on only to God.

Lord Alton concluded his House of Lords debate on the plight of Nigeria with a wake-up call: "Are we to watch one of Africa's greatest countries go the way of Sudan? We must not wait for genocide to happen, as it did in Rwanda. Ominously, history could very easily be repeated."[40]

As for me? I feel sorry for my country. There is no way a nation can ever be built upon impunity. And where you have impunity, even good people will be driven to take the law into their own hands.

And where that happens, how long can their goodness remain?

---

40 *Hansard*, House of Lords debate, 28 June 2018, volume 792: https://hansard. parliament.uk/Lords/2018-06-28/debates/B694EEEC-7D52-4FBB-97E9-20C52519C332/Nigeria?highlight=nigeria#contribution-C14327EC-E2AA-475E-9B23-4DCEF5E8451B

DEFENDING THE LAND?

Since the troubles began in 2001, there has been an existential question that no one is willing to confront. How do ordinary Nigerians defend their land against these armed aggressors?

Back then, I had managed to avert violence by appealing for restraint on the polo field. Years later, I wanted to return to what I had said, to urge the people not to retaliate. I have never retaliated and I never will. I have seen the power of God to save me in difficult times, and until my time is up, I will just keep forgiving. And that is what I was teaching. But the killings and destruction were so widespread that people were beyond listening to any preacher.

And I cannot blame them for that.

The non-violent posture taken up by the church in the north-east was the reason those churches were overrun by Boko Haram. Non-violence had ensured the terrorists' success.

The places where Boko Haram failed were the places where the church had taken up arms to defend itself: in Maiduguri and a handful of villages in southern Borno. For all the years Boko Haram was operating in Borno State, there were Christian villages which defended themselves. And until today, Boko Haram has failed to conquer them.

We brought a young girl who had been displaced from that area into one of our schools. She was all kinds of trouble. She didn't want to learn; she wanted to do one thing only – to go back to fight Boko Haram.

§

To begin with, I couldn't countenance this notion that Christians should defend themselves. It is not that I am opposed to self-defence. I am an ex-soldier. But I have seen what mobs with guns are capable of. I feared that if arms got into the hands of an untrained militia, the day that anger burst, this militia could never be controlled.

This has been seen all over the world. Anywhere there is an unregimented army, the line between self-defence and criminality wears thin. So, I preached against self-defence, as I had in the past. Only this time, no one was listening.

By 2011, if you tried to preach non-violence in church, the people would heckle you. They could even stone you. The times had changed.

The people were within their rights. Constitutionally, Nigeria allows its citizens to defend themselves and their property if they are in danger. And clearly they were. Federal and state governments had shown themselves incapable of or unwilling to defend their own people. So the people were exercising their constitutional right to defend themselves and their land against armed aggression.

But I insisted from the pulpit that self-defence must never slide into criminality or vengeance. Those who defended themselves must never turn into aggressors.

God knows, we must take care when we let slip the dogs of war. Violence with vengeance becomes impossible to contain.

But I could no longer tell Christians to stay where they were if their life was in danger. The line had to change from just stand still and trust God, to defend yourself if you must – but keep the law and keep yourselves under control.

The people would have to defend their own hearts. And this was the harder task by far. Whatever they did, they would have to learn to trust God more than ever in their lives. I preached this to my church and to my pastors.

Becoming a bishop has not turned me into a pacifist. Turn the other cheek, bless those who curse you, put down the sword – these are not pacifism. These are to do with Christian character. You must look beyond selective verses and take the whole counsel of Scripture.

Nations are called to protect their own citizens, and Christians must participate in that call. That will include taking up arms to protect the poor and defend your sovereignty. It will include killing the enemy before the enemy kills you.

As a Christian, I will never take up arms without legal backing. I will never choose to become an aggressor.

But if a government fails in its responsibility to defend its own people, it will create a moral vacuum into which groups like Boko Haram and citizens' militias will rush. When the government fails to protect its citizens it is, in effect, licensing untrained vigilantes to carry out extrajudicial justice, while the lawmakers, the military and the police look on. This is what has happened in Nigeria.

The effect of this is that children, old people, women, and unarmed civilians are being hacked to pieces in their beds. By refusing to restrain murderers, the government is forcing people to rise to defend themselves.

How, then, are we as pastors to uphold order? How can we say, "Peace, peace," when there is no peace?[41] And what peace can there be if we encourage our people to take up arms? This is our dilemma.

I used to be licensed to keep a double-barrelled shotgun for hunting. But Gloria never knew that. I know the danger of having any kind of weapon. It is even more dangerous for young people who are excited at owning firearms and put their hope in those weapons. None of my children ever knew that I was licensed to have a gun. I have since disposed of it.

If there had been a gun in my house when the attackers hurt Gloria, Rinji would have used it. And with more than thirty attackers, he would have been overpowered. He would have been dead. And so would Gloria and several others.

A double-barrelled shotgun is no match for a Kalashnikov. When your first two bullets had gone, you would have no time to reload. The tactic with firearms is to kill or be killed. I have seen many soldiers killed, and all had arms to protect them. The only question is, who will die first?

---

41   Jeremiah 6:14.

If I were still a soldier and had to fight, I would. But I am not. And I believe that God will defend me.

I am ready to die, but I believe that until my time is up, I will not die.

I put my trust in God who can blind the enemy from killing me if it is not my time. And yet, if my time is up, it wouldn't matter what arms I had to protect me. If death is going to come, it will come. It is wonderful to know that our days are numbered in the hands of the One who keeps us.

However, I recognize that not everyone has this kind of faith. Each must act according to his own faith.

So because of this, I cannot say that people should not defend themselves. Because there are times when we do need to keep weapons, just as Nehemiah did. Once your enemy knows that you are armed, he may steer clear, because he too loves his life.

I know only too well that whatever I say on this issue, I will be blamed. If I tell people to stand back, they will be killed. If I tell them to take up arms, they will kill others.

There are people who have been overrun because I said to them, "The government will provide protection. Don't take up arms for yourself." My media team, who were quickly there on the ground, took pictures of the women, children, and babies who had been slaughtered at Dogo Nahawa.

These families were slaughtered because their husbands followed my advice. Until I die, I will carry that guilt. I will carry that weight.

SPEAKING TRUTH TO POWER

There are times when the people of God must speak truth to power. Whatever the consequences. Someone must call for change. If not us, who?

I had an early baptism of fire in 1985 when the Commission for Education decided to build a mosque right next to an Anglican church – St Michael's in Zaria. They had already begun to bring tipper trucks to the site. I wrote to the Minister to say that if they allowed the mosque to be built, there would be chaos. They would be calling for blood to flow.

But they chose to read my letter as an incitement. The government set up a high-powered Commission of Inquiry. They believed I was the one threatening bloodshed and they gave me twenty-four hours to come before the police commissioner, the commander of the army, and others.

The elders of the church, who were senior and respected figures in society, followed me to the chamber. I was surprised to see them, but they came because they didn't want this small boy to be intimidated.

The commission tried to turn them away, but they insisted.

I did have a trump card – the Ministry of Education's plans, which had somehow found their way into my hands. One of the directors of the Ministry had written a letter to say that whatever the Christians tried to do, they were going to build the mosque anyway. And the director had signed it.

The language was provocative, and the mosque itself was a provocation. So I brought out the signed letter and said, "I'm not the one who's inciting bloodshed. It's one of your officers in the Ministry of Education." And I read out the letter.

That mosque was never built. I learned very early that, if you are prepared to say the truth at any time to anyone, then God will give you a means of escape, unless your time is up. I am no longer afraid of these powers. If you don't challenge them over injustice, you will live under oppression.

So I started raising my voice on national matters in 2005. The government was not paying pensions and people were dying.

Then after the attack against Gloria, I redoubled my efforts to take a stand against impunity. That was when the world began to listen. I didn't plan it this way, but what I wrote after that began to have some impact. The Archbishop of Canterbury and the US State Department started referencing my website. Many Christian advocacy groups did the same.

Being the awkward squad can be pretty uncomfortable. But I have seen God vindicate me in the church, and I have seen God vindicate me in society, when I have challenged military and political powers. People have warned me, "Ben, if you do that, you're dead."

If we don't, we're dead anyway. This nations need salvation from the hands of unjust leaders. It doesn't matter whether those leaders are Christian or Muslim, what we are looking for is just governance. We need governors who will care for the people.

It was Christians who helped vote out another Christian, Goodluck Jonathan, and who elected Muhammadu Buhari, a Muslim. Goodluck Jonathan was a disappointment. He gave too much trust to his governors and overlooked the true feelings of the people.

For example, the Chibok girls had disappeared for three days before anyone informed Goodluck Jonathan the children had been abducted. And it was a good deal longer before anyone from the government spoke out. People felt the president had abandoned them. And Chibok was just the tip of the iceberg.

It began earlier, when Boko Haram started to systematically wipe out Christian communities in Borno State. They drove out and uprooted the headquarters of the Brethren Church. They forced nearly 2 million people to flee Borno. But Goodluck Jonathan refused to believe the Christians were being killed and would not go to them.

The killings in Plateau State all happened while Goodluck Jonathan was president. Christians reasoned that if he could not protect them, then why should they continue to vote for him? That was his undoing, and I took the opportunity to tell him so.

Goodluck Jonathan invited me to preach on the tenth anniversary of 9/11 in his presidential chapel in Abuja.

Security for the president was thick. I was screened repeatedly before getting into the compound. They even checked my Bible. Security men had eyes everywhere. Some were in plain clothes, others in black suits and sunglasses. These were the ones who were meticulously watching the president. Others just paced up and down. It was all in stark contrast to the utter absence of security in Plateau State.

The chapel at his villa was a converted squash court. It could seat more than 200 worshippers. It was white, well-lit, and air-conditioned. It had an organ and an altar, and on the wall was a plain wooden cross. The effect was both simple and beautiful.

Most of Goodluck Jonathan's Christian ministers were there. They included security ministers and top military men. I had a sermon that I intended to preach, but I didn't know they would be praying for America that day. I picked up on the prayers from one of the chapel leaders.

I stood to preach from a lectern and addressed the president and his ministers. As Goodluck Jonathan was in church, he was without his trademark fedora.

"I thank God, Mr President, that the chapel is praying for America. I offer my condolences through the president to President Obama."

And I continued: "Please, Mr President, give me permission to put matters into perspective for you. Four days before 9/11, a young girl was going home in Jos on a Friday afternoon. This was a girl who had always gone home on that same route. But on this day, the Muslims decided that she had desecrated their prayers.

"Mr President, from that day on, till today, as I'm speaking to you, Christians, local people, Beroms and indigenous are being killed. Four days before 9/11 till this minute, people are being killed, Mr President.

"In America 3,000 people were killed. I can tell you that the conservative estimate at this time is that 15,000 people have been killed in Plateau State, up to now as I'm talking.

"If you want to know my opinion, Sir, I will tell you. You pray for America, but for Plateau State, you don't care. I am speaking on behalf of those who have died and have yet to die on Plateau. You people sit here, and you don't care."

I was indignant and cross. I was shocked that the Christian church, the church of Jesus in Nigeria, appeared more concerned about America than its own people.

I was aware of the strength of my words and the danger of what I was saying. And at that moment, I didn't care what would happen. People had said privately, "Goodluck Jonathan doesn't care." The President needed to hear that. I had my chance and I took it.

I continued: "Listen, if after the service, anyone of you raises the issue of Plateau State with me, believe me, you will hear what you don't like and you will get what you don't want. The matter of Plateau State for me is deeply personal and extremely emotional. In the last ten years as a pastor, I have conducted more funerals than weddings and christenings combined."

After the service, some ministers protested, "Ben, we didn't know."

I said, "Well, you guys are just sitting in your air-conditioned offices in Abuja. How would you know?"

Our own newspapers had reported it, but they simply didn't believe it.

Goodluck Jonathan was very gracious. After my sermon, he wouldn't let me go immediately. He drove me to a Sunday school and asked me to bless the children, and he told his security guy to bring me over for lunch to talk with him. The following Monday, he ordered his Chief of Defence to rejuvenate the Special Joint Task Force to step up security in Jos.

When I speak truth to power, when I feel I've done the will

of God and spoken out as God has asked me to, I feel comforted. I feel bad for the people who have died, but I feel encouraged in my spirit that I have spoken. God alone will prove my words true or false and stand by to accomplish them in the hearts of people for the sake of justice.

In the case of Goodluck Jonathan, after we spoke, he acted.

As security became improved, tensions reduced radically. After 2011, a crisis in one part of the city would no longer affect the whole. Before then, if a bomb went off, the whole town would catch fire. Now, life would go on and people would continue with their business. A measure of trust was beginning to build.

Even though the investigations into the crisis were kept under wraps and the guilty went unpunished, we struggled hard as a community, both Christian and Muslim, to restore trust and order.

Yet, after this crisis had passed, what I feared took place. Armed robbery became rampant. Those who had lost everything still had their weapons, so they laid hold of them and looked around for someone to rob.

§

At times this mandate feels too much of a burden for one man. That same year, the communities called on me to say, "Ben, please talk to government, speak on our behalf, things are getting bad." I got calls and visits and letters and emails. I was inundated.

I began to say, "Do I look like the governor of the state? Who am I in Nigeria?"

I would say, "I'm tired of talking. You talk, they're not listening to me."

People looked at the figure and not the man. They didn't understand the struggle I was going through as a person.

But over time, I have learned to stop getting angry when people come to me with unrealistic expectations of what they think I can achieve. I have learned to listen and to hear, and then to say what I should say. And of course, that means speaking out on corruption.

Corruption continues to be the blight of Nigeria. No, not just Nigeria. Corruption is the blight of Africa. Corruption is everywhere. Nigeria languishes in the Global Corruption Index, in 148th position – among the worst of the worst.[42] The money doesn't even stay in Africa. It goes to banks abroad.

According to the African Union, some $150 billion is leaking away from Africa every year. Over thirty years, more than $200 billion was siphoned out of Nigeria alone.[43] Nigerian money has leaked to Switzerland, France, Germany, the US, and Britain. Much of it is swilling around in foreign banks and private accounts.

Yet, for every willing taker, there is a giver. Britain gave loans to the Nigerian government while it was still a military dictatorship.

Why did Britain give loans to a dictator and then complain about corruption? What did they expect? They knew those monies would go back to British and foreign banks. If the international community is serious about fighting corruption in Africa, they should refuse to let officials open accounts with foreign banks.

I have my suspicions that a lot of aid money is spent on foreign arms. That money is certainly not being found on the streets of Nigeria.

In 2016 Christian politicians from northern Nigeria held a huge conference in Abuja and I was the main speaker.

Money had been going into banks for months and accruing interest that went to the ministers. People were not getting paid and were suffering. They were getting into trouble and falling into debt, and the value of their money was depreciating. Teachers had not been paid for a whole year and classrooms were falling into disrepair.

---

42 "Corruption Perceptions Index 2017", Transparency International, 21 February 2018: https://www.transparency.org/news/feature/corruption_perceptions_index_2017?gclid=Cj0KCQjwiJncBRC1ARIsAOvG-a46CgBi59wH_mg3B6GmFUblyIL03baD0IaII88xJPe0a_ZmniC0FnYaAhUyEALw_wcB#table
43 "Cleaning up Corruption in Africa", Democracy Works, 31 October 2016: https://democracyworks.org.za/cleaning-up-corruption-in-africa/

I decided to print my speech in the form of a booklet, because I didn't want anybody doctoring what I said. Unknown to me, my speech was taken live by four national television stations.

I called for ministers to be held responsible for helping the poor in health, education, and finance. I argued that if any of those ministers short-changed in any of those areas, they should be hanged or jailed for life. They should never see the streets of Nigeria again.

§

Gloria was not always so sure about the wisdom of speaking out on matters of politics.

She once complained, "You're speaking up about the evils of society – but who is listening to you? You are running a one-man army!"

I said to Gloria, "We must not tolerate injustice. We wouldn't tolerate injustice in the church and we mustn't tolerate it in society. That's what we are called to do – to rise up and defend the poor and the widows and to make sure that society is run for the good of everybody."

She wasn't convinced. "What you are saying is pretty strong. Don't you think they might consider killing you one day?"

"They won't kill me," I replied. "They're not idiots. If they killed me there would be an international outcry. Instead, they are more likely to try to buy me off."

But no one has ever tried. They know that if they offered me money, I would announce from the pulpit how much they had tried to give me – and I would name the man who tried to give it. I will not be bought off.

Corruption is repulsive to me. I may fail, but if I do fail, then I have told people, "Please point it out to me and I will repent." Hold me to account.

But yes, Gloria was right – as usual. They did try to kill me, and her too.

They failed.

So while we can, we speak out.

CHICKEN WINGS

lie. According to the press, there was an attempt to buy me off – to bribe me and other African bishops – with chicken wings. You see, sometimes, even in the church, we have to speak truth to power. And the church doesn't always like it.

This so-called bribe in 1998 began a journey that led to my appointment in 2019 as General Secretary of GAFCON – the Global Anglican Future Conference. GAFCON exists to uphold the authority of Scripture in the heart of the Anglican Communion.[44] But more on that later.

My first Lambeth Conference was in 1998. The troubles in Nigeria had been taking their toll. I had arrived in England hopeful of meeting Christian brothers who would comfort and encourage me. I was searching for solidarity among my fellow bishops, trusting some could share my journey. I had arrived at Lambeth full of hope, but I left insulted, wounded, and feeling unwanted. I am not a man who is easily offended, but I was not alone in my feelings on that occasion.

The attitudes I and my African colleagues encountered from some of our fellow bishops took us aback. Some clearly looked down upon us as less well educated. One even described Africa's Christianity as "only one step up from witchcraft". The attitudes we encountered bordered on racism.

So how had matters come to this?

What brought them to a head was the issue of homosexual practice. Some bishops were arguing that homosexuals must be accepted in the church and welcomed into full ministry, right up to bishop.

But the central issue was even deeper than that. It grew out of a fundamental and painful difference in how we perceived the Word of God.

---

44   About GAFCON: https://www.gafcon.org/about

Could the Bible, this disparate collection of poetry, history, and letters, written by so many authors, so many years ago, really still be described as God's inspired, authoritative, and final Word on human behaviour? I, many African bishops, and some bishops from the West believed so.

By an overwhelming majority, Lambeth passed Resolution 1.10.

It upheld, in the light of Scripture, "faithfulness in marriage between a man and a woman in lifelong union and... that abstinence is right for those who are not called to marriage".[45]

One of our American brothers later sniped that we Africans had been bought off with chicken wings to vote for this.

I'm sorry to say, but your Western chicken wings are simply not as tasty as ours!

Despite Resolution 1.10, some in the US went on to consecrate a bishop who had divorced his wife and moved in to live with a homosexual partner. When others in the church took issue with that, they were asked to leave.

It brought about a rift in the Episcopal Church in the US.

Labelling homosexuality as a cultural practice, rather than a sin, had put these bishops at odds with the Word of God. And it had made homosexuality a defining issue. It felt as though the West was trying to impose a single agenda item on the entire world.

Yet in Africa, we are wrestling with existential issues that demand our undivided attention. We are struggling with massive corruption. We are struggling with a superficial presentation of the gospel that is failing to change lives. We are struggling with every kind of evil.

At Lambeth, we represented those in the Sudan who were being bombed in the Nuba Mountains, the hunger-stricken Anglicans of northern Kenya, and the persecuted Christians of my own Nigeria.

---

45   https://www.anglicancommunion.org/resources/document-library/lambeth-conference/1998/section-i-called-to-full-humanity/section-i10-human-sexuality?author=Lambeth+Conference&year=1998

To lead us out of troubled waters, we chose to take our compass bearings from Scripture, rather than cultural relativity.

To some of the Anglican bishops, it seemed that their African brothers were out of touch. But from where we stood, facing our daily matters of life and death, it felt the other way round. Our brothers in the West appeared indifferent and unaware.

Their continual refrain was that Africans hate homosexuality. But they would never tell you, for example, that I intervened to save fifteen homosexuals who were sentenced to death in Bauchi under Islamic law. I called the Primate of Nigeria, Peter Akinola, and he called President Obasanjo and the fifteen were rescued.

God makes it clear that He abhors sin and every type of evil. If we were to play that down, if we were to sanctify every cultural norm, can you imagine what Nigeria would quickly become? It is the gospel, not human nature, that is the hope of our nation.

At Lambeth, what we could not agree upon was that homosexuality is sin. And we could not agree upon that because we could not agree upon the authority of Scripture, which declares it so.

It is in the authority of Scripture that we are motivated to mission to save sinners.

It is in the authority of Scripture that we have the hope of eternal life.

It is in the authority of Scripture that we believe Jesus is coming again and there will be a day of judgment.

If we refuse to uphold the authority of Scripture, then we no longer have a mission.

And it was concerning mission that there came another disappointment at Lambeth. Ten years earlier, in 1988, the Lambeth Conference had declared a decade of evangelism for the whole Anglican Communion. That resolution caught fire throughout the world. The plan was to report on its progress at Lambeth 1998. But instead the office of Deacon of Evangelism was scrapped and the report was never taken. Mission had been relegated.

No, Lambeth 1998 had wounded many. And there had been

neither apology nor healing. So some of the bishops decided to gather in Jerusalem to pray at the first Global Anglican Future Conference. This was approved by Peter Akinola, the former Anglican Primate of Nigeria, who had by now retired.

Jerusalem was a stark contrast to Lambeth. The music, the fellowship, and the preaching were good. And all the regions there agreed to sign what became known as the Jerusalem Declaration.

The Jerusalem Declaration highlighted the place of the Bible and the teaching of Scripture, which mandated us to pursue the mission of the gospel.[46]

I am a mission-minded man. I was saved and my testimony is clear. I was called by God to preach the gospel as a rural evangelist. My heart, until I die, is offered entirely to the poor of Africa and Nigeria, to the widows and the orphans. That is where my heart is.

Africa is the playground of religious fanatics. It is torn by war and has become the dumping ground for the West.

Most Africans have not got their fair share of the good things this world can offer. We don't have good roads, good hospitals, or good governance. We are way behind.

So I am in an urgent drive to help Africans live and die for what really matters – the gospel of Jesus Christ. This gospel is a life where you don't lie, you don't cheat, you don't sin, and you live a holy life. You live righteously, and you live a life of love and peace in contentment with what little you have. Even if Africans don't get the things of this world, at least they can have what Jesus offers on earth.

On 1 January 2019, I was appointed General Secretary of GAFCON.

Some portray GAFCON as dangerous, divisive, and schismatic. I believe GAFCON is none of these things. GAFCON should be applauded for rescuing those who would otherwise have left the Anglican Church.

---

46   https://www.gafcon.org/resources/the-complete-jerusalem-statement

Let me be clear. I do not envisage a split with the Anglican Church. Not in my time. I think all brothers and sisters who hold on to Scripture will be able to do so within the Anglican Communion.

I have hope in the present Archbishop of Canterbury. I know him. If Justin Welby had been in post a decade ago, perhaps the churches might not have gone this far. We are watching to see if he can stop, or at least reduce, the damage that has been done to the Anglican Church.

As General Secretary of GAFCON, I want the church to be awakened in its responsibility to bring the gospel to the world, to faithfully proclaim Christ to the nations. It is the gospel mission of the Acts of the Apostles, a mission that is deeper than words.

Words come to teach and proclaim Christ crucified, but it is the life that we live in Christ that is the greater part of that proclamation. And I am going to pursue that. I'm going to reach out towards those in the struggling parts of the church, whose voices are not being heard, who wonder, "Who cares?" We are going to speak on their behalf for justice to the various nations of the world. We are going to stand with them, side by side.

We will live with them and share with them what little we have got, beyond mere money.

We will encourage them to continue to study the Word of God. We believe God's Word is the only instrument given by God for the salvation of all mankind. We are going to increase the depth of Bible knowledge and theological education, and strengthen the church and its leadership.

We are going to pursue vigorously the help of the Holy Spirit, which enables us to deal with the demonic and evil powers of this world that militate against the children of God.

And we are going to build a robust women's ministry. In the developing world one woman may have six children. If she believes in Christ and is firmly rooted in the Word of God, then, boy, she has saved six children already!

These children are the youth of tomorrow. Seventy per cent of those who live in Africa are aged thirty-five and under. It is the young who will form an army of missionaries of the gospel of Jesus Christ. They're the ones!

If you look back at the mission movements of 1799 and 1902, the missionaries were all young. In each wave of those earlier missionary movements, it was young people who dared to take the gospel and go and live and die with people in the leprosariums. It was the young who helped the blind, the physically challenged and the unreached. So I want to get the young people enthusiastic about the gospel and passionate about the kingdom of God.

§

When I look at Islam, I can see much that Islam can teach us – if the church is willing to learn. All things work together for good. And the church needs to learn from the passion of militant Islam. Let me be clear – I love their passion, but I don't want to kill! I want to bring life. I want to bring people to know the Lord, to love the Lord, and to live a life of love and freedom.

So why should the church be any less passionate than Islam? Why is the church not preaching the gospel of holiness, righteousness, and justice?

The Muslims have their loudspeakers everywhere, waking people at 4 a.m. to pray. Meanwhile, the Christians are sleeping! What's stopping us from praying? What's keeping us from our devotional life to God?

Before a Muslim can lead a mosque, he must be able to recite at least sixty chapters of the Koran. But we Christians are ordaining people who cannot recite a single chapter of the Bible. We should learn from them.

The Bible is so wonderful! It is the Word of God, it builds us up and frees us and enables us to live for God – but we have abandoned it!

I love Islam's emphasis on practical righteousness. They want to do what is right, and they want to enforce it – that's the whole thrust of Sharia law. Should a Christian who loves the

Lord need to be forced to do as he ought? No! So why are we not passionate about doing what is right and true and just for everybody – without coercion?

God has His ways. And I think with Islam, God is waking us up, if only we would see it.

As for each of us, we may never be like Ajayi Crowther or Wilberforce, my great heroes of the faith. But we must not just sit down and do nothing. If our faith is genuine, it must not only be faithful, but fruitful. We are called to bear fruit. And fruit will follow if we are committed to the Lord.

So the aim of this, my story, is to ignite a passion within each of us to wake up and do something, instead of merely believing and hoping that someone else will get around to it and we will all be OK.

Look around: we are not OK.

Everybody must rise up to play his own unique and special part, if this world is to change.

Appendix One

LETTER TO THE WORLD

To my many friends in Nigeria, the United Kingdom, the US, and the West. Thank you for indulging me by reading my story. I hope it has helped you to share a little of my heart for this great nation of Nigeria that I love.

If so, I would ask you to bear with me a little longer, as I share my prayer requests for my country as well as my hopes and prayers for your own.

TO NIGERIA

With your permission, may I begin with my own beloved Nigeria?

There is a future that I can see for Christians and Muslims together in Nigeria. That future is one where the people come together to decide what kind of country they really want. They must come together and work together to overcome the suspicions that have grown widespread.

There is a need for Nigeria to be restructured, because those suspicions that are tearing our nation apart are growing ever deeper. If the government wants the people to be united, and to build and to grow, then the government must provide the structures that will make for the cohesion and the building of our nation.

Unless there is change, I'm afraid sections of our country could turn to violence and tear themselves away.

Biafra is still calling for independence. The people of the Niger Delta feel aggrieved, cheated, and short-changed. They are blowing up the oil pipes. Boko Haram is demanding a Sunni Islamic nation. And Shia movements are demanding an independence and freedom of their own, with their own form of governance.

These pillars of disunity sprang up during the Babangida military regime, which drew Nigeria into the Organisation of Islamic Cooperation (OIC). It was this act of national disunity in 1986 that paved the way for more than 100 churches to be burned in Zaria the following year, without arrest or prosecution. That regime flung open a doorway to a theology of hate that considered itself above the law.

And through that doorway marched the Shia movement of El Zakzaky, that saw itself as a nation within a nation and demanded an Islamic state in Nigeria.

And that in turn prepared a foundation for fundamentalist movements such as the Izala Society and Boko Haram.

All this was sown during the Babangida regime. They should have seen the implications for the building of our nation. But they did nothing, and in doing nothing, paved the way for the destruction of Nigeria.

All these grievances are symptoms of the ill-health spread by various regimes as a result of their inability to respond to the needs of the people.

There are more than 300 tribes in Nigeria, speaking more than 500 languages. The fault lines are many. The potential for division is huge. The fears of all these different entities that make up our one nation Nigeria must be allayed. If Nigeria is to remain, Nigeria must come together.

Without question, the gospel is the hope for the country.

I see hope in the Middle Belt, where the gospel is being proclaimed. There is hope wherever there is a remnant, no matter how few, who hold on to righteousness and justice and who are willing to sacrifice their lives for the good of others. That is the meaning of the gospel, and it is a beacon of hope for Nigeria.

I have seen God work with a remnant. He doesn't need a movement of millions. And I know of more than a few, across tribes and states, from Fulani, Hausa, Yoruba, and Igbo, who are faithfully holding the torch and sacrificing, who are laying down their lives to uphold justice and righteousness in Nigeria.

Committed Christians are coming together across the nation to discuss seriously how to save their country. Nearly every tribe is represented by vibrant, committed Christians who share that concern.

And in that there is great hope.

TO THE NIGERIAN DIASPORA

Beyond Nigeria, there are many of our people around the world who have left their country to pursue a better life in the West. They have worked hard, they have earned their money, they are living well, and they are comfortable.

But one day, they will look for a home in Nigeria to return to. This is inevitable.

A time will always come when people begin to remember and search once again for their roots. If the current parents don't, then their children or their grandchildren will. No matter how long a people live in a foreign land and how integrated they become into that nation, one day, someone will tell them they don't belong. And at some deep level, that will be true.

Israel has benefited, because its diaspora considered the plight of the nation and returned to Israel to build the land. In India, we see the same thing. Most nations that have been built and have progressed have profited from the experiences of their children in the diaspora, those who have looked back and have gone back to rebuild their mother nation.

This is the history of the world, whatever the nation. People come back and bring their expertise and say, "This is how we can do things. Together, we can do it."

Nigeria's children will always be welcomed home.

But it pains me to say that many Nigerian churches in the diaspora appear blind to what is happening in Nigeria today. Please open your eyes and your hearts to a people who are still your own.

And be sure to open your hearts too to those who have taken you under their wing.

Wherever the children of Nigeria find themselves, they should become missionaries to their host cultures. You must move beyond serving your own kind and your own self-interests and embrace a wider mission. If you fail in this, your gospel will become inbred and weak.

And if you import Nigeria's little local crises into any foreign land, you will dilute the bloodline of the only answer to every crisis, the gospel. There are some matters that should be left behind forever.

Wherever you find yourself, your mission is to your hosts.

It is great that the Nigerian churches are large and growing, but God is not interested in numbers. God's interest is in crossing the human boundaries and barriers to remove the walls that separate us. He does so in order to demonstrate the love of God and from that create one man.

Jesus told the story of the Samaritan who crossed over to help someone from another tribe. Real love will always cross over. It is at this point of crossing over that love is tested. Love is never self-interested or self-serving.

If you fail to reach your host culture, then what happened in North Africa will happen to any church anywhere. The church will be wiped out by catastrophe, persecution, or economic collapse. People will run away, and the church will die.

So to the black-led churches in the UK, I wish you well, and I say this: my brothers and sisters, please read the Scriptures again and attend to your gospel mission.

TO WESTERN NGOS

To the Western nations, I would say, please forgive our occasional reluctance to accept funding from relief agencies. Please forgive it, and try to understand it.

It is not ingratitude, but a concern that your aims and ours are not always the same. Nor is it down to a lack of accountability on a continent that is rife with corruption.

Forgive my plain speaking, but relief organizations are often controlling and out of touch with what is happening on the ground. Their bureaucratic systems just take over. We set something up and they come in from their air-conditioned offices, pay an occasional visit, then ask others to do the work for them and do it their way.

They will often hire their own staff who bring a different vision and a different set of goals. For instance, they may not be interested in the gospel or outreach.

Instead of just working with us, they try to control that work and redirect it and refocus its aims, until it ceases to be what we set out to do.

Sometimes money from NGOs and governments comes with so many strings attached, and with so much control, that to get involved would make our work far less effective. The bureaucracy just gets in the way.

As a bishop and rural evangelist, I know my people and I know what I'm doing. I care for my people, while some agencies appear to care only for their figures. If agencies want to help, they should try to help me do things better, rather than try to change what I do.

But when I say such things, they consider me unaccountable.

The truth is, I am a missionary and it's my calling to be accountable. I keep records. Money does not come to me as a person, it comes to the diocese for projects. Every year, I am audited, along with my whole diocese, by external chartered accountants who are not members of the Anglican Church.

Often, agencies want to claim every penny for every single item for every single child. Fine. But I don't want to be paid to serve my people. That's the difference. So some agencies will not support me, because they don't trust that.

I want to help my people as I see their needs, and I don't want those needs to be determined by people in Abuja or London whose main concern is filling in their reports.

All too often, aid seems to be a bureaucratic box-ticking

exercise, and as long as people can fill in the forms accurately the aid will continue to flow.

Yes, you're right. Corruption is everywhere. And Nigeria is one of the worst culprits. Much of this could be avoided if NGOs would support churches directly. On the whole, transparency and accountability is the basis on which the church operates.

The church is also more likely to recover any money that goes missing. It happened to us, when money was siphoned out of my own organization, the Centre of Excellence for Gospel Health and Development Services.

We set up an investigation and found that one of the NGO staff, in cahoots with one of mine, had embezzled more than 6 million Naira.

I set up my own board of investigation, as did the NGO. I dismissed the member of staff and sent the money back to the NGO – before we recovered it in the courts.

Large sums of money given to Nigeria by NGOs and governments are being siphoned off by the corrupt. True.

My solution to this is that NGOs should support churches with a proven track record of transparency and accountability. The church is less prone to corruption. Let us use our own systems that work for us, instead of imposing your own. Our systems of accountability and our track record make it more likely that the money you so generously give from overseas will go to help the poor in Nigeria.

TO THE UK

To the UK, Nigeria owes such a debt, an enormous debt, not of money, but of love.

My father was a senior civil servant, carrying on the tradition of governance brought to us by the British colonials.

The toys my father bought me from England were so sturdy and well-built that I was able to pass them on to my young ones, who passed them on to theirs. Even my British-made second-hand tricycle somehow survived the rigours of Benji, so I could hand it on to generations yet to be born.

In 1965 my father was transferred from Minna to Bauchi. When it came to bringing me back from boarding school, my father bought me a first-class ticket for a train. All his staff had to do was take me to the stationmaster who received me and settled me in my cabin. I travelled for more than six hours to Jos on my own, with the help of an attendant who looked after me in the cabin. I was just ten years old.

This was just part of the legacy left by the British colonials. It displayed their organizational ability, efficiency, and honesty – virtues that I believed Nigeria possessed for itself until my grown-up days, when I found my country had shifted in every way from the old colonial way of doing things, which was at least honest and efficient.

But an even more important legacy of that era, for which I am eternally grateful, is that of the missionaries, the missionaries who came to my home and brought health, education, and the gospel.

These were not civil servants, but young people who sacrificed everything for us. This same gospel that we preach today in Nigeria was brought to us by missionaries from the United Kingdom at their own cost. For this, I am forever indebted to Britain.

I will never forget what these Englishmen did for us. I am the third generation to benefit from them. The English I now speak and write, my father taught me, because Christian missionaries had taught him. Because of them, I can today communicate and preach the gospel.

The sacrifice these missionaries made has become my legacy and my inheritance. And this is what I teach today: sacrifice for others. British Christians laid down their lives for the sake of the gospel in Nigeria. Most of them died and their graves are with us. I will not betray that trust. How can we ever forget Britain?

My life now is worth nothing if I'm not preaching and living the gospel, whether in Nigeria or anywhere the Lord puts me.

The most dangerous person on earth is an ungrateful person, and I choose not to be an ungrateful person. I value what these missionaries did. Some were from well-to-do families, some were not. But whatever their background, they laid down their lives for Africans and tribal people they did not even know. Only eternity will explain and reveal the extent of their love for Nigeria.

Whatever Britain may think of me, I will always love Britain.

So as a friend of Britain, may I say this: I see in the UK a need for youth evangelism. I see also a need for Bible literacy. People should go back to reading the Bible to find out what God says about people, instead of listening only to what people say about God and His Word. The UK should go back to reading the Bible for themselves to hear what God is saying.

I also believe that families in Britain should look once again at their family lives, and return to how the Bible shows families should be.

Family breakdown is becoming a fashion. I believe the family should stay together; they should struggle through relationships together and be patient together. They should learn to make sacrifices for one another and to stick together, no matter what. They should not be looking to find a way out at the least provocation.

The hurt of separation will last far longer than any hurt that may come from sticking things out and struggling through. Family breakdown must never become the fashion. It must be the other way round – family build-up.

TO THE US

When I look at America, I see a need for the gospel to be set free from politics.

Despite the separation of church and state, there is a tendency for the culture to consider itself to be Christian. But when any culture is assumed to be Christian, it can easily be absorbed into politics. Politics will always seize authority over culture. For that reason, politics will try to take over Christianity and the gospel, if we let it.

The gospel must always be disentangled from politics and from any cultural narrative, in any nation, at any time and anywhere. Christians must critique their own theology and question its authentic biblicality. And the culture itself must come under the critical eye and examination of the Word of God.

This was the contention of the early apostles. When it was cultural to say that Caesar was Lord, they said, "No, Jesus is Lord." That brought them into inevitable conflict with the political powers.

Christians in America should be willing to come into conflict with their politicians. Agreeing with politics is what legitimizes the various theologies that have been a disgrace to the gospel. It baptizes those theologies, whether they are racism and apartheid, or the killing of witches or homosexuals. The politics of hate do not belong to the gospel.

Politicians will say anything to please others and get their votes. Christians must learn to stand up for the gospel, rather than agree with politicians. Christians must always stand up for righteousness and justice. That is the position of God Himself.

God is neither of the left nor of the right. He will never take sides with injustice or unrighteousness. So Christians in the US must speak truth to power.

FOR THE SAKE OF THE GOSPEL

The US and UK have been great missionary-sending nations. The Christian world that has received its faith from you is grateful. I would like to begin to repay just a little of that debt.

I have a desire in my heart to see the raising up of a new missionary movement, whose headquarters is Jos. I see this with the eyes of faith. I am raising up young men and women with adequate educational abilities, and training them in world mission.

I have already sent a few on short-term mission to England. I thank God that wherever these young men have been, they have been loved, respected, and understood.

My dream is to send young people from Nigeria to go and evangelize other young people in Europe. I am sending them to teach the Bible and the gospel that we ourselves were taught 200 years ago.

I hope it will not be long before we can begin to partner with Britain and the US to send missionaries. I see missionaries from Nigeria and other nations going all over the world, side by side. There is a world movement of missions now: it is no longer coming from only one direction, the West. We are returning the favour.

I want to ask the Christians in the United Kingdom to remember the histories of their parents and grandparents who laid down their lives to take this same gospel to all the world. We must rise to that gospel, live that gospel, and preach that gospel.

I would plead that Christians in the United Kingdom get on their knees to pray. And then get up, courageously, ready to live the gospel and preach it by their lives and by all that they do.

You must carry this gospel with your whole heart to your children, to your relatives, to your parents, to your friends, to everybody. You must agonize in prayer for them and share this gospel.

Inevitably, when you do that, suffering will come your way.

Do not think that you will be insulated from this way of suffering. Christians around the world are suffering for this gospel: why should that pass you by? One way or the other, it is coming. It is going to come with time. But it is better to know you are suffering for the gospel than to suffer for no gospel.

Our time is now. The fear of persecution has gone. The tyranny of death has been defeated by the cross of Jesus Christ. And by His resurrection He has assured us that we must live the life of Christ.

If we die, we die to go to be with Christ. If we live, we live for Christ. So the fear of death means nothing. In any case, we will all die one day, but it is better to live for Christ and to die to be with Christ.

So we must recapture again the heart of the gospel, a gospel we will live for and die for and pass on to our children.

PLEASE PRAY FOR US

As for my country, please pray for Nigeria. Pray that God would bring some help to the suffering communities, particularly in the north-east: not only Christians but the non-Christians and Muslims as well. They have been devastated. They are poor, and there is hunger in the land.

The killer herdsmen have driven people from their farms. They cannot harvest. So our prayer request is for God to bring a mighty intervention on behalf of the suffering poor.

Then pray, please, for Nigeria's government, to take up the responsibility of executing justice for all, protecting lives and the property of everybody, without favour or selection. That's the only way to bring about a nation where people will be patriotic, give their best, and be able to live freely to serve one another.

I want to serve my people. My nation has blessed me. I'm so grateful for being a Nigerian. So I want to give something back before I die. But if there is no security, there can be no justice, and without either in the land there will be no opportunity to give.

I am asking God that out of these ashes will rise a wave of an uncommon, unseen revival, likened to the kind of revivals seen in the 1700s in the United Kingdom and surpassing them.

Because so much blood has been spilled on a land of Christians, and so many churches destroyed, I would like to see a revival that would sweep over Nigeria and, indeed, all of Africa: a revival that will take the gospel back to Europe and America.

So pray for us, please. Pray for us that we may not be so pained as not to pray, because people who are suffering sometimes get engrossed in those sufferings and prayer becomes difficult.

Please pray that we will never give up on prayer. But pray most of all that out of our sufferings will come the kind of Christian faith that will be admired, both on earth and in heaven, depicting the love of Jesus Christ, a faith that is fervent in both preaching the gospel and living the gospel. A faith that will invest our all in the mission of the gospel of Christ. That is our prayer request.[47]

---

47   Several paragraphs are adapted from an interview with Ben Kwashi on Clayton TV from Word Alive '11: https://www.clayton.tv/new/0i0/690. Several others are from an interview with Paul Robinson of Release International, filmed on location in Nigeria.

Appendix Two

LETTER TO CHARLES

Dear Charles,

This book is for you, dear friend, to help you on your way. But before I say another word, let me first introduce you to my other friends who are reading this, so they can get to know you too.

Friends, meet Charles.

Charles is a modern man in his thirties with a degree under his belt and the whole world before him. There is only one Charles, but I know many like him. Charles is the extra-special Everyman who has inspired and motivated me to tell my story.

Charles – and I'm sure he wouldn't mind me saying this – has a deep sense of dissatisfaction within.

His job alone is not answering that call. And nor, sadly, is the church. Charles is comfortable in his church and content to be a Christian, but he is not finding fulfilment there, either. I see that in his eyes each week as he takes his place near the back, polite but never fully present.

(Sometimes I tease him that the only reason he comes to church is to find a wife. I see him looking…)

When it comes to serious Christian commitment, Charles is not sure he wants to take the plunge, because all over the world, he sees Christians being persecuted.

So Charles asks himself: "What could *I* do?" He believes he could do *something*, but what, exactly, he's not so sure. He sees no part for himself in stopping persecution, which happens over *there*, nor does he feel any burning need to go out on mission – though *somebody* should, of course.

So many missionaries have gone into the world over so many years, but when Charles looks around it is clear so little has changed.

My friend Charles is an honest man and a realist. He knows there is more in life for him, and he is truthful enough to admit that underneath it all he has yet to find real happiness.

And that simply won't do.

So Charles, may I offer you a little friendly, fatherly advice? If you receive it, I believe it could change everything. In any event, it is well meant, and I hope it will help.

FIRST THINGS FIRST

Charles, if you have read about Jesus but He doesn't yet seem close, then I would say that the early stages of getting to know Jesus are like getting married... (I know. We'll get on to the burning question of finding you a wife in due course.)

You discover your wife each day over a period of years and get to a point where you can say, "I think I'm just beginning to understand this woman!" That can take twenty-five or thirty years – sometimes more. Believe me! You can't just get married and immediately know your wife.

Christians are like the bride of Jesus. There is a growing intimacy that comes from walking with God and getting to know Him. Don't rely on your feelings. If you don't feel His presence, keep going. Keep reading the Scriptures, keep up your devotional life.

God will reveal Himself to you as you walk seriously with Him, because God does not reveal Himself to people who are not serious with Him. So, you will need to be serious and intentional about how you seek Him. People who seek Him will always find Him. They will.

It is as though God is hiding. He doesn't want to show off, but He's there to be found. He wants to be your Saviour, your Lord, your helper, your protector, and your defender. He was like that with Abraham, Jacob, and Joseph.

Israel had to learn to walk with God. They would fail and lose Him, then seek Him again. And He would reveal Himself and they would come back. It's exciting! But it's a long journey. You cannot discover everything about God right away.

Perhaps you suspect your faith is not authentically your own, but a thing in the background you have received from your parents. If so, Charles, I would urge you to do what Jesus said to Nicodemus.

Nicodemus was a high-ranking theologian who had always been a person of faith, or so he thought. But when he saw Jesus, he realized his faith wasn't working. It was shown up as mere religion. He confessed to Jesus, "Your faith is a living faith, it's a walk of faith. How come *I* don't have this kind of faith?"

Perhaps that is really your question: how come your faith is not alive and vital? How come it's neither exciting nor adventurous? How come you're not experiencing Jesus?

Charles, this means you are in a good place! You are at the point where you need to be born again. You need to be intentional and consciously make Jesus your own; you need to ask Him to be your Saviour.

Tell Jesus that you thought you were on this journey, but found out you did not really know Him. Tell Him you're sorry about that, but now you are turning around. Admit that you are a sinner and you have failed. Ask Him to help you by coming into your life.

Exercise your faith right now in a genuine way. Receive Jesus by faith and He will come into your heart.

From today on, decide you are going to trust Him and walk by faith in Him. And as you do that, He will come in the power of the Holy Spirit, by faith. He will!

Excellent!

Two things are at work in you now, Charles: your own faith as you actively trust God, and God Himself, who will fulfil His side of the promise. He promises that when anyone – anyone – calls on His name, He will come and save that person.

As you reach out to Jesus in faith, He will come into your heart and live with you, and you with Him. As you place your faith, belief and trust in Him, He will respond. This is what I did in 1975.

THE STRENGTH TO CONTINUE

How will you know it is real? My own faith decision was confirmed as I began my walk of faith with the Lord. After a couple of months, my life was changed and people could see the difference for themselves.

I began to hunger and thirst for God's Word. I attended Bible studies and they made sense to me. I prayed and it made sense to me. I chose to walk away from sin. I had the capacity to stand up and say no to the things that I knew were wrong, and say yes to the things I knew were right.

Now an adventure is not an adventure without some obstacles to overcome. And saying "No" means some people could well be upset with you. A few may even oppose you in doing what you firmly believe to be right.

From the beginning, some people were jeering at me. But I got a new boldness. I was able to stand up and be different. And that position has served me well for more than forty years.

What gives me the strength to continue is, above all, my quiet time with God. I'm very grateful to my Muslim neighbours. They usually wake up at 4 a.m. to call for prayers, so it is a good time for me to wake up too, and listen to God and study His Word.

This has become a part of my life. It began slowly, but now I find myself walking with God, talking with God, crying out to Him, and listening to Him, mostly in the early hours of the morning. I will wake up much earlier than the family to make sure that I have this precious time of talking with the Lord Jesus and listening to His Word.

Sometimes, during that devotion, I will receive a clear message for my diocese, my wife, or my children, and I will write it down. This is when I settle issues and decide exactly what I am going to do, whether it's hiring or firing or going out on mission.

Everything about my life, including marrying Gloria, was the same. (Charles, take note!) When I ask the Lord for His guidance, I don't often get immediate answers, but that pushes me to keep on praying. It may take days or weeks until an explanation comes.

But I can wait. Because the Jesus I know is passionate about me. He is there, He is real, He saved me, and He called me. He is in the business of sending me and walking with me through this life. He wants to talk with me and He wants me to give Him time. If I don't, things turn sour.

For example, one day when I went to play basketball, He showed me that rain had fallen on the cement and had turned it into sand at the edge of the court. He showed me clearly that unless the sand was swept away, someone running could easily slip on it and get injured. He told me I should go and take a broom and sweep it.

I saw all that and said, "No, nobody will go to that edge." The game started and I was running. The ball came to me at that exact corner. I held it and was getting my balance to take a shot when I slipped on the loose cement. I fell and bruised my knee.

Nobody had to tell me after that.

I ran back to my house, got a broom, and swept it up. I said, "Lord, You showed me and I'm sorry. Thank You it happened to me and not somebody else."

I've never actually seen Jesus – not yet. Once I saw an extraordinary flash of light. It came soon after Gloria's attack. I received that as an assurance. If the intention of all of these things had been to make me discouraged, be angry, and nurse malice, then it failed, because I have seen the Lord, and I know I am on track.

His fragrance to me is indescribable. I don't want to leave that place of His presence, to get up and do anything else. I enjoy it so. Sometimes tears come down my cheeks. It is heaven. There are times when I'm flat on the floor, full of contentment. It is *shalom*, God's life-giving covenant blessing. It is real life! It is full life! I'm living a full life of joy and peace.

When I read the Scriptures, I read of Christ who was alive, of the person of God who lived on earth. But the resurrected Christ is indescribable.

So how could I begin to describe Him to you?

Discover Him for yourself! Make it your life's work! He is absolutely worth it.

Jesus rebukes me when I am presumptuous, when I sin, and when I fail. When I sin is when I really learn about His presence, because it is no longer there. I feel His absence terribly, and I long for Him. I go back to Psalms 8, 51, and 139: "Lord, Lord, please!"

It's so good when He forgives me and comes back and I am walking with Him again.

When I'm doing what is wrong, I know it.

And when I'm doing what is right, but everyone else thinks I am wrong, I know it is they who are wrong, because He is with me.

I hear His voice saying, "Keep on, Ben; keep on."

In these morning moments, I read devotionals from different fathers of the faith. Or I will just be quiet in the Lord. I use that opportunity to bring my prayer requests.

I bring my problems to Him too. These may be the killings, or difficulties with staff, or people who haven't understood me, or whom I haven't understood.

Whenever I have a problem, a prayer request, or a need, I write them down. It keeps my hope running that God will answer me, some day.

WHEN GOD IS SILENT

But sometimes people ask me, "When I pray, it's as though God isn't there. How can I learn to hear God speak like you?"

I learned how God speaks from other Christians. There are those to whom God speaks directly through Scripture. Others hear voices. To others God gives definite signs and events that direct their way. Sometimes He shows me pictures. This is how

God guides me. But whatever the way, I know He wants to speak to me.

The important thing for you, Charles, is to *want* to hear God. There is not a person who truly and sincerely wants to hear from God to whom God has not spoken. He is a speaking God. He talks to His people. He enjoys it – if we will only learn to listen.

Sometimes it may feel as though God is hiding Himself, but you have to search for Him. The longing you have for God is one of His chief ways of showing you how genuine you are. Sometimes He keeps a distance to see what you will do, and then He will reveal Himself to you.

When God speaks to me, I feel so happy. It's like when you're solving a puzzle and the puzzle just fits and you feel, "I've got it!"

I say speaks, but it is more of a perception, a strong inner feeling that He is talking. I have yet to hear His audible voice, but when God speaks in this way, we can tell it is God, because the voice of Satan is always one of doubt and accusation, so we can tell the difference. Once you hear doubt and accusation, you know that's the voice of the enemy.

Fear will never allow you to move forward in anything. Fear will keep you in a state of uncertainty and doubt that you are going to fail. That's what fear does.

But the voice of God gives you confidence and takes you out of fear. It's almost like being reckless. But it's a confidence. It's an assurance.

Nevertheless, sometimes He does appear to be silent. And that is frustrating. We need His guidance and we seek it, and – silence! Have you ever found this, Charles?

Sometimes His silence is a calling to trust and step out in faith.

That's how it was when I was sent to Jos.

If God has already given you an assignment and He is silent, Charles, then His silence may be because you have already been told what to do. Go and get started, and God will back you up.

Or if the assignment has not been made clear to you and God is silent, then you should refuse to move until that assignment has been made clear to you. It will be one or the other.

In my case, when I stepped out and people obeyed me, it just had to be a miracle! It wasn't me they were obeying, but God. When I saw this, I understood I was on track.

At my enthronement service, I preached first and foremost to seek God's kingdom. Unless God is glorified, whatever you do will crumble.

Once you are clear, without any doubt, that you are on track with the kingdom, that you want to establish the rule of God on earth among men and in the hearts of people, then no matter how hard the wind tries to blow you in different directions, Charles, just keep your rudder and your compass pointing the right way and you will surely get there.

The wind might delay you, but it should never distract you from your destination.

Sometimes God's guidance will come directly, through His Word or somebody He has sent – and you will know. You will never go wrong if you stick to the Bible. Read the Word and obey it.

Above all, Charles, you must trust God. He is in charge of your life and all your circumstances. He is in charge of all the responsibilities He has given you. And if He is in charge, then you must never turn first to men or anybody else to help you. Go to God first. This act of faith shows God that He can guide you and trust you to obey Him.

I have kept certain words that were said to me by different people I've met over the years. I remember my teacher saying to me, "You've got to be sure of your calling, because some days are going to be hard, some exciting and some joyful. But most of the days will be hard, and the only thing you will have left when everything else has collapsed is that God has called you."

I've held onto that for more than thirty years, and I am not surprised by whatever comes. God has called me, and I hold on to Him for that.

ON FINDING A WIFE...

So, Charles, on to the issue that troubles you most. It troubles me too! You are unmarried. And when you admire yourself in the mirror to shave, you really can't see why! You need a good wife. And God knows that.

Your wife may not be perfect in the way you wish, but she will be perfect when it comes to putting you through the ringer and bringing out the best in you.

She may not be the sweetest natured, nor the finest to look at, nor the woman of your dreams. But give God the right to give you His very best and He will take great delight in turning your dreams upside down.

When I was about to begin my ministry, I went up a mountain with two good friends who were also in need of wives. And there we shouted our hearts out to the Lord without fear of frightening the cattle or being arrested: "Lord, God, give us wives! *Please,* Lord!"

The three of us now have great women. So cry out to God for the woman of *His* dreams, rather than yours. And let Him give you the wife of His choosing, in His good time, just as He did to me.

God will choose for you, Charles. If you honestly lay that choice before Him, He will help you. He knows who your real match is.

God may not give us what we want, but He will give us what is best for us. I am still learning that.

Back then, Gloria didn't look like the kind of woman she would become many decades later. She was timid and rural, and too serious for her own good. So God gave her somebody who complemented her, who relaxed her, who could get her to do the kind of things she would never have thought of doing.

It drew out the best of my love for her, because I have to love her to get the best out of her. Getting angry with Gloria because she wasn't a Western-educated, civilized city girl would only lock her in. But the more I loved her, the more she came out, until she went way beyond me.

If you let God have His way, then He will do something wonderfully creative. You and your wife together will become a new person, and that new person will wildly exceed the sum of your parts!

Where would I be without Gloria, Charles? I would be dead. You'd better believe it.

She travelled once for five weeks. For five weeks, the waste that went on in my household! Because I was always in the office, the children would come: "Daddy, Daddy, what shall we eat?"

And I would say, "Kill a ram."

In five weeks, we ate two rams, two goats, and one pig. The gas cylinder was exhausted. The children would be boiling water and forget and go playing, until the gas was gone.

When Gloria came back, she said, "Ben! In five weeks you did that?"

I said, "Gloria, isn't that the way you do?"

She travelled again, for two days. In those two days, we ate just meat.

Arbet, who was about five, ran to her: "Mummy! Since you travelled, we have been enjoying!"

She said, "Really? What have you been enjoying?"

"We have been eating meat, just meat! Every day, morning, afternoon, and evening."

Boy, was I in trouble! I don't think I was wired to raise a family. But all six children were taught at home by Gloria, to read, write, and do maths and social studies until they were ready for secondary education.

We have brought out the best in each other. To anyone looking for a good wife, my advice would be: be honest with yourself and with God. You will see many girls that you will love, some at first sight; you may see many you will admire for their figure, their intellect, and their abilities.

Put all of this to God in prayer, but do one thing and one thing only: submit to the choice of God. Listen to your heart honestly. If your heart is being led to the quality of this girl, who may not be all you want her to be, but to whom God is leading you, go for it.

My father said to me, "Never tell a woman you love her unless you mean it!"

So if you have said to a girl you love her, until she says no, pursue her. If she says no, then walk away. Until then, keep going until you get a yes.

Remember, Christians never get desperate – they just get determined. Get determined to lay hold of God and lay hold of His promises, and to never settle for less. Remember Abraham and Ishmael?

HOW TO HOLD ON TO YOUR JOY

Always keep your heart in a good place with God and with others. Over time I have learned that you cannot hold on to malice and expect your ministry to flourish. I have learned to forgive as quickly as I can. It is tough, but I intentionally make up my mind to say I have forgiven, so I can keep a clear conscience.

My dad once told me, "Malice or a bitter heart will eat up all your dividends."

Some injuries are painful and you will carry them for days, but I consciously tell the Lord in prayer, "I forgive." This has taken time to learn, because serious offences have come my way. I have been humiliated – and publicly sometimes – but I have intentionally decided that I will forgive.

Charles, you should do the same. The One who has forgiven you demands it.

The result of this is that I have been blessed with joy and peace in facing whatever difficulties come my way. When those difficulties arrive, I'm not suspicious of anybody or anything.

Difficulties are just that – difficulties. They usually come from Satan, and I am ready to surrender them to the Lord. Lift your eyes to the Lord, push those difficulties to one side, and press on through.

If you want to know how I have kept going, it is my joy. I will not allow my joy to be stolen.

Charles, with all the suffering of human beings going on around you, strive to keep your perspective. You may not be able to help them all, but you can help at least one. And that will give you joy. Helping another will help you find a way through your own moments of suffering.

Yes, sometimes you will feel burdened and weighed down by it all. He knows that. So He gave us a verse that reassures me in a way few can understand: "Cast all your anxiety upon him because he cares for you" (1 Peter 5:7).

No matter how great a burden you are carrying, make sure you always remember Matthew 11:28: "Come to me, all you who are weary and burdened, and I will give you rest." God is more willing to take your burden than you are to lay it down.

I have learned to do this.

I go to my room privately and cry out. I weep before the Lord, whatever the difficulty, whatever the burden. I cry and cry. Don't be too proud to cry out to the Lord, Charles. Let your tears flow.

This will touch the heart of God, because He wants to help His children.

It is during these periods also, as I lay down my burdens to the Lord, that I receive encouragement.

All burdens are intended to discourage. I may enter my prayer room with a weight on my shoulders, but when I come out, I will often find something comes my way to make me happy. It may be my wife or my children or a friend. They don't know what I'm going through, but something will happen to take away that burden.

At times like these, other people cannot help me. So I don't trouble them with my burden. Only God can help me. As God helped Jesus in the Garden of Gethsemane, He will help me, and He will help you too.

And when the burden goes away, and the Lord answers your prayers, write it down. And don't forget to run and say thank You.

Always remember, Charles, there should be thanksgiving even within the request. When you cry and beg and plead, also declare: "I have faith; I trust You, Lord; I thank You. I know You will answer. I am grateful."

Don't let anything steal your joy. That joy that we see ahead encourages us to press on. Nothing must touch that. If you guard your heart and your mind with the peace of the Lord, that joy will drive you on. Walking with God is an adventure. Keep going!

MONEY AND ACCOUNTABILITY

So what about when your leaders don't understand you? Ideally you should have spiritual covering within the church. But if you do find yourself alone, then turn to God and say, "You are my covering," and take the risk.

However, if your pastors have a leading from God and are cautioning you, you would be wise to heed their caution.

When I got to Jos, everybody thought what I did was foolish. I disbanded the standing committee and the diocesan board. And I declared I would remove every member of all the cults from the church. As a result, people removed their money. The coffers emptied and the funds ran out.

You will go through trials. But if you keep your heart strong and your faith strong, these trials will be turned to times of spiritual growth.

This is what I found when I was accused of being corrupt. That story spread throughout the church. Sometimes, we have to overcome a test of the heart. My test was to stay silent and let God vindicate me, to depend on God.

God knows our circumstances. There are times when He will provide the resources through others around you, and there are times when you will be alone. If you have a calling and a ministry to fulfil and there is no help, support, or encouragement to be found, then you will need to rely fully on God. And that is a good place.

God is the one who will raise others to support you. They will offer what money cannot buy, with their presence, their counsel, and their prayers.

And when you do handle money, you will need the wisdom and the generosity of God, along with a healthy fear of the Lord. And that will mean making yourself accountable to others.

This is how it works between Gloria and me. She has the generosity and I have the wisdom.

Gloria is always thinking of ways to help other people. Once she had to drop somebody at the hospital and saw a woman who was crying. Her husband was going to die because she did not have the money to pay for his treatment. Gloria didn't know her name and had never seen her before. But she took all the money she had and gave it to the woman.

Later, Gloria was running a conference for women. A woman came forward to give her testimony. She pointed at Gloria and said, "This is the woman who saved my husband's life."

But I have only myself to blame if Gloria wants to help people. She has seen the man she married doing the same. She doesn't need to ask my permission. Gloria so trusts in my love for her, that she would go into debt to help another person, knowing that I will pay.

So I have learned how to combine my wisdom with her generous nature. When Gloria asks for money for shoes for the second time (because she has given the first pair away), I say, "Gloria, please, I beg you, let it be for shoes…! I will follow you."

Her heart is always to reach out to love, but without necessarily imposing the discipline a person will need in order to stand. So I will stand for justice while Gloria will stand for compassion.

She is generous to a fault, but she is also frugal. And Gloria has trimmed me down to prudence, thriftiness, and reasonableness. She is a plumb line for me that I need to measure up against all the time.

So Charles, you should also listen to your wife (when God is finally able to entrust you with one!). Listen to your wife in areas of personal accountability. It can be hard to find people who will tell you the truth, but your wife will. She will see you, she will know you, and she will understand you.

Sometimes she will say, "Have you prayed?" Now, would you lie? It can be the Spirit of the Lord just popping into her mind to remind you. Listen to your wife. She will play an important part in your accountability.

The Bible says the heart is deceitful above all things, so you will need to make yourself accountable, Charles, to prevent yourself from falling into a trap.

You must be accountable, first and foremost, in your spiritual walk with God on a daily basis. That is the thermometer for your entire future. If you can get your prayer life right, you are also likely to get your sex life right and your finances right. Keep a journal of your walk with God and your Bible studies.

Then listen to your friends. True friends will share their concern for you if you're not doing so well. Let them challenge you. Even as a bishop, I let my friends challenge me. Make yourself accountable to your friends.

And listen to your children. Children? Well, if you're asking God for a wife, Charles, children will usually follow.

My oldest daughter, Hannatu, says, "Daddy, that sermon was very long and there was a lot of Ben." She is very critical of me.

At other times, Nanminen, my youngest, says, "That sermon was great. I'm sure you must have prayed, because I was crying." Listen to your children.

PARENTING

One of the earliest lessons I learned was that finding a life partner, a wife, was a serious business. And after that came raising a family for God. Parenting, by the way, is a full-time job.

So as someone who has brought up 400 children (at last count), I think I have earned the right to offer one or two suggestions...

One thing I can say for sure is there is no blueprint when it comes to bringing up children. I searched out materials that would be helpful. I read a lot of James Dobson, and what the

Bible had to say on the matter. I watched a lot of teaching videos because what I feared the most was that my children would turn out to be just as much trouble as me.

I love children, and wanted to do a good job of raising them. My father was a fine gentleman, but I came to know Jesus Christ in Lagos, not in his house. I wanted to raise a Christian home.

But despite all those Christian books on parenting, when my own children came along, it was another story entirely. God was gracious enough to guide me through. I learned from each child that came along. They taught me a lot.

Each was unique. I learned from Hannatu, who was brilliant and never failed an exam. I learned from Rinji, who, like me, would fail exams because he was too busy playing to take anything seriously. I refused to get angry with him. Now he has a Master's degree and is working on another. I could see myself in Rinji, and understood him.

Then there is Pangak, who was so engrossed in machines that he had no time for human beings. Pangak turned out to be an engineer, of course.

Then there is Arbet, who liked to learn everything by the book. But there are things about human relations no book could ever teach. Arbet clashed with his professor in Ukraine and had to start his medical training all over again in Belarus.

Nendelmwa is just a darling. Wherever she goes on earth, everybody loves her. She is gifted and knows just what to do with children. She is just like her mother. She will work from morning till night because she has a servant heart.

I'm also learning from Nanminen, who is very charming. What do you do with a charmer? You can't get angry with him, even when he does things wrong.

Learn from your children as you parent them.

And I have learned this: you can – you really can – control your temper.

How do I know?

Rinji is like me: he will never read a manual. Rinji just knows stuff.

I bought a brand-new battery shaver that I had never used. Rinji was curious, so he pulled it apart and turned it into a fan to keep him cool at night.

I heard this buzzing. We had bees in the next compound and I was worried they had invaded our house. I turned on the light and caught Rinji at it.

We had a rule that we wouldn't shout at the children at night after prayers. We would go to sleep and settle things in the morning.

So in the morning, I collected my shaver. I said, "Good morning, you idiot." Rinji had forgotten all about it. But I was very angry. I let him have it.

"Do you know how much this cost?"

I was scorching his ears when the phone rang. It was my friend. I became immediately jovial and pleasant until I put down the phone. Then I got stuck back into Rinji. "Do you think this is a toy?"

Then the phone rang again. It was my younger sister. I was as nice as could be. And just as I was dropping the receiver, the Lord said, "Ben, see, you are in control of your anger."

And I realized it was true. If I was truly angry, then why didn't I continue venting my anger on the phone? How could I switch so easily from being jovial and pleasant to being angry? I realized I could choose not to be angry. The choice was mine.

I said to Rinji, "Silly. Don't do it again."

He burst into tears. "Daddy, I'm sorry, I won't do it again."

We hugged and I broke down and we prayed. And that was it. That was for me an everlasting lesson. Rinji became a blessing to me. I learned that I can choose to be angry or not. I can choose to be in control of my temper and my moods. My boy had become my teacher.

Many times I've been slow to learn. My stubbornness was almost the death of Arbet.

When Arbet was a little boy, he was grizzling and whining in the car. "I want my dinner, I want my dinner!"

He went on and on until it became really irritating. I tried to reassure him, "We're going to get dinner in a minute."

But no: "*I need my dinner!*"

So we stopped and I offered Arbet his dinner, but he pushed it away: "I don't want it!"

The moment we got back in the car, his whining kicked up again: "I want my dinner!"

I was furious. We were on a busy trunk road full of traffic. I slammed on the brakes and Arbet leaped out and ran across the road. There were cars everywhere. I was terrified he would be run over.

I yelled, "No! Stop, son! Stop, stop!" I ran to him and snatched him up and held him. He could feel my concern and became quiet.

I sat him down and said, "Why are you whining? Please don't." He said, "OK, Daddy."

The Lord taught me another everlasting lesson. He said to me, "Never, ever, show your anger to your child." I could have lost him. He was just a child who was growing up.

This was a lesson in endurance. You need to take your time.

The devil was using my irritation against me. I have learned not to let him. Oh, we all get angry with our children, but we should not express that anger in a way that will drive them away and into danger.

Never, ever, curse your children. Bless them all the time: "This one has troubles, Lord, he is telling lies. I used to tell lies too, but Lord, You forgave me and You changed me." Sometimes, when they are asleep, go over and bless them.

It's a lesson in parenting, but it's also a lesson in leadership. If you can raise your children successfully, then you can raise your church. God had rebuked me. I was wrong.

Here's the thing: your children will never do what you ask of them. You could give them a million instructions a day, but they will only do what they see you do. The girls copy Gloria and the boys copy me.

I never hesitate to be open to them. I tell them my secrets: fear God, work hard, study books, and keep the faith. There is no secret about how I live in the house. I am an open book.

I learned from my father to love being at home with my wife and children. I love my children way beyond any disagreements. My children are absolutely sure that I love them. We discuss most family things. Nothing is a life-or-death issue for us; nothing will break our relationships, not even school results.

The rhythm of our house is consistent. Everybody will pray together every morning, every evening, and at meals.

So, Charles, here is my counsel to you: raising children does not happen by accident. Have a clear intention of how you plan to raise your children. They will learn the things you approve of, and the things you disapprove of. But what you do and how you live must be a fit with what you believe is good for you, your children, and your community. Use Scripture in the raising of your children for that purpose.

Educating children is very important. If you neglect their education, then drugs, bad habits, or anything will come and steal them away. You must teach them the value of education.

Teach your children to be courteous to everybody, whatever their station in life. Courtesy will open doors to anybody and everybody. If you are humble and well behaved, you are more likely to get a job.

Teaching your children to welcome people is also important. When Nanminen was three, I was out of the house when my friend came to call. Nanminen said, "Uncle, come and sit down."

He went and held his arm. "Mum and Dad are not in, but they will soon come back. Uncle, what will you drink? Tea or coffee?" This was a three-year-old. He had learned that our family welcomes people.

Your children will learn to love people if they see *you* loving people. Your children will learn to love the Lord, if they see *you* love the Lord. And they will learn to believe your faith, if they see *you* practise your faith at home.

Most important of all is the way I love my wife. The children can see it and they like it. It is real. I talk about Gloria with the children, all her madness and her ministry, and they laugh. We talk about her with much affection. They cannot disrespect her. They dare not.

Once they see that I love my wife, they listen to her. Unfortunately, they vote for Gloria more than they vote for me. Everything is about Gloria for the children.

All these things begin in the home.

Charles, you are the watchman of your children. You can never sleep when you have children. Believe me, Charles, I know.

If I had only a single life lesson to pass on to others, the most important lesson of my life would be to pick one child, who would never ordinarily have had an opportunity in life, and struggle through bringing up that child for God.

That life is God-given, and nobody can tell what their future will be. It is a great privilege to have an opportunity to be a blessing to another person's life.

GET GOING!

So Charles, I will draw my letter to you to a close.

My own life story springs from a background less successful than yours. But of this I am sure: God has worked in my life. And He is looking for more people, like you, Charles, to give themselves to His work.

God will use whatever you give Him, just like the young boy with the five little loaves. He must have wondered how his own paltry offering could feed 5,000. But this little boy gave the little he had anyway. And Jesus took it and blessed it and broke it and fed a multitude.

Whenever you offer to God, Charles, He will take it, bless it, break it, and use it. God has a place for you, because there is a place of need in this world for any life that is offered up to God.

So now I have warmed to my theme, and you have learned my life's lessons the easy way, let me look you in the eye and be a little more direct…

Charles, I notice week after week you sit at the back of the church, tied to your mother's apron strings. So let me say, young man, if you don't lace your boots and trust in God and get to work, two things will happen. One, while you are lagging behind, God will move on, and the very apron strings you thought would guide you and give you fulfilment, you're going to lose those as well.

Two – and this is the worst part – you will finish your life accomplishing nothing, because life's accomplishment is not about what you can do, but what you let the hands of God do with you.

So if you're looking to man or to money, you will accomplish their goals, not yours, and certainly not God's. You will die miserably. And if that is not bad enough, you will have sold a sub-standard faith to your family and those who follow you.

Charles, you must learn to free yourself from all apron strings and embrace God fully. Not knowing what tomorrow may look like, you must take the plunge and embrace the risk.

In a little over forty years, I can say that risk has been worth it, and I commend it without reservation or hesitation – even for a moment. Not just because of my experience, but because of the stories of others who lived this life 300 years ago.

They had nothing and God was their everything. He picked rags of people such as Ajayi Crowther, who were former slaves. Not only did He do everything for them, but because of all He achieved through them, their names will never be erased from the history of humanity.

So, Charles – make a choice.

How do you want to start and how do you want to end? It is no use you being a Christian, with all the investment of education you have and the privileges you have enjoyed, if all that can be said about you is that once upon a time there was you, and that was all.

There's more to life than that. There is an unknown adventure ahead that is by far the most exciting part of your life.

That adventure begins by taking that first step into the unknown. That first step is a step of faith, and a living faith is the only true faith.

So, get going, Charles, get going!
What are you waiting for?
Your friend,

Ben

HOW YOU CAN GIVE

If you wish to make a donation to the work of Archbishop Ben from the UK, please send cheques made payable to:

Ben Kwashi Nigeria Fund
Release International
PO Box 54
Orpington
Kent, BR5 4RT

You can also donate online via
www.releaseinternational.org/give.

Alternatively, you could make a cheque payable to *Open Heavens Foundation*, write *Ben Kwashi* on the back, and post it to:

Open Heavens Foundation/Ben Kwashi
3201 Preston Hollow Road
Fort Worth
TX 76109
USA

Thank you.